THE
RECRUITER'S
HANDBOOK

A Complete Guide for Sourcing, Selecting, and Engaging the Best Talent

SHARLYN LAUBY

THE
RECRUITER'S
HANDBOOK

A Complete Guide for Sourcing, Selecting, and Engaging the Best Talent

Society for Human Resource Management
Alexandria, Virginia | www.shrm.org

Strategic Human Resource Management India
Mumbai, India | www.shrmindia.org

Society for Human Resource Management
Haidian District Beijing, China | www.shrm.org/cn

Society for Human Resource Management, Middle East and North Africa Office
Dubai, UAE | www.shrm.org/pages/mena.aspx

SOCIETY FOR HUMAN
RESOURCE MANAGEMENT

This publication is designed to provide accurate and authoritative information regarding the subject matter covered. It is sold with the understanding that neither the publisher nor the author is engaged in rendering legal or other professional service. If legal advice or other expert assistance is required, the services of a competent, licensed professional should be sought. The federal and state laws discussed in this book are subject to frequent revision and interpretation by amendments or judicial revisions that may significantly affect employer or employee rights and obligations. Readers are encouraged to seek legal counsel regarding specific policies and practices in their organizations.

This book is published by the Society for Human Resource Management (SHRM). The interpretations, conclusions, and recommendations in this book are those of the author and do not necessarily represent those of the publisher.

SHRM books and products are available on most online bookstores and through the SHRMStore at www.shrmstore.org.

The Society for Human Resource Management is the world's largest HR professional society, representing 285,000 members in more than 165 countries. For nearly seven decades, the Society has been the leading provider of resources serving the needs of HR professionals and advancing the practice of human resource management. SHRM has more than 575 affiliated chapter within the United States and subsidiary offices in China, India, and United Arab Emirates. Please visit us at www.shrm.org.

Library of Congress Cataloging-in-Publication Data

Names: Lauby, Sharlyn, author.

Title: The recruiter's handbook : a complete guide for sourcing, selecting, and engaging the best talent / Sharlyn Lauby.

Description: Alexandria, Virginia : Society for Human Resource Management, [2018] | Includes bibliographical references and index.

Identifiers: LCCN 2017053969| ISBN 9781586444655 (pbk.) | ISBN 9781586444679 (epub) | ISBN 9781586444686 (mobi)

Subjects: LCSH: Employees--Recruiting. | Employee selection. | Personnel management.

Classification: LCC HF5549.5.R44 L377 2018 | DDC 658.3/11--dc23

Printed in the United States of America

FIRST EDITION

PB Printing   10 9 8 7 6 5 4 3 2 1

61.14516 | 17-0958

Table of Contents

Acknowledgments

I've always said that a book never happens alone.

I want to thank the wonderful people who helped me make this book happen. First, a huge thanks to Tony Lee, Matthew Davis, and the team at SHRM for giving me this opportunity. I also want to thank Shirley Raybuck for her design expertise, Holly Alexander for being a fantastic editor, and Kate Mertes for indexing all of the content.

It's been wonderful working with everyone. I learn something new with every book, and this one is no exception.

A huge thanks to my clients and colleagues who contributed their expertise. You didn't have to answer my request, but I'm sure glad you did. I'm very fortunate to have such giving professionals in my network. And I know readers will find your insights valuable.

Last but certainly not least, all my love and admiration to my husband, Keith. Writing a book becomes a "family activity" in the Lauby household, and he's a great sport about it. I owe him one very long vacation.

Thank you all and enjoy the read. Cheers!
Sharlyn Lauby

Foreword

Finding, interviewing and hiring employees have always been a challenge and priority for any size company, in any industry and in every country. What's different today is that we have an ever-growing skills gap, a more fluid job market, and emerging generations that have a different set of expectations.

After the 2008 U.S. recession, companies are hiring slower and the amount of jobs available in the economy has been steadily increasing, while employee retention has been declining at a similar pace. Almost two-thirds of companies are unable to find skilled candidates and almost one-fourth of employees are planning to change jobs. To add to the complexity, companies have to account for four generations of employees, who have different needs and are divided by trends in culture and technology. Millennials and Generation Z account for about half of the workforce, yet at the same time the proportion of Baby Boomers is growing and aging past retirement. Catering to these generations will become increasingly complex and stressful for recruiters and HR leaders. These four trends are all interrelated and have created a global war for talent that has companies altering their employer value proposition, prioritizing employer branding and redesigning their offices and benefits to appeal to all types of candidates.

Compensation matters. The one thing that has remained constant in my over ten years of workplace research is compensation. Regardless of your age, gender or ethnic background, cash has been king. The one subtle difference today compared to years past is that the conversation has moved from trying to make as much money as possible to "fair pay". With access to salary data from PayScale.com, and the no longer taboo conversations about pay between workers, companies need to focus first and fair pay before even thinking about benefits.

Flexible workplaces attract candidates and keep employees. One of the most profound changes I've witnessed since 2014 is the prioritization of work flexibility over healthcare coverage, following two global millennial studies I worked on with Randstad. After fair pay, all of my peers want a more flexible work environment, which includes a modern office design, to the ability to telecommute, casual dress, job sharing, additional maternal and paternal leave, and flexible hours. Gallup reports that the average workweek has expanded to 47 hours and with smartphones, we are working outside of office hours, resulting in a desire to have more freedom and flexibility. As further evidence, about a third of our economy is gig workers, and through several studies we found that the top reason they choose to freelance is for flexibility. It's a clear sign that companies need to create flexibility programs and then market them in their recruiting initiatives.

Technology isn't a substitute for good managers. Professionals today want to work at organizations with well-developed cultures, pay and benefits, and empathetic leaders. Don't think for a second that all the hype around new technology developments, including chatbots and artificial intelligence, will solve all of your recruiting problems. The most effective tool for recruiting and retaining talent is human interactions, having managers that support internal career development and learning initiatives and a culture where employees feel safe to share new ideas. While a machine might help remove unconscious bias in the recruiting process, don't ever hire anyone without first meeting them! A bad hire can cost you money, time and productivity, that you can't afford to lose when growing your business.

The candidate and employee experience defines company culture. Creating positive candidate and employee experiences will become increasingly critical to securing your place on the "Best Place to Work" list. How you treat your candidates and employees will impact your revenue more moving forward. After conducting a study with CareerArc, we found that a poor candidate experience sways consumer behavior and increases the likelihood that they will post negative reviews online that become part of your company's permanent record. By being more thoughtful around how often you communicate to candidates, and the culture you create for your employees, you will see higher profits.

While there are a lot of recruiting challenges ahead of you, there are also great opportunities to reinvent how you manage the hiring experience and engage your employees. I first connected with Sharlyn Lauby back when she interviewed me in 2010 about personal branding for her popular blog, HR Bartender. Today, we both sit on the Kronos Workforce Institute Advisory Board and I continue to learn from her experience and focus on helping companies with their recruiting and employer branding strategies. In "The Recruiter's Handbook", Sharlyn reveals everything she knows about recruiting from more than a decade of experience, in a simple format that can benefit any company and help you sustain an advantage in the ever-competitive talent war!

Dan Schawbel, *New York Times* bestselling author of *Promote Yourself* and *Me 2.0*, Partner and Research Director at Future Workplace

Foreword

In the Preface to Sharlyn Lauby's *The Recruiter's Handbook,* she emphasizes that this can serve as your single resource guide to the world of recruitment and talent selection, and once you thumb through the pages and the topics outlined in the Table of Contents, you'll know why. The author does an amazing job of covering the full spectrum of hiring considerations—from employer branding and the candidate experience to recruitment ethics and the changing legal landscape, from social media sourcing and reference checking to onboarding and succession planning.

The Recruiter's Handbook never fails to keep you, the reader, engaged, excited, and motivated about how you can drive cultural change by raising awareness of your organization's talent acquisition function. There's so much involved in hiring top talent—recruiters, operational hiring managers, marketing and social media outreach, success statistics and efficiency metrics, and yes—even checklists and tools to ensure you're mastering the content and applying its principles long after you put the book down.

Even more compelling, though, is the fact that the book is structured in a way to make its contents easily accessible, no matter what the particular hiring challenge you're facing. For example, look no further if you need a resource to guide your recruitment in the areas of veteran, disabled, or even ex-offender employment. (Yes, this last category is turning out to be a bright and shiny star for many organizations in need of particular talent while looking to help society get some of its most vulnerable members up and running and in full contribution mode once they're available to work.) Likewise, if you're looking to explore global recruitment or build strong apprenticeship, mentoring, or internship programs, *The Recruiter's Handbook* offers powerful content to launch your initiative.

Even more fundamentally, what style of interview works best—one-on-one, panel, video, or collaborative hiring, and how do you effectively employ resources and tools like candidate assessments, reference checks, and background checks without inadvertently violating the law? Likewise, how do you self-audit your own practices to ensure that your front-line hiring managers are engaged, your candidates are motivated to join your organization from the very first online ad they read or from their first site visit, and your new hires are effectively integrated so that they can minimize learning curves and make full-scale contributions as quickly as possible?

No, there are no guarantees in the world of recruitment and selection, just like there are no guarantees in life. But what *The Recruiter's Handbook* offers you is a tried and true, tested, and authentic tool kit to help shorten the learning curve, avoid legal pitfalls, and build trust in the new hire relationship. Trust stems from healthy and selfless career discussions that can and should become part of every hiring manager's interviewing strategy. In essence, you can move the career and professional development paradigm to the pre-employment stage and turn all your new hires into true believers—in you, in your organization, and in their own ability to effectuate change. In tight or loose labor markets, in good economic times or bad, the people you invite aboard to join your team bring with them new life-blood, exuberant energy, and a fresh set of eyes to (literally) take your organization to the next level. What could be a better use of your time or a better skill to build than maximizing the talent of newly hired employees?

Every manager knows that it's better to manage to people's strengths than to shore up their weaknesses. What Sharlyn Lauby does so well is help you identify and attract the type of performers who are independent, can think on their feet, and find new and unique ways of adding value to your organization over time. Everyone knows a good hire once that person starts: they're positive, energetic, and they go out of their way to get to know people, learn about the organization, and find new ways of reinventing things to make life easier for everyone. Unfortunately, most managers also know how difficult it can be to make one poor hire. A lax attitude, apathy, or an entitlement mentality can likewise show up fairly quickly in terms of that individual's aura or reputation. Think how much stronger you'll be as a recruiter or as a frontline operational leader if you can get this hiring skill down pat right now!

Being an effective hiring manager is a talent that keeps on giving. It's the first step in the leadership trajectory that will help you stand out as a rarity among your peers: *attracting, developing, and retaining* top talent is the arguably the most crucial element of leadership success. Look to *The Recruiter's Handbook* to help you focus on that first verb—attracting—but look also to the wisdom that connects the attraction to the development piece. Developing happens right away in the orientation and onboarding program and should continue throughout the employee lifecycle. Ultimately, if you get those first two verbs right, then the natural consequence—retaining—will surely follow.

You can give your organization no greater gift than the benefit of a talented, motivated, and high performing team. *The Recruiter's Handbook* is your tool and guide to help you get there. Make this your talent acquisition bible, use its tools and templates as roadmaps to your own success and the success of your team, and remember always that when you hire right the first time, you can focus on your people's career growth and development while they find new and exciting ways of making your company a better place. Congratulations on finding your way to this excellent book and resource: now's your opportunity to catapult your own career potential by tapping talent and growing people's careers to add to your company's overall performance and profitability.

Paul Falcone, bestselling author of *96 Great Interview Questions to Ask Before You Hire*

Preface

There are lots of recruiting books on the market—which is exactly why you should have this one. Emphasis on the word "one." We're going to discuss the role of recruiting in-depth later on in this book, but in short, recruiting is a highly visible process to hire the people that make your organization successful. Many people touch the recruiting process, and even more have an opinion about how it should work. For that reason, we all need to have a single resource guide to keep us focused—you know, that go-to book that makes you try a new approach or reminds you to use a proven process. A book you can give to others, so everyone in the organization is on the same page about the recruiting function. That's the goal of this book.

Who Will Benefit from This Book?

Saying that everybody would benefit from this book is probably overdoing it. However, there are some specific workplace scenarios in which this book will bring real value.

Individuals new to the recruiting function. As human resource professionals, we all have to start somewhere, and often it can be learning the recruiting function. Recruiting is the first impression applicants and candidates have of the organization. It's a great opportunity for new recruiters to understand recruiting strategy and how the work they do affects the organization.

New hiring managers. A recruiter's partner in the hiring process is the department manager. At some point, hiring managers need to learn how to effectively and efficiently bring the best talent into their department. Instead of simply providing small snippets of information about how to hire or glossing over the big picture, we have an opportunity to educate hiring managers on the value of the process.

Before we go on, some might think since we're talking about individuals who have a "new" role that we're focused on Millennials. Not completely true. At some point, everyone needs to learn recruiting. I've worked for many organizations in which everyone was a member of the recruiting team. Just like everyone was a member of the sales team. And I'll admit that there are times when we might need to *unlearn* bad recruiting habits we've developed over the years. This book isn't focused on generations. Rather, it is focused on the candidate and employee life cycle along with career development for the individuals involved in the recruiting process.

The Employee Life Cycle Is Changing

Organizations are starting to look at the classic employee life cycle with a new lens. In the past, we thought of the employee life cycle as the journey an employee takes while he or she is employed with the company—recruiting, performance, succession, development, and transition. Today the focus is shifting to a more employee-centered design, similar to the concept of "flipping training" and real-time feedback. Employees are much more involved in defining their career path. This new employee "cycle" allows organizations to create an employee experience that is more engaging, which translates into an attractive employment brand and candidate experience.

HR departments of one. Solo practitioners have to know a little bit of all things HR. This type of role can be fun and offers a tremendous amount of variety. (Translation: you never get bored.) But it also means that there are times when we need in-depth information from outside resources. Books like *The Recruiter's Handbook* can provide just the right answer at just the right moment in time.

Experienced recruiters who manage the talent acquisition function. Sometimes experienced recruiters get distracted by shiny new things that promise to solve all their challenges. This book offers a focus on the basics. In addition, experienced recruiters can use a resource to share with individuals new to recruiting. What a great way to coach and mentor a colleague—by giving him or her a resource to use every day.

How to Use This Book

Don't let the word "handbook" in the title fool you. This book isn't a remedial guide. It's also not a legal guide. We will mention a few laws, but given the ever-changing legislation landscape, it's best to stay on top of changes by contacting your friendly labor attorney. The goal of this book is to help you build a strong recruiting foundation for your organization.

Staying Current with Legislation

Business is constantly changing, and with change come legislative developments. But staying on top of what laws are being proposed and enacted on the local, state, and federal levels can be a full-time job. If you weren't aware, the Society for Human Resource Management (SHRM) has a Policy Action Center that serves as a resource on public policy issues affecting the workplace. You can bookmark the website—advocacy.shrm.org/home.

Another place for regular updates regarding legislation is your local or state SHRM affiliate. Most chapters and state councils have a legislative affairs director who is up-to-date on pending legislation. In addition, chapters and state councils regularly offer legal updates to members. For a list of membership councils in your area, visit shrm.org/communities/volunteers/membership-councils/pages/default.aspx.

The book is divided into eight sections.

I. **Recruiting Responsibilities:** In this section, we will focus on the recruiting function itself and its importance to the organization. If companies want their recruiting teams to be successful, they need to fully understand their role. We'll also talk about ethics and recruiting.

II. **Candidate Strategies:** A common piece of advice when you're speaking to a group of people is "know your audience." In recruiting, that means "know your candidate." This section focuses on building a candidate experience that achieves your recruiting goals.

III. **Organizational Recruiting Strategies:** Successful hiring doesn't mean throwing spaghetti against the wall and seeing if it sticks. It's about having an intentional plan. In this section, we'll discuss how to develop the company's recruiting strategy.

IV. **Sourcing Strategies:** The number one question in every recruiter's mind is, "Where do I find the best talent?" Everywhere is not the answer. It's all about finding your niche. This section offers suggestions for sourcing qualified candidates, the key word being "qualified."

V. **Selecting the Best Candidate:** Remember that the candidate is interviewing the company. Organizations need to create a hiring experience that makes people want to work for their firm. The goal is to hire the best. This section outlines how to create the right selection criteria.

VI. **Extending the Offer:** There's more to finding talent than the interview—background checks, drug screening, and social media have become part of the process. This section focuses on the do's and don'ts of extending job offers.

VII. **Onboarding:** A new hire's welcome to the company happens before his or her first day. Organizations can no longer separate the recruiting and onboarding processes. In this section, we'll talk about how recruiting, training, and operations can partner to build a successful onboarding experience.

VIII. **Evaluation:** Once organizations have a recruiting strategy, it's important to regularly monitor outcomes—both in terms of the process itself and the candidates being hired. We'll discuss the metrics and how to make adjustments based on the numbers.

You can read *The Recruiter's Handbook* in sequence to understand the process and how each piece builds on the previous one. Or you can go straight to the chapter you're trying to learn more about—like sourcing. Use the book in a way that works best for you because that's how it will provide the most value.

FIGURE 1.1: Components of Recruiting

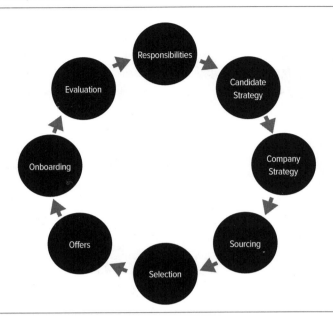

What to Expect in Each Chapter

Recruiting isn't one-size-fits-all. This book provides lots of resources that you can use right away or refer to for some creative inspiration. In each chapter, we will deliver real-world case studies. There's no better way to learn than from people and companies that have "been there, done that." Also, at the end of each chapter, we'll offer guidance and best practices from human resources, recruiting, and business professionals on how you can take your recruiting game to the next level.

At the end of each section, we'll recap the top takeaways—so you can stay focused on implementing your recruiting strategy—as well as a list of actionable, practical tips and resources to make your job easier.

Every organization has a recruiting function, and every person needs to know something about recruiting. This is your handbook to finding and hiring the best talent for your organization. So let's get started! In the book *Good to Great*, author Jim Collins talked about getting the right people on the bus. The start of any successful recruiting function is understanding who the recruiting team is and what role each person plays in the process.

SECTION I
Recruiting Responsibilities

In Section I

This section is focused on the recruiting function. Most of you already know what recruiting is because you picked up this book. But if you're like me, you might have learned recruiting informally.

I'm one of those human resource professionals who doesn't have a degree in HR and was hired to do an HR job. I learned about recruiting, employee relations, etc., on the job. Later, I went back to school, learned about the models and theories and got my professional certification.

So it doesn't hurt to make sure we all have the same level of expectation where the recruiting function is concerned. Especially since we might have learned the recruiting function through different routes. Let's define it.

CHAPTER 1:
What Is Recruiting?

Before we can launch into a conversation about how to be an effective recruiter, it's important to define "recruiting." The way we do business is changing all the time, so common definitions will naturally change along with it.

To make things simple and, since this book is being published by the Society for Human Resource Management (SHRM), we'll use its definition for recruiting, which is "the activity of identifying and soliciting individuals—either from within or outside an organization—to fill job vacancies or staff for growth."

Recruiting versus Talent Acquisition

One of the clarifications we need to address is the relationship between recruiting and talent acquisition. I'm guilty of using these terms interchangeably, but there is a difference.

SHRM defines talent acquisition as "the process of attracting and recruiting the best talent available for the organization." The goal of talent acquisition is broader in scope. It's to "ensure the organization has the right people, with the right skills, who are in the right job, and are working against the right requirements."

Using these two definitions, recruiting is a component of talent acquisition. Another way to phrase that is talent acquisition drives recruiting, similar to how marketing drives sales. The other key words to focus on in the definitions are "activity" and "process." Recruiting is an activity, meaning a major piece of work to be completed. Talent acquisition is a process, which involves several activities, including recruiting.

For this book, we're going to talk about both talent acquisition and recruiting. To be an effective recruiter, you need to know a little about talent acquisition, even if you're not regularly involved with talent acquisition strategy. This strategy affects the work of recruiters. And there might be times when you need to push for a change in talent acquisition strategy to deliver results. More on that later.

Recruiting's Place in the Employee Life Cycle

In the preface, we talked about some of the changes that are taking shape with the employee life cycle. While the cycle is changing, recruiting is still firmly ensconced in the process. In fact, if there's a change in the employee life cycle that involves recruiting, we could argue that recruiting has been replaced with talent acquisition.

Regardless of what the unemployment rate looks like, organizations have found that the best way to attract and hire talent is by building relationships with candidates. In this book, we'll talk about the specifics, but the best way to hire premier talent starts before a person becomes an employee.

For recruiters, understanding the role of talent acquisition and recruiting in the employee life cycle is important. The way a candidate becomes an employee sets the stage for the other components of the life cycle. For example, if a candidate is sourced using social media tools, the candidate might logically assume that the organization embraces employees using social media. If the employee started work and discovered the opposite, he or she might become disillusioned with the job and the company. Recruiters should be conscious of their place in the employee experience and strive to complement it—not contradict it.

Recruiting Ethics

We can't talk about a process without discussing the ethics involved. Ethics are the values and standards that drive our behavior. When it comes to talent acquisition and recruiting, we have an ethical obligation to treat candidates with respect throughout the recruitment and selection process. To ensure that we maintain an ethical process, we can refer to two models:

Procedural justice focuses on the fairness of how decisions get made. An example of a question recruiters might ask about an organization's recruiting and hiring process might be, "Are the steps taken to make the hiring decision fair?"

Distributive justice focuses on the perceived fairness of the outcomes. "Is the final hiring decision itself fair?" would be a question recruiters can ask.

Recruiting, like many other business processes, can face challenges. At times recruiters will be asked to accelerate the process. Or cut corners. Organizations don't make these requests to intentionally question the ethics of a recruiting professional. They make these requests so they can get someone hired. Recruiters must understand their ethical obligations and make sure they do not compromise their ethics.

The bottom line: A recruiter's goal is to bring people into the organization quickly and ethically.

Organizations must recruit. There's absolutely no way around it. Successful organizations develop talent acquisition strategies to drive their recruiting efforts. They understand the role that recruiting plays with candidates and employees. Recruiters work with the other business functions to create alignment between hiring and performance management, succession planning, training, etc. All of these activities must be accomplished in an ethical fashion to maintain the credibility of the recruiter, the function, and the organization.

Bringing people into the organization is necessary, almost self-explanatory. But why is recruiting so important? Let's talk about value in the next chapter.

CHAPTER 2:
Why Is Recruiting Important?

By definition alone, we know that recruiting is important. But outlining the reasons has value because there will be times when we have to convince the organization to recruit, even when no job openings exist. There will also be times when we will ask for resources to support recruiting and need a justification for doing so. Understanding the reasons that recruiting is important to the organization helps recruiters get the job done.

Recruiting Is an Essential Business Competency

Competencies are defined as the ability to do something. Organizations establish competencies as a way of establishing performance expectations and standards. For instance, recruiting is a competency in the Society for Human Resource Management (SHRM) Competency Model. That means, to be a successful HR professional, you need to know recruiting. What's interesting about recruiting in the SHRM Competency Model is how it aligns with the behavioral competencies.

Let me step back for a minute and give you a quick overview of the model. It's composed of eight behavioral competencies and one technical competency. The one technical competency is HR Knowledge, which includes the areas you would expect such as recruiting, compensation, labor law, training, and performance management. The eight behavioral competencies are the following:

1. **Business Acumen** is understanding the organization's operation, functions, and external environment. Recruiting is always looking at the needs of the business as well as the availability of resources to make good recommendations and decisions.

2. **Communication** involves crafting and delivering information. This isn't simply delivering presentations. Communication is about listening, responding, and effectively transferring information to others. Recruiters use their communication skills to tell stories about the company. They listen to candidates and new employees. And they are responsible for both written and verbal communications at every level of the organization.

3. **Consultation** is the ability to work with internal stakeholders to evaluate business challenges and develop solutions to address those challenges. Recruiting involves a tremendous amount of strategy (see number 1), and consultation skills are necessary to get everyone to recognize and buy into programs.

4. **Critical Evaluation** is the ability to collect and analyze data. There's a science to recruiting. It's true that recruiting involves a significant people component, but the data are what drive strategy. Recruiters must be able to read the numbers so they can make informed business decisions.

5. **Ethical Practice** means maintaining high levels of personal and professional integrity, as well as acting as an ethical agent for the organization. Recruiters must make sure they use proper processes to source and hire talent. They must also educate hiring managers on proper hiring and selection.

6. **Global & Cultural Effectiveness** recognizes that we are borderless when it comes to attracting, engaging, and retaining talent. Recruiters are responsible for making sure bias doesn't enter the selection process. They are expected to understand the importance of diversity and inclusion and encourage it throughout the organization.

7. **Leadership & Navigation** is the ability to navigate the organization and accomplish HR goals. From a recruiting perspective, that means finding the best talent and bringing it into the organization.

8. **Relationship Management** is the ability to create and maintain a network of professional contacts both within and outside the organization. This is obviously a huge component of recruiting. Building relationships is essential to developing a talent pipeline.

Recruiting is an important part of the human resource function and the business. Years ago, when I first started my career, I thought recruiting was one of the most boring activities in HR. Then, one day, the vice president of HR asked me to lead the company's recruiting efforts. For a split second, I thought it was some form of punishment.

Then I learned what recruiting was all about. I learned it was hard, and it involved lots of planning, strategy, and metrics. It might be tempting to think of recruiting as simply the interviewing part. Recruiting is so much more. It's a process that needs to be respected, because it has an impact on the entire organization.

The Impact of Recruiting on Other HR Functions

We know recruiting has an impact on the business. Good hires are good for business, and bad hires are, well, not good for the business. Since recruiting is the first step in the employee life cycle, recruiting has an impact on other HR functions. You can see it in looking at the competency models for other HR functions like training and performance management.

The Association for Talent Development (ATD) has developed a competency model, similar to the SHRM Competency Model, for talent development specialists. It includes competencies that crossover into recruiting. For example:

Change Management is focused on applying a systematic process to shift individuals, teams, and organizations from a current state to the desired state. Recruiters and learning professionals might work together to develop a new onboarding process.

Knowledge Management is the activity used to capture, distribute, and archive intellectual capital for collaboration. Not only will learning professionals want to capture the knowledge of recruiters, but they will partner with recruiters to make sure knowledge management is covered in onboarding.

Training Delivery allows recruiters and learning professionals to partner in delivering formal and informal training to new employees—in orientation, onboarding, and new-hire training programs like ethics, anti-harassment, and technical skills.

Coaching applies a systematic process to improving others' ability to set goals, take action, and maximize strengths. Sometimes organizations hire individuals with great potential with the plan to develop them internally. Recruiters look to their colleagues in learning to help new hires who need initial training and development.

Performance Improvement focuses on analyzing employee performance gaps and closing them. Let's face it; sometimes hires don't work out. Recruiters may be asked to conduct confidential searches while learning professionals are working on performance improvement plans.

Another functional area that aligns with recruiting is total rewards. WorldatWork is a nonprofit human resource association focused on compensation, benefits, and work-life effectiveness. Its model connects external influences like the economy, labor market, and regulations to the competencies necessary to attract, motivate, engage, and retain employees:

Compensation must be both internally fair and externally competitive to attract candidates and keep employees.

Benefits provide security for employees and their families. They are also a powerful recruiting and retention tool.

Work-Life Effectiveness encompasses practices, policies, and programs that encourage employees to achieve success at work and home.

Using both models, it's clear that recruiting cannot operate in a silo. Recruiting is not just about filling the job requisition or opening. Recruiting is important because it drives what happens in other functions:

- If recruiters can't fill open positions because compensation is too low, they need to involve other stakeholders.
- If a hiring manager wants to extend an offer to a candidate knowing the candidate will need immediate training to learn a new computer software, then training needs to be involved.

- If the organization is worried that a significant portion of its workforce is of retirement age and the loss of historical knowledge could hurt future product development, recruiters need to understand.

These are just a few of the examples. Recruiting is important because it touches the business. It also touches people.

First Impressions Matter

Of course, businesses are made up of people, so by association recruiting impacts them both. Independent of that fact, recruiting affects individuals and their actions. We'll talk in a later chapter about the candidate experience, but for a moment, let's think about the three groups of people the recruiting process affects.

Candidates are the first and most obvious group. According to Glassdoor.com, the majority of job seekers read at least six reviews before forming an opinion of a company. Sixty-one percent of Glassdoor users report that they seek company reviews and ratings before making the decision to apply for a job, and 69 percent of active job seekers are likely to apply for a job if the employer actively manages its employer brand (that is, has an online presence, maintains it, and is responsive.)

What takes place in recruiting helps form that opinion about the organization. Recruiters shouldn't be surprised if the organization wants a say in the recruiting process because recruiting impacts the company reputation. The reverse is also true. How the organization conducts itself on social media can affect recruiting, and recruiters might want to offer some feedback.

Employees are the second group affected by the recruiting function. The goal is to turn candidates into employees. How well recruiters and hiring managers do their job has an impact on employees. Maren Hogan, founder of Red Branch Media, wrote in an article for TLNT.com that one-third of new hires quit their job after about six months and that referred employees have a 45 percent retention rate after two years.

How recruiters find candidates and bring them into the organization matters. It has an impact on the employee's future with the organization. Organizations aren't looking to hire employees so they can quit in six months. Rather, they want employees who will stay and grow with the company. Recruiters should expect the entire organization to be involved.

Customers are the final group. Organizations never want to lose a candidate *and* a customer at the same time. In a survey from *Recruiting Daily*, 23.8 percent of survey respondents stated that a positive candidate experience with an employer made them more likely to increase their relationships with employers' respective "brand alliances, product purchases or networking." Conversely, 11 percent had poor enough candidate experiences to cut all ties with a company.

Recruiters impact how people feel about the organization, which drives whether individuals recommend and purchase products and services from the company. What recruiters and hiring managers do affects the bottom line.

A Weak Recruiting Function Impacts the Entire Business

There's a well-worn saying that "people are a company's greatest asset." It's true. Don't let the fact that it's old and a cliché water down the message. Even with the talk of robots and artificial intelligence replacing humans, executives realize that talent is the ultimate competitive differentiator in the modern economy. Organizations need people to think up the ideas, build the products, sell the products, service the customers, and keep the operation going. The only way they're going to get people to do all that is by recruiting.

Over the past decade, we've seen rising and falling levels of unemployment. The one thing that's remained constant? Recruiting and retaining talent continues to be a top challenge for businesses. And the stakes are high. In an article in *Harvard Business Review*, 83 executives were asked to put a price tag on how much money they lost each day on a variety of issues. Guess what the top issue was. Yep, hiring the wrong employee was ranked number one with survey respondents, saying their companies waste approximately $9,000 a day.

That's why recruiting is important. Because when mistakes are made, they're expensive mistakes.

SECTION I: 3 Key Takeaways

- Recruiting is highly visible and the first step toward employee engagement and retention.
- Everyone in the organization needs to be trained in recruiting.
- Recruiting impacts the customer experience and, ultimately, the bottom line.

5 Resources to Make Your Job Easier

1. As part of its Effective Practice Guidelines series, the SHRM Foundation has a resource titled *Talent Acquisition: A Guide to Understanding and Managing the Recruitment Process*. It can be found under the "Our Work" section of its website.

2. For more information about the SHRM Competency Model, check out the book *Defining HR Success: 9 Critical Competencies for HR Professionals* by Kari R. Strobel, James N. Kurtessis, Debra J. Cohen, and Alexander Alonso.

3. Don't forget the SHRM Policy Action Center to stay on top of legislative issues impacting your profession.

4. SHRM's Resources & Tools web page offers sample recruiting job descriptions. Great if you need some creative inspiration in writing one.

5. Speaking of SHRM's Resources & Tools, the web page also provides sample hiring policies and procedures. They can provide a starting point for drafting your own.

SECTION II
Candidate Strategies

In Section II

Recruiting is all about the candidate, so let's start with a discussion about the first things a candidate sees and experiences: the company brand and how the company interacts with the candidate.

Organizations can have the best applicant tracking systems and a terrific company culture, but if they fail to engage candidates, candidates are not going to apply. So let's talk about how we get the candidate's attention. Hopefully, in a positive way!

CHAPTER 3:
Employment Branding

 CASE STUDY
CapTech Aligns Career and Consumer Branding

CapTech is a national technology firm offering a full suite of services including management consulting, systems integration, and data management. It has been counted among *Inc.* magazine's 5,000 fastest-growing private companies. Being a rapidly growing firm in a competitive industry, it knew it needed to show that the company was in tune with the market.

Because CapTech spent a significant amount of its recruiting efforts on unique-to-fill positions, it realized that building connections with passive candidates was important. The goal of firm leadership was to make it easy for the company to connect with potential candidates and easy for the candidates to stay engaged with the company.

CapTech's strategy was to build a talent network using social recruiting tools and mobile portals. It gave the company the speed it wanted to post new jobs and connect with applicants. Its philosophy was that the employment brand must align with the competitive nature of the business.

If you visit the firm's website (www.captechconsulting.com), the CapTech company culture comes through loud and clear in its messaging—"Others Talk, We Listen."

The success of aligning employment and consumer brands was tremendous. According to CapTech, it received hundreds of mobile submissions and employment applications via social networks like Facebook and Twitter. To stay competitive, CapTech tracks results and adjusts its recruiting strategy as appropriate.

Stories like this one from CapTech remind us that brand identity is key to our recruiting success. But what exactly is an employment brand, and how can organizations make sure they're developing one that candidates will be attracted to?

What Is Employment Branding, and Why Is It Important?

According to Wikipedia, the term "employer brand" was first introduced back in the 1990s by Simon Barrow and Tim Ambler in the *Journal of Brand Management*. Since then, I'll admit, the term has been abused, but the concept is still essential to business. Employer brand (aka employment brand) is the impression people have about working at the company.

Conceptually, a company's employer brand is like a consumer brand, how someone feels about the company's product or service. We can look at brands like Apple and Starbucks that don't even include their name in their logo, and we all know who they are, and we have a perception of their brand. Marketing executives will agree that the consumer brand is important, and recruiters should say the employer brand is important as well.

When it comes to employment branding, the challenge for recruiters is realizing that the company's consumer brand and employment brand are two different things but that those two different brands must align with each other. When these two brand strategies align, people say, "I love the brand, and I want to work for the company."

The challenge happens when people love one but not the other. For example, can you think of a company for which either of the following is accurate:

- You would buy the product in a heartbeat but never work there in a million years.
- You'd love to work there but would never buy the company's product or service.

To ensure alignment, it's critical for HR and talent acquisition to develop an employment brand as strong as the company's consumer brand. The payoff for a company with a positive and identifiable employment brand is a steady pipeline of qualified candidates.

Next-Gen Employment Branding: Having a Single Brand

Some people say that employment branding in the traditional sense we just discussed is gone. Same with consumer branding. Personally, I think that line of thinking might be driven by company culture. Organizations that insist that employer branding is dead have an opportunity to merge the two together and create one company brand—a brand that will be used to attract and retain customers, candidates, and employees.

Some might argue that their organization already has one brand. Under that one brand, the organization creates specific marketing materials to attract customers but different collateral to attract candidates. Also, some organizations create marketing products for employees, like T-shirts, that promote the company and instill pride. But what we're talking about here is one strategy that addresses all audiences at the same time.

A couple of years ago at the Great Place to Work conference, I had the opportunity to hear Blake Irving, CEO of GoDaddy, talk about creating a singular brand. He shared that the organization was moving away from that type of "one brand with three different types of marketing collateral," to a single brand that integrates all its messaging and marketing collateral. The example he gave was a campaign titled "GoYou. GoDaddy." You can search for the video on the Internet. The goal of the campaign was threefold:

- If I'm a customer, I know exactly how GoDaddy is going to support me and my business.
- If I'm a candidate, I understand the GoDaddy culture—the everyday hard work that's expected to keep customers' business dreams alive.
- If I'm an employee, I'm proud to be a part of the GoDaddy customer's success.

One brand. For multiple audiences. For GoDaddy, a huge benefit of this approach is that it reaches people who might be looking at GoDaddy for more than one reason—for instance, the customer who might want a job or the employee who's thinking about starting a hosted website "side hustle."

To build a singular brand message, human resources and marketing must collaborate on what their single message will be and how the organization should convey one brand. This single message cannot simply be a mashup of "here's what we can do for customers" and "here's what we can do for candidates." It's going to be a challenge to blend messaging, but it can be done. One approach organizations can consider is to start by creating a more traditional brand structure, especially if they don't already have one, and then look at a singular brand as the next iteration in organizational brand development (Employment Branding 2.0 if you will).

Regardless of the brand strategy your organization uses, the point is to have a *successful* brand. Because when it works, it will elevate the entire organization. In the GoDaddy example, everyone sees how they fit. And that's what engagement is all about—engaging customers, candidates, and employees.

 CASE STUDY
Building a Global Employment Brand

mYngle is the leading multilanguage global platform for live online language learning. Marina Tognetti, mYngle's CEO, started the company after facing challenges with her own language learning.

At the time, she was a corporate director with eBay. She knew how to market, manage, and run companies. She knew how to be successful in the digital space.

Tognetti saw that the China market was booming and wanted to be a part of it. She knew if she wanted to do business with China, she needed to learn Chinese, but learning the Chinese language is hard. She bought CDs and DVDs and became very frustrated with the language skills courses that were offered to business executives. So she took matters into her own hands and founded mYngle.

mYngle offers over 40 languages to its customers. When mYngle was founded, Tognetti wanted to set the firm apart by offering not only the traditional language instruction options but the hard-to-find ones as well. She says: "Where language instruction services are limited is in the tier two languages (e.g., Japanese, Chinese, Russian) as well as Asia Pacific languages (Indonesian, Malaysian, Thai). mYngle wanted to make sure that customers could get all their language needs in one place. So, we offer the more common languages like English, French, German, and Italian, along with the hard-to-find ones."

Diversity is a core value at mYngle, and the company employs a global staff across three offices: its corporate office in Holland, a customer service office in the Philippines, and a programming office in Vietnam. Tognetti explains why diversity is an essential part of its brand: "mYngle is a language company. We offer a service that represents diversity. People want to learn languages because they want to communicate with someone who is different than they are. Languages bridge diversity."

mYngle feels its competitive advantage is bringing people from different cultures together and using their corporate values to set its business apart from others. Many language schools are local. Tognetti says learning a language is about more than just grammar. "Language is about more than sentence structure. It's about the cultural perceptions of different words. Our instructors also teach the context of the word. You can understand the sentence and not understand the person. It's also equally important to learn how to listen in different cultures."

The organization also sets its brand apart from others by delivering its courses online. Tognetti says mYngle is focused on their strengths. "We don't try to do it all. Our advantage is not having an education background. Unlike many educational institutions, mYngle understands the student is the customer. We've built the company around the customer and their needs—language instruction that's flexible, personalized, and immediately useful on the job."

As you can see from mYngle's story, building a global brand includes the same components of building a local brand: understanding your customers and aligning your business with their needs.

3 Steps for Creating an Employment Brand

I view the process of creating an employment brand like a traditional gap analysis. There's no sense in creating new processes when proven ones will work just fine.

Step 1. Assess where the organization is right now. Don't sugarcoat it. If your brand reputation stinks, just admit it. That's why you're doing this exercise in the first place. You can use existing documents and resources to get some sense of your current employment brand. Here are a few examples:

- Employee satisfaction survey results.
- Stay and exit interviews.
- Glassdoor.com reviews (or reviews from similar sites).

FIGURE 3.1: Employment Brand Cycle

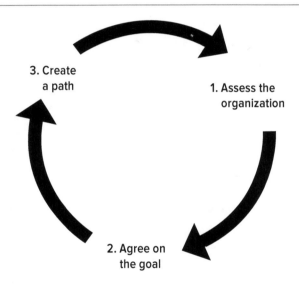

If you don't feel that you have enough information available, focus groups could help fill in the blanks. You could ask employees to describe their work experience in three words. That would tell you a lot! Another way to obtain the same information would be to send out an online survey to employees. You could then import the results into a spreadsheet and easily tabulate them. Then consider turning the results into a word cloud (www.wordclouds.com) or a one-page summary of charts. A visual summary would be a very powerful picture of the company's current brand.

Step 2. Agree on where the organization wants to be. To me, this is the most difficult step. What makes a brand powerful is when everyone agrees on the qualities they want the brand to represent. Otherwise, it's just confusion. Let me share an example using personal branding. Ever met someone that seems to do "everything"? I have. The person says that he or she is a "human resource professional, recruiter, brand strategist, blogger, evangelist, and HR technology expert." That person is wearing a lot of hats. And if he or she is managing to be exceptional at all of them—fantastic. But as someone on the outside, it's hard to know what the person is really good at. Or when I should refer a piece of business to them.

Now, apply the same thing to companies. Having a "mile wide, inch deep" business strategy could cause candidates to be confused about your brand. So companies need to spend some dedicated time thinking about *what they want to be known for*. If candidates only remember one thing about the organization, what do you want it to be? That might be a good question to ask the senior management team.

Step 3. Create a path to get from where you are to where you want to be. Step one will produce brand findings that you absolutely want to keep, as well as some you want to change, which is perfectly fine.

It will take time for organizations to make a complete transition from where they are today to where they want to be. That's fine too. The goal is to always be moving toward your desired state.

For organizations with an established brand, this three-step process is also a great way to conduct an employment brand audit. Make sure what you're hearing in step one aligns with step two. If you're starting to hear a disconnect, that means one of two things:

- The organization isn't living up to its brand promise.
- The brand promise is changing.

Either way, recruiting professionals need to raise the issue because it directly impacts their ability to source and select talent.

Once an organization has created its employment brand, it now must make sure the rest of the world knows about it.

How to Establish Your Employment Brand

A company's brand starts with its mission, vision, and organizational values. I'm a firm believer that organizations need to let their mission, vision, and values drive their culture. In turn, culture drives strategy—including talent strategies, like branding.

The biggest challenge when it comes to mission, vision, and values is living them. More times than I care to admit, I've seen organizations adopt hip, trendy values because they think that's what it takes to attract customers and employees. They would be wrong. Candidates come in for interviews, see the mission and vision of the company, and think "Wow! This is the place I want to work." Then they are hired, and reality sets in. The words painted on the walls and printed on business cards are simply for show. There's a disconnect between the published values and company reality.

A LinkedIn survey reported that approximately 65 percent of working professionals say disagreeing with the company's mission or values is a deal-breaker when considering a future employer. Honestly, that should be okay. Companies should want to hire employees who agree with their values.

Organizations need to be honest about their real values and own them. I remember being interviewed for my first human resource job. My soon-to-be boss told me, "We're a work-hard, play-hard environment." She was right. That's exactly what the company was. She didn't say it was balanced. She said the company did everything with gusto. And guess what? I took the job and loved working there. So companies should not be afraid of telling candidates what they are and what they value. Candidates will appreciate the honesty because it sets the right expectations.

That's what branding is about—setting expectations. For candidates, it's communicating that "this is who we are as a company, what we believe is important, and how you can expect to be treated if you work here."

Monitoring Your Employment Brand

If you want to get a sense of whether the organization is living its values, you can visit rating sites like Glassdoor. For example, a Glassdoor rating shows:

- From employees: pros and cons of working at the company.
- From employees: advice to management.
- From employees: some salary ranges.
- From candidates: the interview process and some interview questions.

You can see how this would be very valuable information to someone who is looking to apply with your company.

It's also very valuable information for the company. If the company has aligned its brand and culture, it will enjoy good reviews that recruiters can use to attract more candidates. If there's a disconnect between the brand and reality, chances are pretty good that it will show up on a rating site somewhere.

How to Respond to Negative Online Reviews

Even the best employers have negative reviews. Not every employee is 100 percent happy. It's not the end of the world if the company receives a poor review on a rating site. But it does raise the question, "Should the company respond?"

First, the company should decide if it's going to respond. While the company may not like the comment, replying may not be beneficial. Next, if the company responds, it needs to be committed to improvement. Otherwise, the reply will sound fake and only make the situation worse.

Organizations that want to keep their negative online reviews to a minimum should consider more proactive measures to solicit feedback from candidates and employees. Examples include surveying new hires about the application process and interviewing them as part of the onboarding process.

Job seekers are doing their homework before responding to job openings. They want to know that the company they're applying to "walks the talk." Rating and review sites offer a glimpse into the answer, and organizations need to be aware of this. If the company is doing the right things, that is, taking care of employees and customers, then the ratings often take care of themselves.

Benefits as a Brand Differentiator

Once the brand has been defined, organizations should examine their employee benefits package to make sure that what they offer employees aligns with the brand. It doesn't send the right message to tell candidates the company values work/life balance and then not offer any programs that support it.

Danroy T. "Dan" Henry, chief culture officer at Bright Horizons, said that benefits are your organization's best chance to deliver on your culture. "You can't just pick a benefit because it seems like a good idea. To get the return on investment, you need to know what problems you're trying to solve—the specific problems your people are having—and respond to those." Henry suggested that having that intelligence from employees will help you can make the right decisions about which benefits to offer.

Is your benefits package authentic? There's a temptation in today's business world to try to emulate the companies that get all the press for being cool. So you start offering nap pods and massages. But if "cool" isn't your brand, you're going to communicate disingenuousness rather than modern. Your employees will see right through it.

Is it something people need? A big part of being a great culture is being responsive. As an example, check your data on your 401(k) participation. Are there a lot of employees on board? If not, you should ask yourself why. Bright Horizons did just that. And it found that a lot of people are so financially stressed these days, they're just not able to think about retirement. They're too busy dealing with today's expenses to keep up. So instead of a gym subsidy, the firm considered offering employees time with financial advisors to ask questions about plan participation. It's an example of how organizations must do their due diligence to know exactly where the stress points are for their employees.

Does it serve your goals? One of the interesting things Bright Horizons learned from its research is that where people work matters. People get excited—and engaged with the company—when they love their employer, even more than if they just love their job. The Bright Horizons research refers to those companies "dream companies," and these dream companies achieve goals like productivity, retention, and recruitment. Henry shared the benefits that make a culture a Dream Company (and the researchers know this from talking to thousands of employees):

- Opportunities to grow careers.
- Assistance to help balance work and personal lives.
- The feeling that the employees' well-being matters to the company.

To choose benefits that fit with your culture and employment brand, look for benefits that provide those three results for employees. After the company's benefits package is in alignment with the employment brand, communicate the benefits effectively to candidates and employees. I asked Henry to share some of the best ways to do this. He emphasized the need to think beyond orientation. "First and foremost: one-time employee-orientation memos are not enough. Same for once-a-year open-enrollment memos. You need to make sure your information is consistently out there." Henry offered two suggestions for communicating benefits:

1. **Keep your language simple.** Let people know where to find everything, and make sure you're targeting people with relevant information. To do the latter, create profiles using employee attributes like age, career history, family circumstances, and professional goals and target specific information to the people who fit those profiles. It's so much better than inundating all employees with all information at all times (and let's face it—they'll delete it anyway if it doesn't apply to them).
2. **Be creative!** Think like a marketer! Go beyond the conventional e-mail. Use snail mail, company meetings, flyers in high-traffic areas, live testimonials, and benefits fairs. And make sure you're finding pathways to all your people—newcomers, veterans, tech-savvy folks, those without individual e-mail addresses, people at a desk in the home office, remote employees—everyone.

To evaluate the effectiveness of organizational benefits, companies can look at utilization analysis to determine how much a benefit is being used. Henry also suggested taking the extra step of surveying employees about their benefits package. "Surveys are great tools to find out what your employees are thinking. But they must be set up to 'listen' for the things you need them to listen for. A truly illustrative survey will be a mix of life and work questions, including very specific questions like, 'What are your sources of work stress?' Doing that will give you important insights into things like how the benefits you have are working, and which ones you might need to add or change." Henry added that bold questions are going to get you the most relevant answers. "For example, a startup tech company might be surprised to find that their Millennials are now having children and are stressed about how much time it's taking them to get from the child care center to the office. Maybe your employees are stressed about paying for a child's college education. You won't know any of that if you're only asking about the company health plan."

As you think about surveying employees about their benefits, be brave enough to ask the tough questions about how HR is doing. HR and talent acquisition play a huge role in bringing the company's employment brand to life. Ask employees questions like, "Is HR responsive enough?" The answers may sting a little, but you'll find solutions.

Finally, don't make the big mistake of using a "one and done" approach when it comes to asking employees for feedback. Be sure to loop back to older surveys to see how (or if) the company's benefits programs are moving the dial.

Use Stories to Share Your Brand

One of the key ingredients to organizational culture is its stories. At Globoforce's WorkHuman conference, I listened to Steve Denning, an expert in organizational storytelling, outline the four principles to effective storytelling:

1. Be true.
2. Be positive.
3. Be succinct.
4. Show growth.

As I think about these principles, I'm reminded of the opportunities we have to engage candidates and employees with our brand using storytelling. It could be said that the principles of engagement are based on truth, positivity, effectiveness, efficiency, and a desire to move forward. So culture, brand, and engagement are very much aligned. There are five types of stories you can use to connect candidates and employees with your organization:

1. **Stories about the history of the company.** Years ago, I worked for an airline, and one of the first stories candidates heard was about the founder. He was the guy "who sold you the ticket, put your bags on the plane, and then flew the plane." We told the story during recruiting fairs, in orientation, and in other settings. The story not only gave employees a history lesson, but it told them something about the company's founding principles.

2. **Stories explaining how decisions are made.** At some point, the same airline was looking to save some serious expenses. Instead of just cutting the budget, it went to employees and explained the situation. It created a suggestion contest that financially rewarded employees for developing ideas that either increased revenue or reduced expenses. The result positively impacted the organization in millions of dollars.

3. **Stories about employees delivering exceptional service.** During a business trip in Tampa, FL, I checked into a hotel that displayed a sign at the front desk warning about mosquitoes in the area and giving recommendations to take precautions; the media was just starting to report on the Zika virus. In fact, the hotel said it would provide bug spray to guests on request. Since I didn't have bug spray with

me, I asked about it. The front desk clerk looked around and couldn't find any bug spray behind the front desk. Instead of telling me that he couldn't find any or the hotel was out of it, he walked over to the gift shop, grabbed a package of bug spray, told the cashier to charge it to the hotel, and handed it to me. I will tell that story for years.

4. **Stories about how employees interact with each other.** Most of the organizations I've worked for have used some form of collaborative hiring in which teams were formed to strategize and recruit. One of the things I've learned is that candidates immediately sense if the recruiting team is truly a team. They can tell by the way the team members interact and by the stories they share about the organization.

5. **Stories about what the world will be like in the future.** I grew up in Orlando, FL, during the time that Walt Disney World was being built. During this time, a television show called *The Wonderful World of Disney* aired, and Walt Disney himself shared with viewers a sneak peek into the construction of Walt Disney World. I remember watching him explain EPCOT (Experimental Prototype Community of Tomorrow) for the first time. Today, organizations have a powerful way to share their stories directly with consumers using mobile, social media, and video.

Stories tell candidates, employees, and customers about the organization. They allow people to see what the company is really all about (that is, the company's brand). Stories create a sense of company "community." And they create engagement.

Conveying Your Employment Brand During the Recruitment Process

One of the first ways we communicate our employment brand is through job descriptions. If a firm is hiring a new position, creating a job description is the first step. If the opening is to replace an employee who is moving up or moving on, it's still a good idea to review and update the job description. However, Tim Sackett, president of HRU Technical Resources and author of the blog *The Tim Sackett Project*, suggested there are two types of job descriptions: legal and marketing. "Job descriptions [JDs] as we know them are dead; it's more of legal document now. The new JD is really a marketing document that helps you attract talent."

Don't panic. This doesn't necessarily mean that traditional job descriptions will go away anytime soon. Traditional job descriptions have multiple uses, some of them being legal; therefore, legal departments will want to have a say in the decision to eliminate them. But recruiters may want to start thinking about a more user-friendly way to share job responsibilities. Sackett said the key and the challenge is creativity. "The biggest issue I see in creating exciting job descriptions and postings is corporate talent acquisition pros feeling like they're not creative enough. They don't have to be great; no one is asking them to write *Harry Potter*. Just add in some of their passion for the company and why they love working there."

Regardless of the approach you take with your job descriptions, I'd like to believe that most organizations realize job descriptions are valuable. In my experience, the challenge isn't convincing people job descriptions are valuable. It's keeping them up-to-date. Sackett agreed that reviewing job descriptions before the recruiting process begins is imperative, even for those positions that the recruiter must fill multiple times in a year:

> Each position, while the basic job description might be the same, filling this one position also fills a dynamic within the team that might be missing. "Okay, we need an emergency room RN, the same as the last ten we've filled from a skills standpoint, but right now on my team I have a bunch of folks who are very analytical by-the-book types, I need a nurse who is more big picture and willing to work around the edges." Those are two very different people, but both need some very specific skills.

Sackett described this job description review session as an "intake" meeting, adding that most recruiters are not handling them correctly:

> I think recruiters hate intake meetings because they do them and never get anything new out of the managers. I think those people are doing these meetings wrong. Recruiters who can work themselves into a talent advisor role, value these meetings as a time to speak strategically with the hiring manager about the makeup of their team, where the manager sees her team in the future, and how this hire fits into that strategy. During these meetings, the recruiter becomes the expert in talent and positions themselves as an important part of this hiring manager's inner circle in developing a world-class team.

So what's the best way to conduct an intake meeting? Sackett offered two tricks that have worked well for him:

Trick #1. Sit in their office and don't leave until they've completed what you ask. You smile when you read this, but if you sit there long enough, I guarantee you they'll review it!

Trick #2. Don't make them do it. Job descriptions are boring, and no one wants to read them. So design something managers would want to read. Develop a job posting that speaks to both the job and the leadership style of that specific manager, that describes the exciting projects this new hire will work on, and that defines your great culture. Turn your boring job description into an exciting marketing document to attract talent. I guarantee that, if you put information in your job posting about the hiring manager, he or she will want to read it completely and give feedback.

I know from experience that Sackett's suggestions work, but it takes time to work up the nerve to actually force the issue—especially if the hiring manager is a member of the senior management team. Sackett offered advice for how to handle hiring managers who want to change the job description after the recruiting process has started:

> If a hiring manager wants to change the job description after we've started recruiting, I usually [want to] have them shot! I know, this is a real problem, but it's only a problem because you didn't first sit down and really dig into this position in the first place to find out what the hiring manager needed—beyond the boring job description—before you started. So, if they [want to change the job description], I let them, because it's my fault to begin with (well, at least 99 percent of the time). If I'm doing great intake meetings, I rarely have a hiring manager ask to change the job description after we've started recruiting. In the rare cases that they do, I know there's a legitimate reason for wanting the change, and I'm fine with doing it at that point.

Besides the manager who feels that reviewing the job description is unnecessary and a waste of time, another dynamic to consider is the new manager who has little recruiting experience. In my book, *Manager Onboarding: 5 Steps for Setting New Leaders Up for Success*, I mention that recruiting is one of those things that new managers need to know when they start recruiting. Managers don't have to know how to recruit on their first day. Training a manager six months or a year before they actually start hiring could be a waste of company resources. And, as Sackett pointed out, a waste of your time:

> What you'll see is [that] the less a hiring manager hires, the more [he or she will] want to change the job description because [he or she hasn't] even dialed it in yet. A good way to deal with these managers is to do some very fast initial surface sourcing of some candidate resumes that you haven't even screened yet and have them give you some quick feedback on what they see based on the initial job description. Once they see what's on the market, many times you'll see these changes come out right away on what they want, and it takes you about twenty minutes to print a handful of resumes for them to look at, which saves you hours in wasted time recruiting.

Job descriptions perform many functions. They're a legal document and a performance document. As Sackett pointed out, they're a starting point to a larger talent discussion on how you're helping hiring managers improve their team and their own personal performance. But for them to be effective at attracting and hiring talent, they must reflect your organization, and they must stay current.

Companies Are Being Talked about on Social Media (Whether They Like It or Not)

Whole books and conferences are dedicated to the topic of social recruiting. This book does not devote much discussion to the topic, but I do want to mention social media as it relates to branding. I'm still amazed at the number of people responsible for hiring who are not social savvy. Social media isn't a fad. It's not going anywhere. LinkedIn was founded in 2002. Facebook was founded in 2004, and Twitter in 2006. Billions of people around the world use these platforms daily.

If you or your company decides not to permit social media, that's fine. But keep in mind that someone in your company's competitive set might. It's also possible that people are talking about your company—good, bad, or indifferent—on social media. For that reason alone, it's worth understanding the concepts behind social media and regularly evaluating your participation levels. Like everything in business today, social media changes regularly, and the reasons you chose to opt out a year or two ago might be the reasons you want to get involved today.

Organizations that want to build their brand presence are including social media in their strategy. They are making it easy for candidates to connect with them on social media and to learn about the company and open jobs via social media.

In the book *A Necessary Evil: Managing Employee Activity on Facebook, Twitter, LinkedIn ... and the Hundreds of Other Social Media Sites*, author Aliah D. Wright wrote that the number one best practice in social recruiting is to be social and sociable. "You cannot recruit where you are not present. Develop a diverse strategy for recruiting across all social media channels to reach a broader, more diverse talent pool."

Another aspect of social media that's great for your brand is listening. Once we create our brand promise, we're often so focused on pushing it out that we forget to take the time to hear what others might be saying about it. Wright suggested developing relationships on social platforms to understand the market. "Listening to candidates, engaging them in conversation, and developing relationships that may later lead to jobs is only the beginning. Their connections and expertise may prove fruitful in other areas as well. Social listening tools, of which there are hundreds, can identify candidates for future recruitment."

The last component to consider regarding social media and branding is maintenance. Wright reminded organizations not to set it and forget it: "Do not erect social sites and ignore them; remember, simply using hashtags such as #jobs and #careers is not enough either. Pay attention to tweet chats (pre-arranged Twitter discussions) related to your industry and the people participating in them. Comment on blogs too."

Social media is a tool that can elevate your brand and provide a medium to engage job seekers. It involves creating a strategy that aligns with the rest of your recruiting efforts and commitment from the organization.

Gamification Adds Fun and Educates Candidates about the Brand

I used to work in the hospitality industry. It's a fun industry to work in, but it's hard work. Let me repeat that—it's very hard work. As a recruiter, I often found that candidates were more in tune with the fun aspect of the industry than the hard-work side. I wanted candidates to understand both. I can't tell you how many times new employees came into HR to resign because they didn't realize what the work was all about. Totally the company's fault, but it's still frustrating and a waste of resources.

Years ago, to give outsiders a glimpse into the complex operations that take place at a hotel, Marriott International created a virtual environment that simulated the real work atmosphere with My Marriott Hotel. The game was a brand awareness and educational tool that gave people a behind-the-scenes look at what running a hotel is like. Here's how it worked: At first, players managed a virtual hotel restaurant kitchen. They bought equipment and ingredients on a budget, hired, and trained employees, and served guests. Points were earned for happy customers and lost for poor service, and ultimately, players were rewarded when their operation turned a profit. After successfully managing the kitchen, they could move on to other areas of hotel operations.

FIGURE 3.2: My Marriott International Virtual Environment

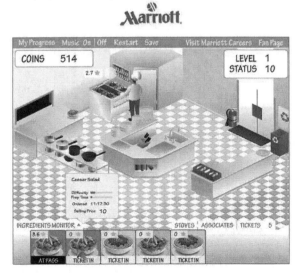

Source: www.blogs.marriott.com/.a/6a0120a73c0f0d970b014e8934ca8a970d-popup

The game was not only fun, but it answered questions for candidates who were curious about what it meant to work for a hotel and what simply went on inside, especially if they had never stayed in one.

Not every organization has the resources or inclination to create a game. That's not the point. The point is that educating candidates about your brand doesn't have to be boring. It can be fun—for them and for you.

Career Portals Are a Candidate's First Impression of the Company Brand

You might be wondering why I'm addressing career portals (aka career websites) at the end of this chapter and not the beginning. It's because the company's brand drives what the company's career site will look like—not the other way around. Here's a quick checklist of what to consider in your company's career portal:

Develop the company culture and branding. People visiting the site want to know what to expect from the brand and the employer. Let job seekers know about the organization and its mission, vision, and values. Candidates not only want to know what the company does but what it considers important. From a talent acquisition perspective, knowing this information helps candidates decide to engage with the organization.

✓ **Give readers welcoming and engaging content.** The way we communicate says something about us. Whether it's job descriptions or a video about the company, the words we use and the phrases we choose allow candidates and new hires to engage with the company. Job seekers want to feel the company is honest, transparent, and relatable.

✓ **Make sure the site is visually pleasing.** There's an old saying that a picture says a thousand words, and it has never been truer. Include images, images, and more images! Not only can recruiters tell people what it's like to work at their company, but they can also *show* them. Pictures of employees having fun doing serious work are priceless! Just remember to keep it real.

✓ **Provide visitors with an intuitive experience.** Technology today isn't about being easy—it's about being intuitive. Candidates shouldn't have to call or e-mail the company to figure out how to upload their resume or how to apply for a job. Having intuitive technology tells candidates that the company put some thought into the user experience, and that thoughtfulness translates into how the company will treat them as an employee.

✓ **Highlight education and training.** Talent acquisition is very competitive, and showing candidates the investment the company plans to make in the employee's success gives the organization a competitive advantage. It also makes for a better workforce and organization. If you want employees to be committed to the organization, they need to feel as though their success is also the company's success.

Finally, once the employment brand is established and the company's career portal is in place, develop a review and maintenance schedule. Just because the site is up and running doesn't mean the process is over. In fact, it's just getting started. The talent acquisition team needs to gather regular feedback from users, review the career site for new features, and plan for updates.

Employment Branding Is More Than a Buzzword

Employment branding isn't dead. It might be a subset of the company brand or integrated into the company brand, but it's there. An employer brand drives what candidates think of the organization and contributes to their decision whether to apply.

So call it what you will, but employment branding doesn't dismiss the value of having a branding strategy and working that strategy.

TIPS
3 Tips for Taking Your Employment Brand to the Next Level

Consumer brands change and evolve over time. Employment brands do the same. At some point, your organization will want to evaluate the relevance and effectiveness of its existing brand. Here's how three talent acquisition professionals defined their employment brand strategy.

1. *Jim Collins is senior director of talent acquisition at Ultimate Software, a leading provider of human capital management (HCM) solutions in the cloud. The company has been ranked seventh on* Forbes *magazine's 2017 list of the 100 Most Innovative Growth Companies.*

> Ultimate Software has a wonderful story and employment brand, boasting numerous awards and a high Glassdoor ranking, but we believe the key to a successful recruiting program is hiring for cultural fit.
>
> At Ultimate, we look beyond each resume to uncover the real "intangibles." Some of the key intangibles we look for are empathy, long-term leadership, situational awareness, ambition, vulnerability, gravitas, and hunger. How does a person work across all functions, and are they smart—while remaining humble? Do they have good judgment? Would they fit well in a diverse, world-class culture?
>
> People who are quick to share credit and define team success as more important than their own success work well in our people-first culture, which is based on trust. The best part is, when we hire these special talents, they refer all their like-minded peers. We truly are passionate about finding the "right fit" for every position, because when you hire someone, you're not just hiring their resume—you're

onboarding the entire spectrum of the person, what has shaped them and what they have overcome to get to where they are.

2. **Alexandra Levit** *is a partner at PeopleResults, a talent and change management firm, and the author of the international bestseller* They Don't Teach Corporate in College. *Her goal is to prepare organizations and their employees for meaningful careers in the future workplace.*

Recent research by Employer Brand International found social media (58 percent) to be the No. 1 channel for communicating the employer brand, but only 21 percent of organizations have mobile-optimized methods for doing so. These numbers, particularly the latter one, are too low. Mobile devices such as smartphones, tablets, and phablets make that information and computing power accessible to users around the world.

As these technologies gain greater and greater momentum, they are profoundly changing the power and reach of the employer brand. Now your job is to use the same digital tools that solicit customers in order to talk about your brand in a way that will attract top talent, which means creating and managing interactive, mobile-efficient career websites, CRM campaigns tied to an email database, a holistic yet culturally appropriate social media and content strategy, and real-time employee feedback and communication tools.

3. **Shaunda Zilich** *describes her job as "selling experience." As GE's global employment brand leader, she is responsible for modernizing its recruitment and bolstering its employer brand across all functions and regions, in all GE businesses, and with all GE employees as advocates.*

If you have an employment or consumer brand that is already established, I would encourage you to incorporate two alternate ways of thinking in each of your recruiting strategies. The first is **to think to yourself in each contact with a lead/candidate ... "Am I pushing or pulling?"** Things like:

- Am I pushing information on "career channels" or am I meeting people where they are and enticing them to learn more? Connect on the "where."
- Am I pushing information about us or am I pulling their interest because I'm showing them we care about the same issues? Connect on the "why."

The second way of thinking I would encourage is to **understand and use methods where candidates/leads like to communicate**. Usually, these methods will be mechanisms that provide:

- Real-time conversation
- Transparent/real points of view (non-polished)
- Interaction/engagement on things they want to talk about

Obviously, chat and text come to mind, but also video, Facebook Live, Instagram, Snapchat, and others can be great channels to connect with talent in this way.

CHAPTER 4:
Candidate Experience

 CASE STUDY
Virgin Media Loses Candidates and Customers

Back in 2014, Virgin Media realized it had a problem. The company had discovered that it had a -29 Net Promoter Score (NPS). The NPS is an index that measures the willingness of customers to recommend the company's products or services.

Here's some background about the company. Virgin Media is a British company providing telephone, television, and broadband Internet services to businesses and consumers. In 2014, approximately 135,000 people applied for a job with the company.

By conducting an organizational assessment, Virgin Media came to discover that the way job candidates were being treated, specifically the way they were being rejected, was having an impact on the company's bottom line.

To understand the scope of the issue, Virgin Media reached out to previous candidates. It discovered that the company had lost 7,500 customers (18 percent of their applicants) because of a direct candidate rejection or poor candidate experience. Virgin Media estimated this translated into a $6.4 million loss.

To turn the situation around, Virgin Media ran a series of workshops to identify the employee value proposition (EVP) of working at the company. This information was used to create candidate experience maps, which outlined a seamless and enhanced experience.

The full initiative is being phased in, but the lesson is clear: organizations cannot afford to lose customers because of their candidate experience. And the cost of losing customers can total millions of dollars.

The candidate experience is every touchpoint in the hiring process. It includes employment branding, career websites, interviews, offer letters, background screening, and more. It's the experience that a candidate has before he or she becomes an employee. And while it's implied that the candidate experience is with your organization, remember that it's also with the vendors that are a part of your hiring process (background screening companies are an example).

It should be obvious that candidates will want to work for companies that provide a positive candidate experience and not work for companies that don't. The candidate experience is an indicator of how a person will be treated as an employee, but it goes further than that. A company's candidate experience impacts not only hiring but the bottom line.

According to the *2016 Talent Board North American Candidate Experience Research Report*, 41 percent of job seekers who give their overall candidate experience a one-star rating (on a five-star scale, with five being the most positive rating) will definitely take their alliances, product purchases, and relationships elsewhere. Conversely, 64 percent of job seekers who give their overall candidate experience a positive five-star rating will definitely increase their employer relationships.

Yet many organizations do not focus on the quality of their candidate experience. A survey from CareerArc reported that nearly 60 percent of candidates have a poor candidate experience, and 72 percent of those candidates share that negative experience either online or with someone directly. The good news is that developing an excellent candidate experience doesn't have to be hard, time-consuming, or expensive.

Creating the Candidate Experience

Use the same three-step process outlined in the last chapter on employment branding to create a candidate experience. Again, I'm all about using proven processes, and the gap analysis is a solid approach:

1. **Assess where the organization is right now.** There's an opportunity to collect information from new hires about the candidate experience. If possible, you may want to obtain feedback from candidates who were not hired—whether that was the candidate's or the company's decision.
2. **Reach consensus on what the candidate experience will be.** This could be a challenge, but it's essential for the organization to agree on how it wants to interact and communicate with candidates. The recruiting function will want to have a say in this.
3. **Develop a plan to bridge the gap.** I'm a big fan of the SMART format (see below) when it comes to goals and plans. It allows individuals and organizations to thoroughly document their activities, assign responsibility, and establish a timeline for completion.

FYI
SMART Planning

Years ago, I worked for a company where, every time something went wrong, the company president held a meeting to discuss how we were going to fix the problem. We had to create something called "a SMART plan" explaining the steps we were going to take. Sad to say, we developed a lot of SMART plans. I thought it was some form of punishment.

It wasn't until I started studying for my human resource certification that I learned SMART plans have been around for many years and were not created as a form of torture by senior leadership. The project management term was first used in 1981 by George T. Doran. SMART is an acronym:

- **S, Specific** represents exactly what you would like to accomplish. Think of it as the who, what, where, when, which, and why of the goal.
- **M, Measurable** answers the question of how success is measured.
- **A, Actionable (sometimes seen as Achievable or Attainable)** outlines the steps needed to complete the goal.
- **R, Responsible (other versions use Realistic or Relevant)** identifies the people needed to reach this goal.
- **T, Time-bound (or Trackable)** establishes the time frame to achieve the goal.

Over the years, I've found the SMART acronym easy to remember, so I mold it for creating meeting minutes and action plans. I can't think of a better way to create a plan to get from point A to point B:

- What are we going to do? (Specific)
- How will we measure our success? (Measurable)
- What are the steps that will help us attain our goal? (Actionable)
- Who will be responsible for each step? (Responsible)
- When will the task be completed? (Time-bound)

SMART plans can be used for individual goals, department plans, and even organizational strategy. You can create an Excel spreadsheet to document your plan and progress.

4 Ways to Improve the Candidate Experience

Organizations with a candidate experience strategy in place realize the work isn't over. You'll want to regularly audit your process to ensure it's working the way you intended. And look for trends that you might want to incorporate. There will always be a reason to improve the candidate experience.

The most obvious way to improve the candidate experience is by treating candidates with respect, so I'm not going to include that in the list. Every organization needs to understand that candidates are interviewing it and making decisions about the quality of the company. The hiring process is a two-way street. That being said, there are a few other tactics that organizations might want to consider:

1. Market the company. The *Talent Board North American Candidate Experience Research Report* noted that most candidates continue to take control of their job search, with 75 percent of candidates conducting their own job search research across multiple channels before applying. Company values and employee testimonials are two of the most valuable types of marketing content for candidates at 42 percent and 36 percent, respectively.

Organizations can include their employee values on their company website and career webpages. They can also add information about their values to the company pages on social sites like LinkedIn and Facebook.

In addition, organizations can use employee testimonials as soundbites in job advertisements or compile them as a video to be housed on the company website or shown at job fairs. The Cheesecake Factory once put together a testimonial video asking employees to finish the sentence, "The Cheesecake Factory is a great place to _____." Employees talked about having "cheesecake in their veins," and "I have a family here," and "The company cares about me."

Recruiters cannot take for granted that everyone knows about the company or that, if the company builds a new career website, people will automatically visit. Recruiters need to make sure that the company message is reaching the places where candidates are. And if employees love working for the company, find a way to share that with candidates.

2. Educate candidates. During the 2017 TAtech Spring Congress, I had the opportunity to hear Lindsay Stanton from Digi-Me and Katie Roth of Aureon talk about engaging candidates and enhancing the experience through educational videos. Aureon is an Iowa-based company that provides business services including temporary and direct-hire staffing solutions. It partnered with Digi-Me to create candidate videos that would not only help promote job openings but demystify the hiring process.

It might be tempting to think that video is expensive and difficult to create. And that used to be true. However, candidates today want the truth. They want authenticity, not a slick production. Don't get me wrong; there are still times when high-quality production value is important. The point here is not to discount video.

Consider adding some video to the candidate experience. It could be about the company, the department, the job, the work environment, and the benefits of working there.

Take it one step further and create a video about the recruiting process. It shouldn't be a secret to candidates.

Want to really kick it up a notch? Consider filming a couple of videos about how to interview well and about the best ways to follow up after the interview. That's information a candidate can use in any job search. The videos can reside on your careers web page. It could be a way to keep job seekers engaged with your company.

One last thing: Don't assume that these suggestions about adding video to the candidate experience are only for executive positions. According to Roth, Aureon achieves a high response rate from skilled trade positions using video. The digital age is changing the experience, and video can create a competitive advantage.

3. Respond to candidates. I've always worked in industries in which candidates could be customers. It made me realize that I didn't want to be responsible for losing a candidate and a customer at the same time. One of the ways we were able to improve the candidate experience at my previous employers was by closing the loop with every person who applied. Please note: I didn't say that every person got the answer he or she wanted to hear or received a personal phone call. But everyone received some sort of acknowledgment.

Forty-seven percent of candidates were still waiting to hear back from employers more than two months after they applied, according to the *2016 Talent Board North American Candidate Experience Research Report*. Plus, only 20 percent of candidates received an e-mail from a recruiter or hiring manager notifying them they were not being considered, and only 8 percent received a phone call from a recruiter or hiring manager notifying them they were not being considered.

The good news for employers is that today's technology solutions allow companies to create standardized responses with personalization options, so candidates aren't left wondering. While they may not receive the response that they were hoping for, they will remember the fact that the company provided closure in a respectful way.

4. Make the company "shareable." Speaking of sharing, it's important for organizations to connect with potential candidates where they are, and that means using social media on mobile devices. In Chapter 3, we talked about the need to have a pulse on what's being said about the company brand on social media. The other piece of keeping the pulse is to use social media as a way to make the candidate experience easier and more like the consumer experience.

But effectively using social media also means having a mobile strategy. According to Pew Research Center, approximately 77 percent of Americans have a smartphone, and that number increases to 92 percent for younger Americans. In addition, half of the public now owns a tablet computer.

I asked Craig Fisher, employer branding leader at CA Technologies, why having a mobile recruiting strategy helps the company brand and candidate experience. "More and more, younger workers will only see your website or brand on a mobile device. If your career site isn't mobile-ready you signal to them that you are not a progressive company! Today's workers want access to the tech they are used to. And it is mostly mobile."

But don't fall into the trap of thinking that mobile recruitment is important only at large organizations. Fisher pointed out that many companies don't even realize that a high number of their job applications either start or are completed from a mobile device. "If a company's career site isn't mobile-friendly or designed with a flexible framework, they are losing valuable prospects. Most currently-employed job seekers search for jobs on breaks or lunch at some point. They are reluctant to use company devices to search, so they use their mobile device. Common sense says to make it easy for them."

The good news is that making your company mobile friendly isn't as expensive as it used to be. Fisher said that most modern web templates use a responsive design that will adjust to the device on which it is viewed:

> Adding a mobile responsive design does not have to be an expensive proposition. Career sites do need to be careful about keeping an applicant's personal information secure. The secure information piece is generally handled by an applicant tracking system. So, the mobile-friendly website is there for a good user experience. Ask your applicant tracking software provider if their application is mobile-friendly. Usually, it is. One of the greatest trends today is a multi-step application where a candidate can start the application process with very little information given and finish it at a later time or step.

And for those companies thinking that once their career site is mobile friendly, they're done—think again. Fisher suggested that artificial intelligence (AI) is the "next big thing" recruiters need to be watching: "Artificial intelligence systems can now chat with job candidates to answer questions during their application process online and on mobile devices. These chatbots are intuitive and can streamline the process for both candidates and employers. The next evolution is interview preparation and eventually even job offers. Don't worry; we'll still need real people to make empathetic decisions. Also, someone has to wind the clocks."

Recruiting Bots Get Hiring Conversations Started

Artificial intelligence bots (short for robots) are assisting recruiters to manage the screening process. They can ask and answer basic questions, helping candidates decide if this is the right opportunity to pursue and find out if the candidate has the minimum qualifications.

For example, a venture-backed San Jose, Calif., company uses a bot named TARA (talent acquisition and recruiting automation) to hire freelancers from a pool of over 50,000 prescreened contractors.

Ryan Healy, founder and president of the enterprise chat-software company Brazen, sees it as the future. In an interview with the Society for Human Resource Management (SHRM), he said, "I believe bots are going to replace the current things that are impersonal, like filling out registration forms or filling out applications." While the technology is new, the initial response is positive.

The Candidate Experience Sets the Bar

Some aspects of recruiting may change based on the job market. For example, organizations may use one type of sourcing strategy when candidates are scarce and another when candidates are more available. The candidate experience shouldn't be sacrificed no matter what the job market looks like. Regardless of how many candidates apply or are interviewed, you want them all to have a positive experience with the organization.

TIPS
3 Tips for Taking Your Candidate Experience to the Next Level

For organizations that have already gone through the exercise of defining their candidate experience, their work isn't done. Experienced talent acquisition professionals are always looking for activities that will take their candidate experience one step further. Here's what three business professionals had to say.

1. *Kristen Brown is vice president of global talent acquisition for Kronos Incorporated, a global leader in delivering workforce solutions in the cloud. Kronos has more than 5,200 employees worldwide and does business in more than 100 countries, and Brown is responsible for leading Kronos's global efforts to attract and hire the best talent in the technology industry. In her time at Kronos, she has led strategic recruitment efforts to support the company's growth to over $1 billion in annual revenue.*

> One of the most important practices for recruiters to "take it to the next level" is to create a candidate experience that mirrors your company culture, and then continues consistently through the onboarding process. Employee engagement starts well before day one—for Kronos, it begins when a candidate evaluates us as a potential employer, and the

emotional connection builds throughout the hiring process. Ensuring consistency in candidate and employee experience—which must include active participation by the employee's future manager—results in a smooth transition from candidate to employee to help drive high engagement on day one and beyond.

2. ***Michael C. Bush*** *is CEO of Great Place to Work, "the global authority on building, sustaining, and recognizing high-trust, high-performing workplace cultures." Previously he served as CEO of Tetra Tech Communications, which he grew from $40 million to $300 million in revenues. He was also a member of President Obama's White House Business Council.*

The recruiters who are going to be most successful moving forward will be those who challenge themselves to bring in a more diverse talent pool, at *all* levels of the company. This is what leaders at top companies are thinking about. People often use the excuse that "it's too hard" to find talented employees across all demographics. However, we work with organizations every day who do it successfully—and our research shows that financially, these companies reap the rewards when compared to those who do not. They understand the benefits that come when you have a workforce that reflects your customer base and your community. They prioritize this in their recruitment strategy, and they are intentional and creative in how they achieve this. Their efforts result in a workforce that is more innovative, more in touch with the customer, and taps into all of its human potential more effectively.

3. ***Kevin W. Grossman*** *is the Talent Board president of global programs responsible for all aspects of the Candidate Experience Awards worldwide. He also produces and hosts "world of work" podcasts including The CandEs Shop Talk, Reach West Radio, and Working Tech. He has over 18 years of domain expertise in the human resource and talent acquisition industry.*

Developing a candidate experience strategy is just one step in improving the recruiting process. To take things to the next level, employers need to integrate consistent communication and feedback loops at each stage. While these aren't new concepts, communicating with candidates, whether about their status or for the purpose of soliciting feedback, is a key differentiator between positive and negative candidate experiences. Research from the Talent Board's 2016 Candidate Experience (CandE) Awards program indicates that 32 percent of candidates who had an overall five-star experience were asked for varying forms of feedback, while 88 percent of candidates with a one-star experience were never asked for feedback—a missed opportunity in today's highly competitive talent landscape. Incorporating proactive communications and feedback throughout the process will help the hiring organization better understand the candidate's perspective and enable recruiters to keep candidate engaged and interested. What may seem like small changes can equate to a big impact on business outcomes as the quality of hire improves along with the organization's employment brand.

SECTION II: 3 Key Takeaways

- Candidates are doing their homework before applying for jobs. Your company brand and candidate experience will tell them how you will treat employees.
- Employment branding is a job seeker's first impression. It sets expectations.
- The candidate experience is directly tied to the organization's bottom line. Never lose a candidate and a customer at the same time.

5 Resources to Make Your Job Easier

1. *A Necessary Evil: Managing Employee Activity on Facebook, Twitter, LinkedIn … and the Hundreds of Other Social Media Sites* by Aliah D. Wright provides an entry into using social media to achieve your HR and recruiting goals.
2. *Employer Branding for Dummies* is a special edition e-book published by Glassdoor.com (free download with registration). Not only does it provide actionable advice, but it shares employment-related research from the company.
3. LinkedIn operates the world's largest professional network with more than 467 million members in over 200 countries. In addition, the network includes more than 40 million students and recent college graduates. Subscribe to the LinkedIn blog for reports and updates about features.
4. Marketing has come up several times in this section. Consider reading a marketing textbook to understand more. My personal favorite is *Principles of Marketing* by Philip Kotler and Gary Armstrong. You don't need the latest edition.
5. The Talent Board (www.thetalentboard.org) provides research, webinars, and workshops on talent acquisition and the candidate experience. You can sign up to receive its newsletter.

SECTION III
Organizational Recruiting Strategies

In Section III

The last section was all about the candidate. Now, let's focus on the company. This section is about the plan that the organization needs to put in place for itself. What does the company need, and when does it need it?

I realized after I wrote sections II and III that they're roughly the same length. Coincidence? I think not. Recruiting is an equal mix of what's good for candidates and the company.

CHAPTER 5:
Workforce Planning

 CASE STUDY
Peter Cappelli Explains Dynamism and the Labor Market

In an article for Human Resource Executive Online, Dr. Peter Cappelli, the George W. Taylor Professor of Management and director of the Center for Human Resources at The Wharton School of the University of Pennsylvania, examined the discussion that finding and hiring talent isn't as dynamic as articles might claim. Some of the trends he cited include:

- Fewer individuals are moving from jobs to unemployment.
- Fewer individuals are moving out of the labor force (that is, into retirement).
- People are not moving geographically as much as they did 20 years ago.
- There's a decline in people moving from one job to another.

Cappelli suggested that the lack of job hopping could be due to evidence that changing jobs isn't as lucrative as it used to be. Years ago, one of the quickest ways to gain a significant pay increase was to change employers. Also, employers do not appear to be as supportive of relocation. Cappelli also concluded that the challenges facing talent acquisition could be isolated to a few industries such as health care and technology.

It's essential for organizations to have a firm understanding of the labor dynamics happening in their business, industry, and key jobs. To be successful, recruiters must know where their future talent will be found.

Workforce planning is the process of aligning the labor needs of the organization with the current workforce. It involves using business intelligence to understand workforce trends and developing staffing plans that will allow recruiters to find essential talent under a given set of conditions. As Cappelli's article suggests, talent acquisition professionals need to understand the labor market if they want to find the best talent.

Workforce Planning and Workforce Development Are Not the Same Thing

While we're talking about workforce planning, let's also discuss the workforce development system. Several years ago, I received an invitation to join the local workforce development board. My first thought was, "What does this have to do with me?" But I accepted the invitation and served on the board for several years. I learned a lot. Let me repeat that—I learned a lot!

In the U.S., workforce development boards (also known as workforce investment boards) work with their economic development counterparts to ensure businesses have access to talent. They also work with schools, colleges, and universities to make sure certain jobs that are essential to the community have available curriculum.

Workforce board funding is incredibly complex. The money comes from the federal government (via each state). The two major sources are the Workforce Investment Act (WIA) and Temporary Assistance for Needy Families (TANF). And workforce spending is specific, meaning that most of the time, workforce boards cannot spend funding on whatever they want or, in some cases, on what their community needs. Each funding stream has very specific rules about how the funds may be spent.

Workforce development could be a part of a company's workforce planning process, but it doesn't have to be. Recruiters should take the time to learn about their local economic and workforce development boards to decide if a strategic partnership makes sense.

6 Steps to Creating a Workforce Plan

Creating a workforce plan is very similar to the gap analysis activities we've discussed in previous chapters. It's an exercise in moving from your current state to a future state. The difference is the information that you collect to conduct the analysis and develop the plan.

Step 1. Create a clear sense of your organization's mission, vision, and values (M-V-V). Also, the organization's goals and objectives. When we're talking about M-V-V, we are referring to the real deal—not some marketing copy that an agency thought would resonate with customers or candidates. People quickly see through that when they interact with the organization.

Step 2. Identify knowledge, skills, and abilities (KSAs). Using the M-V-V, determine the organization's staffing needs in terms of KSAs. I have a confession to make: sometimes, I use these terms interchangeably. Truth is, I shouldn't. Knowledge, skills, and abilities are three different things. And it's important to know the difference—even though the difference can be subtle.

FYI
The Difference between Knowledge, Skills, and Abilities

Knowledge is the theoretical or practical understanding of a subject. For example, an employee might have knowledge of the ADDIE model (as in Analysis, Design, Development, Implementation, Evaluation) used in instructional design. This doesn't mean the employee knows how to be an instructional designer. It means he or she knows the model.

Skills are the proficiencies developed through training or experience. Using the ADDIE example, the employee has demonstrated skills in applying the ADDIE model when designing training programs. Skills are usually something that has been learned. So we can develop our skills through the transfer of knowledge.

Abilities are the qualities of being able to do something. There is a fine line between skills and abilities. Most people would say the differentiator is whether the thing in question was learned or innate. I think of organization and prioritization as abilities that can help employees develop their instructional design skills.

I believe that the reason we sometimes use the terms interchangeably is because they are all career "must-haves." During the hiring process, candidates are asked about their KSAs. Managers use KSAs when they are considering employees for transfers and promotions. Companies use KSAs when they create and update their replacement and succession plans.

With all the talk in the media about the skills gap, employers need to understand the difference between knowledge, skills, and abilities because the way an individual obtains them can vary. And if an organization is trying to figure out how to solve the skills gap that exists within their workforce, then talent acquisition and learning professionals must link to the right solutions.

For instance, if the issue is knowledge, then HR might want to create an in-house library where employees can check out books on the topics. But if the challenge is skills, the answer might be training. And if abilities need to be improved, perhaps managers can develop personal action plans that give employees the opportunity to refine their abilities.

There are times when it's fine to use the terms interchangeably and others when we need to emphasize the exact term. Regardless, they're all equally important.

Once the current KSAs have been identified, prioritize the findings and display them in a simple format, such as a table:

PRIORITIES	CRITICAL REQUIREMENTS	KSAs	SKILL LEVEL

Step 3. Conduct an environmental scan. This is a systemic process that researches and interprets data to identify potential risks. Traditionally, the scan would include labor market data, economic data, demographics about the workforce and community, and the political environment. Often an environmental scan also includes information about the company's industry and competitive set. An environmental scan gives organizations insights into possible challenges in fulfilling their recruiting strategy and possible shifts in future skills.

Step 4. Analyze your current staff. This step involves an analysis within an analysis. A staffing analysis is a systemic way of determining the organization's staffing needs. Basically, it is a piece of your workforce plan (which is on some level, an analysis).

To conduct a staffing analysis, you use the same skills as in workforce planning: data collection and critical evaluation. The difference is in the data you're collecting and evaluating. A lot of the information we've been collecting with the workforce plan is external or not attached to a person. With a staffing analysis, however, the focus is internal and attached to specific employees. Staffing analysis software is available, or you could create an Excel spreadsheet.

EMPLOYEE	KSAs	SKILL LEVEL

Step 5. Identify the gap. At this point, you can see where the organization currently stands in terms of its mission, goals, and priority of knowledge and skills. You also know the skills of your current workforce. The third element is determining what's taking place in your industry, competitive set, and community—which cannot be ignored. Even if the company doesn't like what's happening in its industry, it needs to consider whether to take those external factors into account or whether those factors do not have a significant impact on its plans.

Step 6. Create a plan to address the gap. I mentioned in the last chapter that I like using SMART plans to document action steps. Same applies here. Organizations can use SMART plans to outline their workforce planning goals, success measures, responsibilities, and timeline. I've included an example at the end of this chapter.

CASE STUDY
Benefits of Using SMART Plans

I've found the biggest benefit of SMART plans is that they allow me to steer conversations in the right direction to answer all the necessary questions. For any goal, we have to address each step: Specific, Measurable, Actionable, Responsible, and Time-bound.

What happens when SMART plans aren't employed? Here's an example: We're in a meeting, and Leonard in operations says, "I'm not happy with the quality of temps we've been getting lately. Let's find a new staffing company to partner with." On the surface, this seems like a fine idea. Everyone agrees.

After the meeting, Jose, the purchasing director, comes to you and says, "I don't have a problem with changing staffing companies, but our agreement includes a money-back guarantee if we're not pleased with the temp's work. Maybe we should follow up with the staffing company." Later, Cecil, the technology director, comes to you and says, "I don't have a problem changing staffing companies, but we should consider hiring directly from freelancing firms like Upwork. It would allow us to find better temporary workers from anywhere in the world. It would mean a bit of extra work for HR, so they might have to increase headcount."

You're thinking—why didn't this come up at the meeting?!

SMART planning keeps the discussion on track. Now when Leonard in operations brings up the staffing company discussion, someone can say to the purchasing director, "It sounds like a good idea. Jose, is there anything we need to know about our existing agreement?" Jose then has the chance to answer.

Same goes for the technology director. You can ask, "Cecil, are there any new solutions that we should consider?"

Now the whole group is informed and can make a good decision. Running the meeting according to a SMART format saved the group time by addressing everyone's questions and comments during the meeting.

SMART goals are particularly valuable in the areas of measurement, responsibility, and timeliness.

Bridging the STEM Skills Gap

The first thing that might come to mind when considering workforce planning are skills gaps. The skills of current employees aren't the skills that will be needed in the future. We see this discussion with science, technology, engineering, and math (STEM) skills.

What's challenging with the STEM skills discussion is that there's no clear consensus that a skills gap exists. A Bureau of Labor Statistics article pointed out two contradictory points:

- The President's Council of Advisors on Science and Technology states the need for 1 million STEM professionals over the next decade and the need to increase yearly production of undergraduate STEM degrees by 34 percent to keep up with demand.

- The Sloan Foundation states that there are no general shortages of scientists and engineers; in fact, it suggests a surplus. Many STEM-degreed professionals are not employed in STEM work.

The reason I bring up this topic isn't to argue either side. Rather, the reason is to suggest that both points of view may be correct. Maybe there's a surplus of mechanical engineers and a need for physicists. Or maybe there's a surplus of petroleum engineers in Florida and a need for them in Texas.

That's what workforce planning is about—understanding the dynamic and creating a plan to address it. Using the engineer examples, organizations have several options. They could hire engineers from areas that have a surplus and relocate them. Depending on the type of work the organization does, it could open a remote location in an area that has a surplus of engineers. It could also work with a local college or university to encourage more students to pursue engineering degrees.

Some organizations are developing partnerships with nonprofit organizations specifically focused on developing STEM skills. For example, Girls Who Code is a national nonprofit organization focused on closing the gender gap in technology. They offer after-school clubs for girls in grades 6 through 12 and summer programs for girls in grades 10 through 11. Since 2013, the organization has helped nearly 15,000 girls learn coding skills. Sixty top companies have pledged to hire Girls Who Code alumni, including AT&T, General Motors, IBM, Microsoft, Prudential, and Goldman Sachs.

Organizations have options, and that's a good thing. Recruiting professionals need to be prepared to present the relevant workforce data and recommendations to bridge any skills gap.

Using Apprenticeships to Close Skills Gaps

Even if your organization doesn't feel it has a STEM skills gap to worry about, other types of skills gaps can impact an organization and its industry. For instance, the hospitality industry has encountered challenges over the years recruiting for skilled positions in the culinary arts. Instead of focusing its energies solely on vocational training, Hilton Worldwide addressed the issue by setting up the first U.S. apprenticeship system in tourism.

Apprenticeships are opportunities for someone to learn a trade while working at the same time, the idea being that the person has agreed to work for a predetermined length of time during which the employer agrees to provide job skills training. While we tend to think of apprenticeships as being associated with manufacturing jobs, an increasing number of organizations are looking at the advantages of apprenticeships. It's a way to get young workers or individuals looking to change careers involved and earn money at the same time. In addition, organizations might be able to receive grant dollars to assist with apprentice training efforts.

Internships Are Valuable
When Implemented Properly (and Legally)

While we're discussing apprenticeships, let's talk about internships. An internship is different from an apprenticeship. Interns are typically students who work for an organization (often without pay) to gain exposure or satisfy an educational requirement. Over the past few years, internships have received a fair amount of scrutiny because of the student's possible status as someone who is working without pay.

Given that some organizations might tend to view interns as "free labor," I asked California attorney Andrea W.S. Paris what businesses need to remember about interns and compensation. She cautioned employers, especially private, for-profit companies, in equating the two:

> At the federal level and in California where I am, the definition of "employee" is quite broad. Thus, anyone who works or provides services to the company is an employee by default, unless that person could be taken out of the employee umbrella because they meet certain tests. The same is true for interns, who should be classified as employees, and therefore entitled to protections such as minimum wage and overtime pay, unless they meet certain criteria. However, volunteers for governmental entities, non-profits, and religious organizations who work without expectation of compensation are excepted.

Paris shared the following six necessary criteria of an internship program's exclusion from the minimum wage and overtime pay requirements of the Fair Labor Standards Act (FLSA):

1. The internship ... is similar to training which would be given in an educational environment;
2. The internship experience is for the benefit of the intern;
3. The intern does not displace regular employees, but works under close supervision of existing staff;
4. The employer that provides the training derives no immediate advantage from the

activities of the intern; and on occasion, its operations may actually be impeded;

5. The intern is not necessarily entitled to a job at the conclusion of the internship; and

6. The employer and the intern understand that the intern is not entitled to wages for the time spent in the internship.

In addition, states may have their own criteria, so organizations need to make sure that they also analyze the internship based on their state's specific criteria.

According to Paris, the general overarching factor in evaluating an internship seems to be which party benefits from the relationship—the intern or the organization. Paris reminded us that if the interns would be considered bona fide employees (however temporary or short the employment duration), then organizations must follow all the laws related to pay, anti-discrimination, workers' compensation, etc., as they would any other employee. Paris said, "But even if interns are excepted from the FLSA or other wage and hour laws at the state level, we are seeing a shift to increased protection of even unpaid interns and volunteers against harassment and discrimination at the state level, including Oregon, New York, California, Illinois, and Washington, D.C."

For organizations considering internships as part of their talent acquisition strategy, Paris offered three things to keep in mind:

1. Identify what the internship program is meant to accomplish and draft a description of the program, including detailed requirements, expectations, and the benefits to the intern. This will help you determine various logistics, including the length of the program, what the interns will do, and supervisory issues. If the organization will be the primary beneficiary of the relationship, for example, to fill staffing shortages or to have lower-level clerical work performed, then the interns are clearly employees and should be treated as such.

2. If interns will be employees, understand the financial and legal impact of the additional employees. Will the interns push your organization over certain thresholds, thereby subjecting it to laws that it wouldn't be subjected to otherwise?

3. Maintain accurate records, of course.

Internship programs allow organizations to find future employees while at the same time give students a sneak peek into their chosen profession. But they must be designed properly and legally.

The Middle Skills Gap Impacts Everyone

There is one type of skills gap that has the potential to touch every kind of organization. It's called the middle skills gap and is defined as those jobs that require more than a high school diploma but less than a four-year degree. In a 2014 Accenture report, the industries affected most by the middle skills gap were finance, telecommunication, health care, and retail.

An Association for Talent Development (ATD) report suggested that the answer to the middle skills gap is training and education primarily in areas like interpersonal skills and communication, including being able to effectively communicate using technology. Those types of skills are becoming ones that we expect of every employee regardless of job title.

Organizations will need to figure out how they will handle skills gaps in areas they've maybe never had to consider before. Will they simply keep positions open until they find a candidate with the skills? Or will organizations offer training programs that allow new and current employees to obtain those skills?

How to Successfully Address Skills Gaps

For recruiters to successfully conduct workforce planning, they need to be able to see trends and identify possible solutions. They need to be able to bridge gaps between where their workforce is today and where they want it to be in the future. Here are some activities that can help:

- **Pay attention to what's happening in your geographic area and industry.** What's happening on a global or national stage might not pertain to your geographic region. Your industry could be affected by external factors not facing other industries. Recruiters and hiring managers need to know their market conditions.
- **Find credible sources for information.** "Fake news" doesn't just happen in politics. If you're going to cite sources for a trend or a solution, they need to be ones that the organization finds credible. The last thing you want to do is cite a source that the CEO questions.
- **Consume news and information.** Being well-informed is one of your biggest strengths as a recruiter. That can be using whatever medium you like the most—articles, videos, periodicals, podcasts, etc.
- **Develop an opinion about recruiting trends for the positions you need to source and hire.** What would be your answer if the CEO asked, "Do you believe the skills gap exists?" Recruiters play a strategic role in the business. It's not unreasonable for senior management to ask these types of questions—and expect answers.
- **Ask questions.** Based on where the trends are heading, recruiters should be prepared to question their hiring processes. Ask questions like "Do the requirements match the job?," "Are all of the requirements necessary?," and "If we can't find a candidate, what's plan B?"

Workforce planning is not about filling jobs. It's about understanding the skills market and developing a plan to make sure that the skills the organization needs are available when the organization needs them. In today's business world, organizations understand that preparing people for work isn't entirely the education system's responsibility. Recruiters must get involved.

 TIPS

3 Tips for Taking Your Workforce Planning Efforts to the Next Level

Workforce plans need to be constantly monitored, evaluated, and updated to reflect what's currently happening in the market. If your organization already has a workforce plan in place, you'll want to keep your eye on future trends. I asked three professionals in the recruiting space for their thoughts on how to stay current.

1. **Steve Browne**, *SHRM-SCP, is executive director of HR for LaRosa's, Inc., which serves pizza and other Italian dishes in Ohio, and a member of the SHRM board of directors. He also recently released his first book,* HR on Purpose!!

> A key to looking forward is to remember not to stagnate. We tend to have a ton of ambition and success in implementing items that are forward thinking because they do shift our recruiting efforts forward. And, then we settle and rest. It takes an incredible amount of energy and effort to move the needle in organizations—especially when it comes to considering talent.
>
> Remember this—the newest place you move to is just the next starting point.
>
> Future trends follow this pattern because what you see ahead of you will quickly become the norm. So, I would recommend that you own that and move forward to set the new norms. Just understand that you need to keep that momentum going to set the norm that doesn't even exist yet. Being vigilant is needed in HR and recruiting because the temptation to stay put soon turns to stagnation, and it's so much harder to push against inertia once things become set in place. Keep moving and look ahead while you also implement. It works!!

2. **Mary Faulkner** *is the director of talent acquisition at a water utility in Colorado. She is also the author of* Surviving Leadership, *a leadership development blog that is a must-read for business professionals.*

> Getting ahead of trends always feels like an exercise in reading tea leaves, doesn't it? There are always variables that could throw all your

planning to the wind. The goal should be to have good contingency plans in place and [to ensure] you have the flexibility to shift your workforce plan quickly. That means having a good mix of buy-build-borrow strategy in your staffing. It also means you have to stay educated about what is happening in both recruiting trends AND your industry—what companies are at risk for layoffs; which companies are moving into your market; how is technology impacting skill requirements.

To really take it to the next level, the best recruiting professionals will approach it like a business intelligence analysis and share that information with your hiring managers on a regular basis. The best-laid plans are only as good as the execution of said plans, and that means hiring managers need to agree with your recommendations. Keep them educated, acknowledge their opinions, and support your recommendations.

3. **Michael Reddy** *is a founder and the CEO of HireSphere, a company "focused on bringing the humanity back to recruiting by building complete candidate profiles and using advanced analytics to identify the best candidates for the best jobs."*

Recruiting has become tougher over the years, with time to fill positions twice that of 2010 according to The Australian Financial Review. To get great candidates requires being innovative. Recruiters need to get ahead of social recruiting trends to find the best candidates faster.

There is a mismatch in the social sites recruiters use to hunt for candidates with where most candidates are active. According to Jobvite, while only about 36 percent of candidates are active on LinkedIn, over 94 percent of recruiters are. About 55 percent of recruiters are using Facebook to find candidates, while 84 percent of candidates are on Facebook. Job seekers are spending much more time on Facebook, but recruiters are not there to communicate with them.

Recruiters need to be sure to communicate in the right ways on social sites. To be effective on social sites, recruiters need to take off their recruiting hats and contribute to the community. This includes being easy to find and creating content relating to their expertise. This includes answering questions, presenting tips and tricks, making comments on posts, etc. This helps the recruiter gain respect within the community and build great relationships. These relationships can lead to great recruiting opportunities.

One company that has done a good job with this is Starbucks. They have used social media well for recruiting, with an emphasis on the platforms that their customers are active on. An example of where they used social media well was an initiative to get children into technology. They were using Facebook and Twitter to encourage people to attend an event for children to learn about tech and how tech is important to Starbucks. The initiative grew because of the strong social media initiative to the point that other companies started using their hashtag causing the initiative to go viral. The event helped Starbucks hire people both for their stores and their main office as well as get many children interested in technology.

CHAPTER 6:
Creating a Recruiting Strategy

CASE STUDY
AT&T Faces a Talent Overhaul

Dallas-based AT&T employs over 250,000 people, most of whom have been with the organization 10-plus years. As such, their employees gained their initial employment skills training during a different era. Now that AT&T is moving from cables and hardware to Internet- and cloud-based solutions, the company and its talent need to reinvent themselves.

AT&T took a long view on talent management, creating a program called Workforce 2020 to identify the skills that the organization would need for the future. It created "future role profiles" for departments and jobs. These profiles identified jobs that needed to be eliminated and consolidated. New performance standards and metrics were assigned for each profile as well.

The company also drafted a communications plan to let employees know about the eventual changes in their positions and what would be expected regarding re-education. Managers were responsible for motivating and engaging employees during this transition. In addition, AT&T partnered with the labor unions they had collective bargaining agreements with for additional training and development. The union was supportive in those efforts.

Since 2013, AT&T has spent over $250 million on employee education and development to help employees acquire the skills they need for the newly created roles within the company. The expectation is that over the next decade, these employees will find themselves changing roles again.

Some industries are moving so quickly that finding talent to support their business is a major challenge. The AT&T case study reminds us that recruiting is about more than finding candidates from the outside. It's about filling the talent needs of the organization. Sometimes, that's better handled from inside the company.

In the last chapter, we focused on workforce planning (that is, the talent that's available for hire). If the talent that organizations need aligns with the talent they have and what's currently available: Bingo! Our job as recruiters is easy. Unfortunately, it doesn't always work out that way.

And that's why we need a recruiting strategy. There's more to fulfilling the talent needs of the organization than just hiring.

3 Recruiting Strategies: Buy, Build, and Borrow

When organizations need to acquire talent, they have three options: buy, build, or borrow. They can "buy" talent—meaning hire someone as an employee. They can "build" talent—which involves training employees to assume new or different responsibilities. Or they can "borrow" talent—suggesting that they would find a freelancer or consultant to do the work. There are advantages and disadvantages to each of them.

Using a Buy Strategy to Find Talent

One of the most obvious advantages of hiring talent from the outside is that you can bring in skills and experience not currently within the organization. For instance, startups might need a professional with experience in getting funding. Or if the organization is launching a new product line, it might make sense to bring in a marketing professional with experience in that area.

Another advantage is having a fresh set of eyes in the organization. If the company feels that something is missing in the collaborative process, bringing in a new perspective could be the answer. Also, organizations looking to make difficult personnel changes might find that hiring from the outside helps usher in a new way of thinking. It's a reality in business that the people who got the company where it is today might not be the people who can take it to the next level.

The downside of bringing in talent from the outside is cost. Top talent is always in demand. If the company wants specific experience and skills, it will have to pay for it. And if the unemployment rate is low, organizations need to be prepared to compete by offering competitive wages and benefits.

Then there's the issue of culture. Even when organizations do a great job with their employment branding and candidate experience, new hires don't know the organization and culture. Organizations have plenty of unwritten rules that new hires need to figure out. Any external hire will have a learning curve.

Every organization needs to have some level of buy in their recruiting strategy, even in organizations that place emphasis on promoting from within. There are times when bringing in a person from the outside just makes good business sense. Examples are starting a new product or service or needing a culture change. However, in both scenarios, it's important for the new hire to understand his or her role. The company needs to set new hires up for success.

Filling Your Talent Needs with a Build Recruiting Strategy

Organizations that focus on building talent can concentrate on building the skills and experience they need. It's an incredibly good use of organizational resources. For that reason, building talent can be less expensive than buying it.

Building talent is also great for employee morale, which can have a positive impact on employee engagement. Employees want to know that the organization is willing to invest in their success. They like to see their hard work (and the hard work of others) recognized.

On the downside, building talent can take a while. Chances are, the skills and experiences you want employees to learn aren't quick to master. That doesn't mean your current employees will be unable to learn them; it simply means that training takes time. It also means that companies need to have a clear sense of what they need. This can be incredibly difficult to identify. Many industries are moving so fast to keep up that they struggle to know what they will need six months from now, much less two years from now. That impacts their ability to develop internal talent.

First and foremost, a build recruiting tactic works best when the organization's goals allow for a long-term development plan. An example is the AT&T case study at the beginning of the chapter. The business knew that over the next decade, it would shift priorities from ABC to XYZ. Acknowledging future priorities allowed it time to identify the skills that employees currently have, the ones they would need, and a path to bridge the gap. It also allowed the company to allocate resources over time to address skills gaps and needs.

The build tactic also works very well when the workforce is stable. Obviously, organizations don't want to train and develop people so they will leave. That being said, this discussion isn't about zero turnover. Turnover is inevitable. Organizations cannot be afraid to develop talent for fear of being poached. In fact, the opposite is true—developing talent is a way to engage and retain employees.

Finally, the build tactic works to help companies develop their succession plan. According to HR People + Strategy, two-thirds of U.S. public and private companies admit they have no formal succession plans in place for senior management. It seems only logical that, if companies aren't planning for the departure of senior executives, they're probably not dedicating significant resources toward succession planning (or replacement planning) for the rest of the organization.

Even if you're sourcing and selecting the best candidates right now, at some point, you may need to consider a build strategy. It's better to think about succession planning now because it takes time to develop people and see the results. For example, Pew

Research reported that 10,000 people each day turn 65. While not all Baby Boomers are leaving at the same time, someday, eventually, they will leave. The best time to think about the future of talent in your organization is when you can address it proactively. Plan ahead and put a build strategy in place long before you need it.

Leveraging a Borrow Recruiting Strategy to Meet Your Staffing Needs

Many organizations, regardless of size, have a need for specialized skills. They don't need it all the time—but when they do, it's important. Instead of hiring a full-time employee, organizations can hire a freelancer, contractor, or consultant. Another option is hiring part-time, on-call, or seasonal workers.

According to an article in *Fast Company*, more than 40 percent of the U.S. workforce will be independent workers by the year 2020. Please note: this is right around the corner. Regardless of the reason for the increase in self-employment (and there are many), organizations have an opportunity to leverage independent work by borrowing talent when they need it.

But using a borrow strategy involves a mindset shift. For years, organizations have associated freelancers as "temporary" or "dispensable" workers. Those days are over. To successfully implement borrow tactics, organizations should view contingent workers as an essential piece of their staffing strategy.

The biggest advantage to borrowing talent is the proper utilization of resources. Organizations can get specialized talent when they need it, at the moment they need it, without hiring a full-time employee. In addition, companies can keep their existing talent engaged. For example, companies don't have to lose the knowledge and experience of employees transitioning into semi-retirement or former employees looking for a "side hustle."

Keeping both freelancers and employees engaged can be challenging. A benefit of successful borrow tactics is having freelancers who are available when the company needs them, but they must feel connected to the organization to stay. Engaging contingent workers means managing them in a new way. Likewise, keeping employees engaged means making sure they understand the organization's strategy and do not feel threatened by a consultant working on a regular basis.

Companies also need to find ways to keep consultants and contractors connected even when they aren't working on a project. Managers must be able to effectively select, engage, and maintain relationships with their freelancing team. Vendor management isn't simply a skill for procurement departments; it's a skill that needs to be developed at every level.

The Ideal Way to Implement a Borrow Strategy

While certain industries (for example, hospitality and retail) have been using contingent workers for decades, using a borrow strategy isn't contained to one type of business. Businesses that have defined peaks and valleys might find that contingent workers are a great way to staff up during busy times and staff down during slower ones.

It can also be valuable to find similar companies that have peaks and valleys the opposite of yours. Helping talented freelancers find other gigs is great for engagement! For example, I worked at a hotel with a defined busy and slow season. We found that the city's local sports teams had the opposite busy and slow season. The jobs were similar in responsibilities, pay, etc. When our employees couldn't get all their hours with us, they knew they could work someplace else.

A tenured workforce is another opportunity to use borrow tactics. There's lots of talk about the benefits of doing some work during retirement. As employees start to discuss retirement, companies can let them know that freelance or consulting work is available. It's a win for the employee who might want a few extra dollars and a win for the company because it gets to keep employee knowledge a bit longer.

The same philosophy applies to anyone who might be leaving traditional jobs to freelance and have more freedom with their time. Organizations do not have to lose an employee's knowledge and skills. It's possible that employees leaving full-time jobs would be open to part-time work arrangements.

Every job is not a full-time job. Part of a recruiter's role is to make sure that the jobs created are truly necessary and provide value. That includes contingent worker jobs.

Companies can develop a well-publicized contingent workforce strategy that supplies the talent they need and helps with retention. But it takes developing a new recruiting mentality and treating freelancers as an extension of the workforce.

Organizations Need to Weigh Time and Resources

The decision to build, borrow, or buy comes down to two factors: time and resources. Organizations with limited time might not be able to build talent. Companies with limited budgets might not be able to buy the talent they need.

Talent acquisition professionals can take the information they've compiled in their workforce plan and use it to develop their recruiting strategy. Companies should think about their current and future skills needs and then plan accordingly. For example, if an organization wants to build its own talent pipelines, then it should start planning for how it is going to do that. It might involve replacement planning, succession planning, talent pools, training resources, dedicated training staff, and other strategies. You get the point.

Recruiting Global Talent

Organizations want access to the best talent and realize that their competitive advantage relies on attracting that talent, even if it means hiring talent outside of the U.S.

The buy, build, borrow strategy still applies in a global setting. However, immigration laws add a level of complexity to the process. According to the Council for Global Immigration's 2016 Employer Immigration Metrics (EIM) Survey, 74 percent of respondents reported that the ability to obtain work visas in a timely, predictable, and flexible manner is critical to their organization's business objectives.

Eric B. Meyer, a partner in the Labor & Employment Practice Group at Philadelphia-based Dilworth Paxson LLP and author of the blog *The Employer Handbook*, says organizations need to consider the country-specific, hiring-centric employment laws in which they are looking to fill positions. "There are questions that the company should ask and, at least, start to answer when developing a global recruiting process. Those could be in relation to U.S. employment laws, the laws of another country, or both! For example, is it efficient to stick to a single hiring blueprint? Or will the company scale with various processes? There's also the issue of continuity; much like when a company expands operations across state lines."

In the same Council for Global Immigration EIM Survey, respondents reported that cumbersome immigration procedures at least doubled the length of the hiring process. And most respondents said that the process required legal counsel. Unfortunately, we don't have time to do a deep dive into global talent and immigration, but if your organization is starting to consider a global recruiting strategy, the Council for Global Immigration has a guide, *Immigration 101: Inside the U.S. Employment-Based Immigration System*. You can download it from the council's website (www.cfgi.org).

Succession Planning

Some activities that have a huge impact on recruiting may or may not be the responsibility of the recruiting function. One of them is succession planning. While this book isn't about creating a formal succession plan, the activity of creating a succession plan does relate to recruiting. And, as such, I believe that talent acquisition professionals need to think about it when developing their recruitment strategy.

By the way, if you are looking for a good guide to building a succession plan, check out *Effective Succession Planning: Ensuring Leadership Continuity and Building Talent from Within* by William J. Rothwell. It includes a CD-ROM with ready-to-use worksheets, assessment tools, and training guides.

I mentioned earlier that organizations seem to be reluctant to develop succession plans. I think the reason is that they're conflicted about whether to tell employees they're a part of the succession plan. There are certainly pros and cons to consider. The Society for Human Resource Management (SHRM) ran a point/counterpoint on the subject in *HR Magazine*. It's an interesting read, and you can find it on its website.

Wondering whether to tell employees that they're part of a succession plan is not a reason to avoid succession planning. And talent acquisition professionals might want to consider weighing in on this topic. Organizations without succession plans rely on the recruiting function to be their succession plan, which means, if they don't have a succession plan, they must account for it in their recruiting strategy.

What if employees don't want to be a part of the succession plan? It doesn't make good business sense to develop a career plan that employees want to be excluded from. Employees need to buy in to being a part of the company's succession plan.

Employees also need to be held accountable for their future. Just because an employee is part of the plan doesn't mean he or she will always be part of the plan. Employees need to be held accountable for achieving their career goals if they want to stay in the succession plan.

Succession planning is just that—planning. And plans change regularly. For the same reason that you should tell employees they're a part of the succession plan, a company should review and update its plan on a regular basis. It's no secret that I happen to be in the "yes, you should tell employees they're a part of the succession plan" camp. But I do understand the counter argument. It can be messy and ugly to tell an employee that he or she is no longer part of the succession plan.

But weigh that against not telling employees and having them resign to accept a position with another company with more opportunity. If that happens, the responsibility for filling their former positions falls to recruiting.

If the organization is still reluctant to tell employees they're part of the plan, one alternative to consider is talent pools. This might be the best of both worlds. Employees know they're being groomed for future opportunities, but the specifics haven't been identified yet.

Creating Organizational Talent Pools

Talent pools are groups of employees who are being trained and developed to assume greater responsibilities within the organization. Often, but not always, they have been identified as high-performing and high-potential individuals.

Talent pools allow organizations to develop employees in areas that align with company competencies and values instead of focusing on developing specific position skills. This allows talent pools to address the biggest challenge with succession planning, which is telling individuals they're part of the plan. Organizations can communicate to a group, "You're the future of the company," instead of telling an individual, "You are our next chief marketing officer."

Talent pools provide the flexibility needed in emerging or developing industries. Some industries are moving so quickly that they don't know what next year looks like, much less what their five-year recruiting strategy should include. That unpredictability can make traditional succession planning efforts difficult and talent pools an ideal tool.

4 Steps for Developing a Talent Pool

Creating a talent pool does take some planning. Here are four steps to developing an organizational talent pool:

Step 1. Review the organizational strategies. Much of the information regarding the strategies has already been gathered as part of the workforce planning activity. The goal here is to identify the competencies needed to make those strategies happen. In the future, the strategies will change, but the competencies may remain the same. An example is critical thinking skills. Regardless of the strategy, critical thinking is necessary.

Step 2. Assess the company's current talent to identify any skills gaps. Again, this information was gathered during the staffing analysis and workforce planning activity. Organizations can accomplish this step using a variety of techniques, including performance reviews, assessments, multi-rater feedback, and interviews. A combination of techniques could prove to be exceptionally valuable. The key consideration is consistency.

Step 3. Create modules or groups of activities that will help employees learn the skills they need. Once the organization identifies the skills it will help employees develop, recruiting can work with learning and development to figure out the process. A combination of internal and external training and project-based learning may be useful. Three activities proven to be very effective include:

- **Management coaching.** Good managers have valued relationships with their employees. They are positioned to deliver open, honest feedback that can help employees change behaviors and improve performance.
- **Peer-to-peer feedback.** Organizations spend an incredible amount of time collaborating. Peer-to-peer interaction is how most employees spend their time. Training employees to deliver timely, specific feedback can make an impact.
- **Mentoring.** Organizations can encourage mentoring relationships to cover topics that don't necessarily warrant a training program—like office politics and negotiation skills. Employees can benefit from the wisdom of experience.

Step 4. Monitor progress and make regular adjustments. Like succession planning and recruiting strategies, talent pools need to be monitored. The organization should conduct regular talent assessments and observe market conditions. Both internal and external factors can prompt a change in talent development strategy.

The talent wars aren't going away anytime soon. Organizations must think about the future. They are not going to be able to find all the talent they need via external recruiting. Talent pools allow companies to develop future talent from within. They also give businesses the flexibility to meet their fluid operational needs.

Replacement Planning

If there's one activity that has more of an impact than succession planning and talent pools, it's replacement planning, although the term is frequently used in conversations about succession planning. They are two different things. A replacement plan identifies "backups" for positions. Traditionally, it focuses on top-level positions, but it can be done for any key position in the organization.

Replacement planning is often mentioned in conjunction with succession planning because it identifies individuals who can assume roles at some point in the future and shows how ready they are for that role. But replacement planning doesn't have to be defined as a subset of succession planning.

Having individuals identified as backups just makes good business sense, for a variety of reasons. As much as we don't like to mention it, employees can become unexpectedly seriously ill or have an accident and be unable to work. The organization needs to find someone to take over their responsibilities—even temporarily.

A certain amount of turnover is healthy for the business, as are certain types of turnover (for example, the dismissal of a toxic employee). Since organizations don't always get to control the timing and circumstances, having a staffing backup plan (aka replacement plan), makes sense. And recruiters will want to have a say in how that plan is developed.

7 Steps to Developing a Replacement Plan

If your organization has a formal succession plan, you might already have replacements identified. Or it could be an added step in the existing process. For organizations using talent pools for employee development, here are seven steps that can guide a replacement planning activity:

Step 1. Identify key positions. While every job is important, certain roles within the organization would significantly impact the business if left open for a long period. According to SHRM, the average time to fill an open position is 42 days. Using that as your benchmark, which positions must be filled in less time? Ideally, we'd like every job to be filled quickly, but identify those that *must* be a priority. Those key positions are a place to start. You should have much of this information from your workforce plan.

Step 2. Identify the critical skills for each position. You're seeing a theme here—you've got this information from your staffing analysis. List the qualities that anyone holding this position must have. Not a wish list: remember this is a replacement plan. If someone had the basic skills, then he or she could learn the other skills or knowledge required for the position.

Step 3. Assess the skills of current employees. Again, your staffing analysis should contain this information. If not, you can obtain it in the form of training records, performance reviews, coaching feedback, and 9-box grids. It might also be helpful to look at the skills of freelancers and consultants who currently partner with the organization or at former employees who might be interested in returning.

Step 4. Match the critical skills to the current skills of employees. This step is when organizations might be tempted to think that backup employees are currently in the department—for instance, the accounting manager is the obvious backup for the accounting director. However, a recent transfer might be interested in returning to his or her former department. Keep the planning activity focused on skills, not current job titles.

Step 5. Pay attention to jobs that don't have matches. This exercise will possibly surface some jobs that need immediate attention—meaning there is no replacement available. It's better to find out this information during a planning activity than when you're trying to fill an opening. This is why recruiting needs to be a part of the conversation so there are no surprises.

Step 6. Develop a plan to address gaps. This plan might include development programs, mentoring, coaching, and contingent staffing—or a combination of all these programs. With replacement planning, the organization doesn't have to identify a single replacement. Use talent pools to develop transferable skills for many positions.

Step 7. Evaluate the plan. On a regular basis evaluate the plan to make sure the company's needs can still be met. For key positions, the individuals currently holding those roles can be tasked with helping identify their replacement and train them. This goal could become part of their performance review.

While organizations are working hard to hire, engage, and retain the best talent, it would be naïve to think employees never leave. Replacement plans provide the organization with the comfort that a last-minute resignation, retirement, or employee illness will not leave the company disadvantaged.

Replacement plans do one other thing. They give the organization a sense of the investment they will need to make should a backup be necessary. Whether it's temporary or long term, employees asked to assume greater responsibilities need support. Regular replacement planning activities make the organization keenly aware of the support the affected employees will need to be successful.

Talent Networks and Communities

One more topic needs to be considered in a company's recruiting strategy: what the organization plans to do when it does not have any job openings. I know what you're thinking—is that even possible?! No job openings?! While I'm of the mindset that the recruiting process should never completely end, the company may possibly want to slow its hiring activities. But that doesn't mean it should stop filling the pipeline.

The reverse is also true. Sometimes candidates aren't ready to apply even though the company has openings. They want to learn a bit more about the work and the organization.

So organizations need to consider creating talent networks and communities. Talent networks and communities are designed to keep candidates interested so when the company has an opening, the candidate is ready to apply. And vice versa.

FIGURE 6.1: Talent Networks and Talent Communities

Talent Networks	Talent Communities
Short-term	Long-term
2-way communication between company and candidates	3-way communication between company, candidates, and community members

An example of talent networks in practice comes from Penn National Gaming, a leader in the gaming and racing industries with over 25 facilities in the U.S. It wants candidates to know that working at its company means "working happy." In addition to giving candidates the ability to apply for jobs using their mobile devices and share openings with their friends on social media, the firm's career site has a button that says, "Not ready to apply? Connect with us!," encouraging candidates to stay engaged with the company.

Recruiting Strategy Involves Planning Beyond the Job Opening.

Yes, talent acquisition professionals have to think about filling jobs. But the truth is, they need to think beyond that—they need to fill a talent pipeline. A recruiting strategy needs to cover all the pieces, not simply filling requisitions. If the recruiting strategy is designed only to fill openings, at some point, the company won't be able to fill openings. Recruiters can fill openings because they filled the pipeline with talented candidates.

The companies that will win the talent wars are the ones that will have the most options. They will build, borrow, and buy talent. They will think about the future by planning for replacements. And companies won't let time or resources dictate their hiring outcomes because recruiters are planning for the future right now.

Example: A SMART Social Recruiting Plan

Here's a starting SMART plan to help develop a social recruiting strategy. The left column shows the individual components of SMART. The top row reflects the first step in the strategy process—analysis.

FIGURE 6.2: SMART Social Recruiting Plan

Talent Networks	STEP ONE	
	Analyze the Environment	
Specific What are we going to do?	1) Determine the goal	2) Choose 1-2 sites to drive traffic to.
Measurable How will we measure our success?	All stakeholders will agree upon the goal for a social recruiting program.	2 websites will be clearly identified as primary drivers for all social recruiting activity.
Achievable What are the steps that will help us attain our goal?	Discuss key deliverables with stakeholders including • Finance (cost) • Marketing (exposure) • Technology (capability) • Operations (hiring results)	Discuss with Marketing a strategy for selecting primary sites. Get recommendations from recruiting team on primary sites. Meet with technology team regarding site maintenance, traffic, and mobile feasibility.
Responsible Who will be accountable for each step?	Human Resources, Recruiting team, Technology department, C-Team	Marketing department, Technology department, Recruiting team
Trackable When will the task be completed?	Q1	Q1

TIPS
3 Tips for Taking Your Recruiting Strategy to the Next Level

Developing a recruiting strategy is important. Keeping it current and relevant is a hard job. If your organization already has a recruiting strategy in place, here are a few things to consider when maintaining it.

1. **Dawn Burke** *is an HR leader, speaker, and writer specializing in new "trench HR" practices, engagement, and workplace culture. Her executive HR and leadership career has spanned the last 20 years. In addition, she serves as the author of DawnHBurke.com and is a contributor to the talent management blog Fistful of Talent.*

> If you want to kick your recruiting efforts into the stratosphere, partner with your marketing department to create targeted "recruitment marketing" campaigns. Not only are talent pools shrinking, but candidates of *all* generations are consuming *and* absorbing content in new ways. Marketing can teach recruiters how to get job ads to the right candidates (quality not quantity!). In addition, marketing can produce visually appealing materials that can be distributed through social channels easily and absorbed quickly by candidates. Do this pronto! I promise you won't regret it.

2. **Marilyn C. Durant,** *M.S., SPHR, SHRM-SCP is president of Durant Resources Group, Inc., a consultancy that provides talent, leadership, and organizational solutions. She's the recipient of the HR Association of Palm Beach County's Lifetime Achievement Award for her service to the profession and community.*

> In my experience, it is about gaining trust with the candidate(s) that you are sourcing in today's virtual workspace. I am currently doing professional level searches in over ten countries for a global client company. We have never met or conducted digital interviews, yet they are fully willing to engage in the process due to the integrity of the approach. The key is seeking the talent out directly through research and social media. Once they respond with interest, respond in a timely manner and stay in communication throughout the process. Get back to everyone whether they are a candidate or not; even in today's digital space. Communication and trust are key. They can be a good referral source down the road and in the end.

Stop acting and sounding like a salesperson and act like a qualified, trusted professional who is genuinely interested in the value that the candidate brings to the table. Sell them on the brand later. This same integrity holds true with the client company. Communication and follow through with commitments is key.

Leveraging technology and social media have made it all possible, but we are all still humans looking for attention and appreciation for what they bring to the table and can better themselves in the long run.

3. **Jayne Mattson** *is senior vice president at Keystone Associates and site lead for the Southborough, Mass., office. In her role at Keystone, she consults with professionals and executives from a diverse range of industries, functions, and organizational levels and specializes in midcareer change, pre-retirement planning, and career self-assessment.*

Improved technology tools, such as video interviews and social media outlets, will continue to drive recruiting strategies. However, until the active and passive seekers recognize the need to keep their LinkedIn profiles and social media presence up to date, the time to find talent will still be an issue. To get ahead of future trends, companies need to be proactive, not reactive in finding talent—combining technology with face to face interaction!

Most people have heard of the "hidden job market" where existing jobs are not published or created because they are going to be filled later in the year. To avoid competition in the job market, job seekers need to uncover these opportunities. Recruiters need to be thinking the same way. They need to know who would be the best fit for their company based on background, qualifications, experience— all based on future needs.

An organization can create future talent networks (FTNs) as a way to build relationships with hidden talent. Each month, the company could offer a session that features a functional area, including the hiring manager who talks about the department and the type of people the company is looking to hire. The recruiter could talk about the culture and what the company looks for during the interview process.

This method will tap into "future talent potential" so that when a position opens up, the company will already have a highly qualified candidate in mind. In the early stages, an employer may want to partner with university career centers so students can learn about it and its roles by participating in an FTN session. Eventually, job seekers could ask questions about the company, its culture, and the opening. Recruiters and hiring managers could engage with candidates and ask questions like:

- Why are you targeting our company?
- What skills and experience do you think is a good match for what we do?

As companies look ahead one to five years and contemplate the kind of talent they will need and where they will find it, hiring managers and recruiters can refer to an existing database or even a taping of any actual virtual meetings to see who they might want to reach out to for an open position. Knowing who is out there *before* they need it is accessing the hidden talent. By shifting the company's recruiting strategies to future and present; a company can tap into talent that companies typically do not even know about because those individuals are not applying for jobs.

SECTION III: 3 Key Takeaways

- Recruiting is about closing the gap. Where are we right now? Where do we need to be? Create a path to get there.
- The recruiting function must partner with learning and development. Sometimes, organizations will need to develop talent from within.
- Once a recruitment strategy has been created, the work isn't over. Revisit and revise it regularly.

5 Resources to Make Your Job Easier

1. The Bureau of Labor Statistics (www.bls.gov) is the principal federal agency responsible for measuring labor market activity. Its mission is to collect and disseminate economic information to support public and private decision-making.
2. The Fair Labor Standards Act (FLSA) (www.dol.gov/whd/flsa) has been the subject of media attention in recent years. This law establishes a minimum wage, overtime pay, and other standards for workers.
3. To learn more about workforce development funding, visit the websites for the Workforce Investment Act (WIA) (www.doleta.gov/usworkforce/wia/act.cfm) and Temporary Assistance for Needy Families (TANF) (www.acf.hhs.gov/ofa/programs/tanf) websites.
4. The acronym SMART has come up several times in this section. If you want to learn more, check out the book *S.M.A.R.T. Goals Made Simple: 10 Steps to Master Your Personal and Career Goals* by S. J. Scott.
5. Even if you're not responsible for the company's succession plan, it's important to have an opinion about it. William J. Rothwell's book *Effective Succession Planning: Ensuring Leadership Continuity and Building Talent from Within* is a practical guide and includes a CD-ROM with ready-to-use worksheets, assessment tools, and training guides.

SECTION IV
Sourcing Strategies

In Section IV

You might be wondering why I've dedicated an entire section to one chapter. Sourcing is a key piece in the recruiting process. To fill jobs, you need applicants. You can have the best recruiting strategy in the whole world, but if you don't get sourcing right, you won't have any applicants.

And sources are everywhere. This section offers some creative inspiration about where you can source applicants. I've assembled the longest list I could find.

CHAPTER 7:
Sourcing

 CASE STUDY
Adidas Group Focuses on a Proactive Recruitment Process
Since 1949, Adidas Group has been a global leader in the sporting goods industry. The company is headquartered in Germany with 170 subsidiaries around the world and a workforce of over 60,000, with about one-third based in the Asia Pacific region.

The firm's recruiters were faced with two challenges. First, the hiring process wasn't effective or efficient. Recruiters were accustomed to using two major sources—job boards and third-party agencies. This wasn't enough, and it didn't produce the quality of candidates they were looking for. The second challenge was inconsistency. Each recruiter had his or her own relationships with agencies, and, therefore, the company brand was being presented differently in each location.

To provide consistency, efficiency, and effectiveness, Adidas built a recruitment hub that allowed recruiters to post jobs in a central location. The company saw an immediate benefit because passive job seekers could find job openings quicker. The hub also enabled Adidas to learn more about the people reading its job openings. These efforts gave it the ability to refine its recruitment messaging and reduce time-to-fill.

There's an old technology term called "garbage in, garbage out" (GIGO). It means if you put good data in the system, you'll get good outputs. And vice versa. The Adidas case study tells us that the same principle applies in recruiting. If organizations want good candidates, they need to have good sourcing strategies. "Spray and pray" recruitment simply won't cut it. It's about quality, not quantity.

Creating a Sourcing Strategy
One of the biggest decisions that organizations must make is what their sourcing strategy will be—meaning what is the most important attribute the company wants in a

candidate. For example, is the company trying to find candidates that fit the culture? If so, that goal would drive the places that the company sources candidates.

I'm a believer that organizations can create a diverse workforce of qualified employees who fit the company culture. I don't believe it's easy, but it can be done. Reaching this goal means companies need to have a diverse sourcing strategy and not focus their tactics in a single direction.

Recruiters must find that magic formula of sources that will allow them to keep the talent pipeline full—because full talent pipelines fill jobs. Developing a sourcing strategy could be similar to a gap analysis. What sourcing strategies is the company using? What types of positions will the company need to fill in the future? How can we get from point A to point B? The good news is that you already know what you're doing, and you've conducted a thorough breakdown of the job to create a staffing analysis, workforce plan, and recruiting strategy.

Unfortunately, a lot of companies look only at their recruiting strategy when something isn't working. That could be too late. Developing a source takes time. During a panel discussion at the TAtech 2017 Chicago Spring Congress, I heard recruiters say that they will give a source upwards of a year to prove itself. Talent acquisition professionals should think far in advance.

We talked in the last chapter (on recruiting strategy) about a couple of sourcing activities that companies need to consider and cultivate on a regular basis: talent networks and communities. Here are three ways to keep job seekers engaged in talent networks and communities:

1. **Send out a newsletter.** A digital newsletter could contain updates about the company and new position openings. It could also display pictures from employee events (for example, a photo of employees volunteering in the community). Mention upcoming industry events and job fairs that you'll be attending. And encourage readers to follow the company on social channels.

2. **Create a contest.** The Home Depot wanted to find a way to thank people for promoting its career site. The company created the Great Giveback Contest: Helping Hands, which awarded gift cards to individuals who helped spread the word about the site. The contest has been around for a few years, and the company has seen a 200 percent increase in participation.

3. **Include recruitment information on the company blog.** If your organization already has a blog, see if you can get space on the editorial calendar. You can write about careers and the great things employees are doing every day. After a while, you can also post links to available job openings with the company.

Let's talk about a couple of different jobs in an organization and how the sourcing strategy might be different for each.

Executive Recruitment

Let's start our sourcing strategy discussion at the top—meaning the C-suite. I asked Mark S. Fogel, SPHR, GPHR, CEO and co-founder of Human Capital 3.0, a boutique HR firm with some very big clients, to share his expertise in hiring and working with executives. Fogel's impact on the profession is well known, and the Society for Human Resource Management (SHRM) has recognized him as the Human Capital Leader of the Year. According to Fogel, "No single executive position is the same, and even the same position is different within and across industries. Revenue size, demographics, profit margins and responsibilities and culture all impact every single role in an organization. Same with being public, private, or non-profit."

Fogel shared an example using major accounting firms. The managing partners for those firms have similar roles in the same industry. Yet they have slightly different business models and organizational structures. A CEO in the same industry could have a significantly different overall span of control and daily responsibilities. This could also be the case for other typical C-suite roles: marketing, finance, HR, operations, technology, and legal.

In some cases, it is even more difficult in matching a CFO or chief human resource officer (CHRO) to a new opportunity because more granular activities and processes, including ones specific to an industry, are involved. An example would be a highly technical manufacturing head of operations or HR trying to go to a technology business where the internal daily activities are vastly different. Yes, the roles are technical, but that's where the similarities end. In manufacturing, the daily activity is ruled by measures like error rate, quality, and fill rates to customers. HR and operations executives are dealing with large workforces of hourly employees, multiple shifts, and possibly several locations.

Contrast the manufacturing environment with a technology company located on a large campus. The workforce is highly educated and includes a significant number of virtual employees and freelancers. The end product is software code versus a physical product. The organizational culture is such that breaking rules is almost as important as following them.

So hiring for C-suite and senior executives is more robust and detailed than for other positions, even at the director or managerial level. The process often involves multiple rounds of interviews, behavioral assessments, meetings with the board of directors, and sometimes completing a strategically oriented project.

Fogel pointed out the ability to source these candidates tends to be more relationship driven: "Senior level executives do not traditionally visit or acknowledge the same job boards or advertisements that junior and mid-level executives may visit. Cold calling is typically not an option. Direct access to these individuals is critical. Therefore, significant time needs to be spent on developing a rich network where introductions can be made directly."

Senior executives have typically established their own network of retained search professionals with whom they regularly touch base. Fogel said senior executives build networks, which positions them well when opportunities arise. "Many are very savvy, establishing networks and attending events and offsite invitation-only conferences to keep their network alive and fresh."

Because hiring executives is so individualized, I asked Fogel how organizations can make sure the executive candidates being sourced are capable. He offered a scenario that makes a lot of sense. A senior-level executive with more than two years at a particular business typically has the technical capabilities for the organizations they work at. Would a business hold a poor-performing C-level executive for two years if he or she couldn't technically navigate the role? In most cases, no. The issue comes up when the executive does not have tenure.

The exception to this logic is skills such as leadership and delegation. Whether an executive has those abilities will come out during a robust interview process with well-structured interview questions.

Sales Recruitment

We've established that all recruiting is not the same and that some recruiting efforts require specialized knowledge. Let's take sales positions, for instance. Not all sales positions are the same, according to Gil "GW" Williams, career matchmaker for the sales and marketing group at Intel Corporation:

> The core skills involved with sales positions are the same, but the knowledge is different based on what you're selling. For example, when Intel started, they were mainly a B2B (business-to-business) organization, meaning we didn't sell to the end user. Intel sold their product through original equipment manufacturers (OEMs) like Apple, Dell, etc. which in turn was used in the product sold to the consumer. A few years ago, Intel revamped their business model to also include more of a B2C (business-to-consumer) line. It was more focused on a vertical (i.e., line of business or industry) and from a technology standpoint. It brings a more end-to-end technology solution. However, this changed our sales structure and the skills we require from sales people.

When Intel had more of a B2B sales structure (and it still has this component), the sales team was assigned a geographic region. That meant understanding that the geographic market was a primary skill for sales professionals. The new structure meant that sales people needed to understand the specifics of the technology line they were selling, like cloud computing, Internet of things (IoT), memory, and perceptual computing.

Williams explained that sourcing sales professionals in a rapidly changing technology environment makes it difficult to keep the talent pipeline filled—a challenge he's okay with. "It's hard to find a sales person to sell innovative technology that's still being defined. But, that's what keeps my job fresh."

He added that part of what makes recruiting for sales positions unique is the hybrid of skills that are necessary for a successful organization. "At Intel, our sales group is comprised mostly of business development managers (BDM) and technical sales specialists. I describe the BDMs as Batman and specialists as Robin. Both are responsible for meeting revenue goals, and both require sales and technology knowledge and skills, but the mix is different. Because their level of engagement with the client is a bit different."

If you're wondering where to find those passive candidates, think about your frenemies, those organizations in your industry that some days you collaborate with and other days you compete with. If you cannot identify those companies, ask your hiring manager. Williams says having conversations with hiring managers is key. "As a recruiter, I need to know the industry, the players, and the market in terms of compensation and benefits. I also need to understand the job. What's on the job description (in many cases) is only ABOUT 40 percent of what the hiring manager really wants. I talk with the manager to make sure I have a clear understanding."

Williams said he's found success sourcing passive candidates. "Recruiting is a hunting game, not a fishing game. The best candidates are the passive ones—the ones who are willing to look at a great opportunity." He added that those are the candidates who are focused on building their careers. "There's a difference between job hopping and career building. Changing jobs every 1 to 3 years is job hopping. Changing jobs every 3 to 5 years is career building."

Which raises the question, can recruiters take steps during the interview process to ensure a candidate has the knowledge and skills to be successful? Williams responded that he feels that candidates should be able to sell themselves and their accomplishments. "Paper doesn't show everything. At Intel, we hold managers accountable for their hires. If they want to check references, that's fine. But on some level, references are a waste of time. Managers need to feel comfortable with the information the candidate told them."

"Extreme" Recruitment

The competition for technology and programming talent is so intense that organizations are using some unique (or extreme) tactics. According to an article in *Entrepreneur*, Deloitte's recruiting representatives are starting to source candidates at hackathons, code fests, and product showcases. They're also eliminating the traditional multistep interview process and personality assessment.

While this approach may not work for all organizations, it does point to three things: 1) companies need to constantly assess what's happening in the job market; they can't wait until an opening exists; 2) companies may have to revamp their current hiring practices to attract the best talent; and 3) companies need to be able to do it quickly, or risk losing talent.

Industry Recruitment

In addition to some organizations specializing their sourcing of candidates based on the job, some industries have such specialized business models that companies within those industries require candidates to have industry experience. I'm not here to debate whether that's true. But in my experience, government, health care, hospitality, retail, and transportation have an element of uniqueness to them. For example, it might be the need to hire tipped employees. Or the need to hire airline employees who are covered under the Railway Labor Act.

Organizations differ in their preferences: some deem industry experience as essential, whereas others say that employees can get the training they need on the job, and still others want outsiders. I've been hired by companies because I *didn't* have industry experience. Those employers felt being an outsider gave me a fresh perspective.

It gets back to the question I posed at the beginning of the chapter: What's the first qualifier for candidates? If it's industry knowledge, then that will drive your sourcing strategy.

FYI
Equal Employment, AAPs, and Diversity

Companies with contracts in the public sector may be subject to laws that require diversity recruiting and reporting, as well as an affirmative action plan (AAP).

As I mentioned in the preface, the law is always changing. We're not taking an in-depth look at laws in this book, but recruiters should still be aware of legal requirements. It will impact your recruiting efforts, particularly in the area of sourcing.

If you're looking for information about affirmative action plans or related topics, I suggest checking out SHRM's Express Request feature. It's free and can quickly provide resources to get you started. You can access it on the SHRM website under the Resources & Tools tab.

Certain professions (such as serving in the government or military) involve tasks and responsibilities that could transition perfectly into new roles. For example, defense contractors regularly source service members because they have a working knowledge of the industry as well as transferable skills.

Military Recruitment

Only 20 percent of employers have veteran recruiting initiatives, according to Futurestep. In addition, 70 percent don't provide training to recruiters or hiring managers on veteran hiring. Veterans are a huge untapped source of excellent candidates.

SHRM works with the U.S. Department of Labor's Veterans' Employment and Training Service (VETS) and the Employer Support of the Guard and Reserve (ESGR). SHRM members have access to the tools that will help them understand the value of hiring veterans and working with employees who are active reserve members. Check out SHRM's Military Employment Resource Page for more information.

A couple of the resources that I found particularly interesting on SHRM's resource page included a step-by-step toolkit for employers, an employment training tool related to traumatic brain injury and post-traumatic stress, and an eLearning course on the Uniformed Services Employment and Reemployment Rights Act (USERRA).

Recruiting Older Workers and Pre-Retirees

Please forgive me for the subtitle in this section. I think we're still trying to figure out the most socially acceptable terminology for this group. Is it mature workers? Aging workforce? Older employees? Baby Boomers? Instead of focusing on the label, I want to talk about individuals who are probably over age 50 and thinking about some aspects of formal retirement, like Social Security and Medicare.

These individuals are thinking of retirement-related programs because of the age eligibility, not necessarily because they are physically or emotionally ready to stop working. In most developed countries, population growth among people over age 65 is outpacing the growth of the traditional working age population (ages 25 to 64). This means, at some point in the not-too-distant future, organizations will have to look at older workers as a source of talent—if they're not doing it already.

SHRM and the SHRM Foundation have launched the Aging Workforce Research Initiative, a research project to recognize the value of older workers. An executive summary, posted on the SHRM website, examines the state of older workers in the U.S., along with recruitment and retention strategies. The results were also reported by industry, including manufacturing; oil, gas, and mining; and finance, insurance, and real estate.

Ex-Offender Employment

According to the Prison Policy Initiative, a nonprofit, nonpartisan research organization, 636,000 people are released from prison each year. It goes without saying that these people need jobs. It helps them to successfully re-enter society and become contributing citizens. And organizations need workers.

I'm not suggesting that organizations compromise safety and security. However, there could be opportunities to create a win-win situation. In the SHRM article "Hiring Job Seekers with Criminal Histories," author Mark Feffer told the story of Davon Miller, who was convicted of distributing cocaine and unlawful possession of a firearm. After his release from prison, he was able to find work in the restaurant industry starting with an entry-level role and working his way up to sous chef and kitchen manager.

Legislation is also playing a factor. An increasing number of states are passing ban-the-box laws, which remove the check box on job applications asking if a candidate has ever been convicted of a crime. The intent of these laws is to require employers to consider the candidate's experience and qualifications before doing a background check. As I mentioned earlier, organizations will want to make sure that they are compliant with the laws in the cities and states where they are sourcing and recruiting.

Employing Individuals with Disabilities

According to the last U.S. Census, nearly one in five people have a disability. In addition, only 41 percent of those ages 21 to 64 are employed. Clearly, there's a gap between the number of qualified candidates with a disability and the opportunities they are being considered for.

In a survey conducted by the Florida Endowment Foundation for Vocational Rehabilitation on recruiting and retaining people with disabilities, respondents suggested the barriers to hiring people with disabilities included the cost of providing health insurance, job accommodations, training, and the lack of management commitment.

Some organizations have found that hiring individuals with disabilities fosters diversity and inclusion, which brings value to both the business and the bottom line. Publix Super Markets is one of those companies. It is the largest employee-owned grocery chain in the U.S. with $34 billion in sales and over 188,000 employees. And, for over 20 years, it has been listed as one of *Fortune* magazine's 100 Best Companies to Work For. CEO Ed Crenshaw explained the company's hiring philosophy: "Publix realizes the need to be able to serve a diverse customer base and have people working for us that resemble that base."

Once recruiters understand the job they are sourcing and the qualifications of their ideal candidate, then they can start identifying the source. One of the first places any recruiter should look is their employees.

Employees as a Referral Source

Employee referral programs are considered a very effective way to recruit quality talent at a low cost-per-hire. LinkedIn's *Global Recruiting Trends 2016* reported that 39 percent of talent leaders rank employee referrals high as a source. However, the same study pointed out that there's room for program improvements.

A big mistake that organizations make is thinking employee referral programs are about referral bonuses. The reality is they're about *culture*.

Organizations that want robust employee referral programs need to make sure they are building a culture that encourages employees to make referrals. Employees can't make referrals if they don't meet people, which means employees need work/life balance to feel as if they can take the time to attend, for example, networking events and association meetings. It means they need to feel good about their job and their work.

Employee referrals don't happen just because you set aside money in the budget. I've worked places in which employees made referrals with no program in place. They were actively engaged with the company and proceeded to tell their friends and acquaintances. The money is just an extra.

Speaking of the money, I've often said that organizations need to pay referral bonuses that align with their cost-per-hire. For example, if your cost-per-hire is $5,000, then paying a $25 referral bonus six months after the new hire starts isn't … well, it just *isn't*. I can't tell you what to offer, but do consider the savings when you are having this discussion. Then build your bonuses accordingly. Employees who provide successful referrals save companies a whole bunch of money. Thank them for it.

I would also challenge organizations to eliminate the so-called waiting period for paying referral bonuses. The employee's role in a referral program is to provide the company with the *candidate*. The responsibility for selection and retention doesn't belong to the employee—it belongs to the manager. Why are employees being penalized by having to wait for their referral bonus? The responsibility of selecting the right candidate, setting the new employee up for success, training him or her, and providing recognition belongs to the manager. If the new employee leaves in 60 or 90 days, then the issue wasn't the referral. The company needs to look somewhere else for answers.

Referral bonuses have the potential to be a very effective recruiting tool for organizations. But the key to their success is in appropriate pricing, timely payment, and placing responsibility for the program where it belongs.

POV
Boomerang Employees Know the Company's Strengths and Weaknesses

Of course, another consideration with employee referral programs are former employees (also known as "rehires" or "boomerangs"). A couple of years ago, I had the pleasure of recording a podcast on boomerang employees with John Hollon, a media executive with broad expertise in talent management. He's also someone who has firsthand experience as a boomerang employee. So I asked John if he would share his thoughts.

John, why should organizations consider boomerang employees? Is there a reason *not* to?
I can see a lot of upside to hiring people who used to be in your employ. Not only can they

get up to speed quicker than someone who doesn't know the organization, but they have a better sense of the culture, working environment, relationships with other employees, and other knowledge that is helpful both to the employer and to them. That's all good.

However, there is a major issue to consider—why did the former employee leave in the first place? Even if it was under good circumstances, organizations change, and the would-be boomerang may simply not fit as well given how the company has evolved. Plus, my experience is that boomerangs don't get much of a honeymoon period the second time around because the company feels they already know them. That means that the normal adjustment period new hires have gets washed away pretty quickly for a returning employee—even if the organization now is very different from the one they've left. That's a recipe for trouble in my book.

Since they've been through the process already, should the hiring process be different for boomerang employees?

The hiring process for a boomerang should focus on whether or not they would be happy, and the company happy, if they returned. Why did they go in the first place? If it was because of some situation on the job, has that changed since they have left? They also need to be brought up to speed on what has changed since they left and how those changes would impact them. My experience is that the more the boomerang is able to be hired for a job that is completely different from what they did the last time around, the higher the probability for success in their return.

Once hired, how can organizations set boomerang employees up for success?

If an organization decides to rehire a former employee, it means they have gotten past why the person departed in the first place and have accepted that they are better off with them than not. So it behooves the organization to do everything possible to make sure they can re-acclimate to the workplace environment and get up to speed quickly.

Companies go wrong when they assume this will be easy given the boomerang's previous experience, and it helps to give them a mentor to guide them—preferably someone they already know from their first tour of duty. The mentor should be focused on helping the boomerang get plugged into all that has changed since they left, as well as getting acclimated to their new job and work environment. Anything an organization can do to help the boomerang easily adjust and get settled will pay off in the long run.

What you don't want is a boomerang hire gone bad, where a good idea gets turned into a terrible experience for all involved. That's why anything an organization can do to make the new job situation as clear and focused as possible will help to maximize the potential for boomerang success.

I think John's comments are a good reminder that we need to move past the mindset that every employee who leaves us is disengaged and disgruntled. Past employees are, or can be, a great source of hire. They can also be a great source for employee referrals, that is, if they feel the company was a good place to work and will treat their referral right as an employee.

Organizations cannot recruit by employee referrals alone, but referrals are an essential part of any sourcing strategy. However, they only work if the culture allows and supports it.

Job Posting and Job Bidding

In addition to referrals, two other processes that allow employees to get involved in candidate sourcing are job postings and job bidding.

Job posting is the process of an organization letting existing employees know an opening exists. Some organizations are committed to posting all openings internally before starting to source outside candidates. The advantages include positive morale because employees feel they have career opportunities. The disadvantage can be a slower time-to-fill because the organization conducts two searches—one internally and potentially another one externally.

Job bidding occurs when employees express an interest in an opening that hasn't occurred yet. Employees can formally let the company know of their desire and qualifications for a position. The downside is that the opening hasn't occurred yet, and there's no guarantee of when or if an opening will happen. The upside is that, if an opening does occur, the recruiting team already has candidates in the pipeline. It's also possible that the employee might be qualified for other similar opportunities.

In both job posting and bidding, organizations need to be conscious of the employee engagement and retention implications of not following their processes. Job posting and bidding can be very positive for morale—inconsistency in the program can have the opposite effect.

The sources we've talked about so far have been quite specific and targeted. A couple of other places to source applicants have a broader reach. I like to think of them as either in-person or third party.

In-Person Sourcing

In-person sourcing includes activities such as walk-ins, college recruiting, and job fairs. I know that sometimes in our technology-driven society it might be easy to forget the days of walking into a company and filling out a job application. Depending on the jobs you're sourcing, this could be a viable strategy.

The key to effective in-person sourcing is writing an enticing job posting that prompts people to show up when and where you want them. We touched on job ads briefly with Tim Sackett back in Chapter 3 (on employment branding) and mentioned the need for a realistic job description. In these situations, if someone is walking in to apply or attending a job fair to apply, the job description needs to be succinct and, dare I say, *sexy*. Recruiters want candidates to hear the one-minute pitch and say, "Ooooh! Where's an application?" versus "Hmmm … let me think about it."

The second key element to successful in-person sourcing is marketing. Not only does the copy need to be well written, but it needs to be packaged effectively and displayed in the right places. You can have the best job posting in the whole world, but if no one sees it, applicants aren't going to show up.

How to Get Your Job Postings in Front of Job Seekers

When it comes to digital marketing, I believe that one of the most mysterious technology terms out there is SEO (aka search engine optimization). Lots of people claim to be SEO experts. Many folks will tell you to do *this* or *that* because it "improves SEO." But honestly, what does that mean?

 POV
HR Professionals Should Care about Search Engine Optimization

A couple of years ago, I had the opportunity to interview Susan Vitale, chief marketing officer at iCIMS, where she talked about SEO in the context of human resources. It was an interesting conversation, so I wanted to share it with you.

Susan, briefly describe for readers what search engine optimization (SEO) is and why we should care about it.

SEO is the practice of improving the visibility and ranking of a website in a search engine's "organic," or unpaid, results. In most cases, the higher a website ranks on the search results page, the more visitors to the website it will receive from the search engine's users.

HR professionals should care about SEO because it is crucial to their talent acquisition efforts. Although traditional recruitment advertising techniques generate visits to your career site, more and more candidates are using major search engines like Google or Bing to find jobs.

One of the first things job seekers do in their quest to find their dream job is to simply run a Google search of their desired job title, plus a location. There are tens of billions of searches performed online, with the majority on Google alone. And, according to DirectEmployers, over 300 million job-related searches take place on other search engines.

The challenge is this: If you were to search for a job opening, there would typically be far too many results to go through (for example, a Google search for marketing jobs in New Jersey yields about 40 million results). Most of the results on the first page are populated by job board sites and websites such as Craigslist. With Google only displaying ten results per page, competition for these spots can be very intense. Companies need to find ways to raise their profile on search engines. Fortunately, all of this can be addressed to work in your favor if you put the right practices into place to make your careers site more SEO-friendly.

I've always found SEO to be very broad in scope. At times, it can appear a bit overwhelming. What areas do you see as having the greatest potential to be overlooked? And, if HR only has time to focus on one aspect of SEO, what should that be?
Mobile optimized career microsites are becoming an important part of companies' SEO strategies for talent acquisition because they help drive traffic to their career portals. Career microsites are small search engine optimized websites that advertise your jobs and point traffic to your career portal. Unlike traditional job boards, a career microsite is like your company's own job board, in that it is fully branded and can include additional information to sell your company.

The real power of the career microsite and the main difference between a career microsite and a career portal is the website address or the URL. A strong URL is a key component in SEO which drives traffic to your site by helping your company rank higher in a standard, non-branded (meaning, not using your company name) Google search. It is an independent website using keywords and the .JOBS domain to support an improved search engine ranking. A company's career portal, however, uses a .com domain and a branded website address. Because of this, the career portal does not rank as high on non-branded searches with any of the most popular search engines like Google, Bing or Yahoo.

The value of the career microsite, therefore, is that in using SEO techniques, your career microsite and your job postings rank more highly in a Google search. This allows your open positions to be found, even if a candidate does not know your company name and performs a Google search using generic job titles or locations.

SEO changes on a regular basis. Every time Google changes their algorithm, search preferences change. Are there 2-3 SEO basics that everyone can and should remember?
A couple of years ago, Google changed its algorithm to rank mobile friendly sites higher in search rankings. This is BIG news for businesses that rely on organic website traffic. It's also important for employers who use their career microsite to attract and hire top talent since Google's new algorithm will bump down sites in search rankings that are not mobile optimized.

Talent recruiters are potentially losing out on due to obsolete technology. We've seen it in our work with clients. The disruptive force of technology has permanently changed the way people apply for jobs and how companies hire, leaving dramatic and lasting effects on talent acquisition practices. From the rise of job aggregator apps to social recruiting to increased video usage among both job seekers and employers, a digital revolution has surely taken place in the industry today. The most basic takeaway for recruiters: if your career site is not mobile-optimized you're already missing out on a massive number of potential candidates.

If a company is doing SEO right, what kind of results should they expect? Conversely, how can someone tell if they're doing SEO wrong?

SEO should be part of an overall employment branding strategy that is driven by the career microsite capable of being viewed on any device. Having a consistent, well-branded company presence online and on social networks will make SEO simpler and more effective. In the end, the number and quality of candidates should increase over time due to higher search rankings and resulting traffic.

Therefore, measurement is also key. SEO is not a "one and done" activity; it is an ongoing effort, so the ability to measure the success of an SEO strategy is necessary to improve it constantly. To ensure positive results, measure and track the candidate sources that are performing best for each type of role, which will enable the company to meet specific objectives and achieve maximum return on investment.

While the research shows an increase in job seekers using their mobile phones to search and apply for jobs, don't panic if your career site isn't mobile optimized. The good news is there are talent acquisition suite providers that can make it easy for companies. They employ a responsive design technique to automatically accommodate the appropriate viewing experience whether the candidate is on a desktop, smartphone or tablet. It's not about doing everything yourself. It's about understanding enough to know when to partner.

Speaking of partners, our last sourcing option is using third-party recruiters. Mark Fogel touched on one aspect of third party recruiting, executive search, earlier in the chapter. But that's not the only kind.

Using Third-Party Sources to Recruit

Not all sourcing must be done in-house. In fact, sometimes it may make sense to partner with an external resource like an executive recruiter, staffing firm, or recruitment process outsourcing firm for assistance.

I'd also encourage organizations not to view using a third party as "we don't have the capability in-house." Using a third party isn't an acknowledgment of failure, it's about using the company's resources wisely. I view it like my AAA membership. If I get a flat tire, am I capable of changing it? Yes. Is that the best use of my time and energy? No. I'd get more done using an outside resource to do that work while I answer e-mails and make calls.

But it's important to understand that not all outside recruiters specialize in the same thing. For instance, I asked a friend of mine, Alan Berger, an executive recruiter with 25-plus years of employment lifecycle experience, to explain what executive recruiters do. The HR search practice he oversees at Steven Douglas Associates is a mix of contingency and retained search from the mid to senior level and is almost exclusively focused on South Florida. According to Berger, "An executive recruiter's job is to build a recruiter/client relationship and help the organization surface viable candidates for their openings. Perhaps the organization wasn't satisfied with a candidate and are looking for more candidates with a better fit. Or the organization may need multiple candidates to move along in the process. I've worked with one publicly traded company that always needs at least two candidates to advance to the final round."

Joan Ciferri, president of David Wood Personnel, explained how using a staffing firm is different from traditional sourcing:

> When a company pays to post a position on a job board their preference would likely be to find a candidate through that posting rather than adding a recruiting fee to what they've already paid for in the posting. That being said, if they are open to working with a recruiter the process of hiring is much easier and time effective for them in the long run.
>
> Many recruiters spend most of their day finding candidates for jobs instead of jobs for candidates. What that means is that clients contact the recruiter with job openings and they recruit for the qualified candidates to fit those jobs. After all, it is the client company who is paying the recruiter to perform.
>
> Staffing firms should be able to share with the candidate more about the job than just the information in the job posting. They should be able to give the candidate insight into the person they will be interviewing with and practice a mock interview. This will help candidates to feel confident about communicating the qualities and experience they have that qualifies them for the job. Staffing firms can also provide testing and reference checking. This makes it much easier for the client to focus on hiring the right person.

Recruitment Process Outsourcing

Recruitment process outsourcing (RPO) is a form of business process outsourcing in which a company partners with an outside expert to design and execute a program that transforms the talent acquisition function. It's a very strategic partnership, whereby the RPO partner recruits on behalf of the client, essentially acting as the internal recruitment function.

RPOs are a holistic solution in that, in addition to providing sourcing and recruiting services, they offer technology solutions like an applicant tracking system (ATS). The RPO provider is accountable to fill all requisitions that fall within its scope of work. It works directly with hiring managers to develop and execute a sourcing strategy and to recruit passive candidates specifically for their openings. All candidates are tracked within the ATS to ensure the client is compliant. Candidates are then hired as employees of the client organization.

I asked Pam Verhoff, president of Advanced RPO, a consultancy focused on building innovative recruitment solutions that are highly tailored to each client's unique needs, what types of positions are ideal for an RPO. Verhoff has over 25 years of industry experience in designing and executing talent acquisition solutions for clients of all sizes, from *Fortune* 100 to startups. She described how an RPO works:

> RPO was first adapted by organizations that had a high volume of one position (e.g., customer service representatives in a call center environment). However, RPO providers have become much more sophisticated and are effective at handling all position types. It's just like you have an internal team of recruiters handling talent acquisition. If the hiring manager is effective at defining what they need within the role, an RPO recruiter is better able to employ the most effective recruitment strategy to fill the role. An RPO partnership does require defined scope, meaning clarity around which positions the RPO provider is responsible for as well as the activities that are outsourced to the RPO provider. It may be a specific location, specific functions or all roles or it may just be the front end of the process, rather than end-to-end. With the majority of our clients, Advanced RPO supports clients end-to-end and fills all openings across the organization.

You may be asking yourself, is an RPO basically the same thing as a staffing agency? And the answer is no. Staffing agencies are much different than RPO providers. Staffing agencies are typically focused on contract staffing (temporary) and individual searches. In both cases, the work is sometimes reactive and transactional. Staffing agencies are also typically focused on very specific functions within a defined geography—for example, accounting and finance in the New York market. As such, they build a database of talent that meets their criteria and then shop that talent out to organizations. Unless it's a direct hire, the candidates who are placed are employees of the *agency*, not employees of the company in which they are working. Both staffing agencies and RPOs are valuable depending on the needs of the organization.

Verhoff explained the unique advantages of working with an RPO:

In my opinion, the greatest advantage of working with an RPO provider is the access to recruitment expertise. Recruiting is an RPO provider's core competency. Therefore, they invest in great recruiters. They also have extensive experience managing recruiting functions for many clients, so they share best practices. Access to an extensive team of experts has far greater return than hiring 1 or 2 recruiters in-house or on a contract basis. A very close second advantage is the scalability of an RPO solution. If you have a spike in requisitions, they apply more resources, and conversely, if the volume drops, they reduce resources. They handle all of the resource management. Pricing models are variable, so you aren't saddled with a heavy fixed overhead tied to recruiting.

Active versus Passive Candidates

Active candidates are those individuals who are *actively* seeking a job. Passive candidates aren't out there telling their friends that they're looking, but they might be persuaded to leave for the right opportunity.

When the labor market is tight, recruiters may have to include passive candidates in their sourcing strategy. Passive candidates can have the skill set the organization is looking for. They may not overinflate their qualifications or requirements, since they're happy with their current position and not anxious to leave.

Recruiters looking to pitch passive candidates will want to think about what they can offer someone in terms of the job, benefits, compensation, and the company. Do you have what it takes to encourage someone who is content with his or her current position to listen to a new opportunity?

Find the Sources That Bring the Best Results

According to a *Talent Acquisition Benchmarking Report* customized by the SHRM Knowledge Development division (February 2017), the top 10 sources being used by organizations are:

1. Employee referrals (84 percent).
2. Company website (82 percent).
3. Social media (67 percent).
4. Paid job boards (66 percent).
5. Free job boards (63 percent).
6. Staffing agencies: temp to hire (48 percent).
7. Informal networking (48 percent).
8. Staffing agencies: direct hire (42 percent).
9. Print advertising (38 percent).
10. On-campus college recruiting and job fairs (tied at 37 percent).

You'll notice that the top sources of hire are ones that the organization controls—employee referrals, company career portals, and social media. That's not to say that outside resources like job boards, staffing agencies, and college campuses lack value. But it does mean that effective sourcing begins at home. Organizations must have their own sourcing strategies in place for outside partnerships to work effectively.

TIPS
3 Tips for Taking Your Sourcing Strategy to the Next Level

Sourcing is like putting together a jigsaw puzzle. It's about finding the perfect pieces that fit together to bring qualified candidates to the organization. It doesn't matter if you work in a huge global organization or a small office—sourcing is a key component in hiring the right people. I asked three professionals who have responsibility for sourcing to share their thoughts on next-gen sourcing.

*1. **Kelly Dingee** is senior talent acquisition manager with Marriott International, an American multinational hospitality company. She is also a blogger for* Fistful of Talent (www.fistfuloftalent.com).

> There are several actions recruiters can take to find and test new sources. Networking with peers, training, and conferences are excellent for jump starting sourcing strategies.
>
> I've also found that 20 years into this sourcing world, the foundation I got from AIRS (www.airsdirectory.com) was solid. And the tactics appear to be unchanging (the Boolean search operator site: for example).
>
> Taking the time to explore new sites/sources and determining how to best leverage them continues to be invaluable. A recruiter that easily runs search strings without a bot, and enjoys research, needs just one luxury to continue to develop new sources—time. Recruiters that continue to get their hands dirty with sourcing will continue to find new sources. Simple key word searches, peer searching candidates, and locating candidate contact information are all tasks that uncover new resources with a few quick keystrokes. Taking just one hour each week to explore functioning outside a recruiter's normal sources and tools can do much to develop a recruiter's knowledge. Team that with a peer that you can bounce ideas off of? It's gold.
>
> Now as I help source executives for Marriott, I'm finding it's key to meet up with my managers and peers to get ideas as well as share

whatever we've discovered in the past week. And more often than not, I'm not looking for new tools to help me find people (except when it comes to contact information, always seeking great tools there), but ways to expedite the process of extracting data en masse.

2. **Dr. Ameerzeb Pirzada** *is the chief and consultant dentist at Z Dental Studio in Pakistan. The office has fewer than 20 employees and provides services in every field of dentistry, including maxillofacial surgery, prosthodontics, and pediatric dentistry.*

As a teacher at my university, I get to interact and recruit a lot of fresh graduate students. It's made me realize that global and college recruiting should be re-engineered for it to succeed.

Young people play a key role in a modern-day practice. Unfortunately, recruiting budgets and processes have been the same for the past decade, even though colleges and expectation of the students have changed drastically, the methods for recruiting remain the same.

Personally, I believe, global college recruiting, taking on college students from remote areas and recruiting students from online universities can change the entire recruiting model and keep you ahead of the curve. Moreover, you may get recruits that may go above and beyond their natural limits to get the job done. On the plus side, global recruiting will make your company stand out; your company will be known as a company that recruits internationally which means more exposure for your establishment.

3. **Ninh Tran** *is chief operating officer and co-founder of Hiretual, an artificial intelligence (AI) sourcing platform built by recruiters for recruiters that serves as a "recruiter's best friend." Before starting Hiretual, he worked for Google and co-founded HireTeamMate, Inc., an executive search firm. He's a frequent contributor to the SourceCon and ERE Media communities.*

Behind every successful sourcer is the mastery of technology, the basic skill of research, and natural curiosity. During the Hiretual beta, our top super user, Vishnu Vardhan at Roljobs, topped 10,443 people sourced and screened in less than one week. Before that, his weekly average was 3,843. He mastered sourcing technology and fully integrated it into his process. Vishnu supported his team of ten recruiters with thirty consistent on-site interviews each week.

To understand technology, you must get your hands dirty trying different things and sourcing methods. Be willing to fail, measure everything, and try again until you achieve more productivity or ninety percent engagement rate. Researching is about searching, again and again, going deeper each time discovering new things and "finding what cannot be found." Build up the expertise of finding clues and making connections where they are unlikely to happen—not just to find the right people but to engage them. Set yourself apart from the rest of the crowd. I highly recommend putting your sourcing to the challenge on sites like Sourcing Games (www.sourcing.games/) and hone your abilities. Natural curiosity is what drives the sourcing experts to ask questions and poke around source codes to find things like LinkedIn uploading its user's resumes to SlideShare.

SECTION IV: 3 Key Takeaways

- Sourcing begins inside the company. Organizations already have many resources available to them, especially current employees.
- Different positions require different sources. There is no one single source that will find all the qualified candidates a company needs.
- Sourcing is also about trial and error. It's about "getting your hands dirty" and always being curious.

5 Resources to Make Your Job Easier

1. If your organization is required by law to have an affirmative action plan, the U.S. Department of Labor, Office of Federal Contract Compliance Programs has affirmative action programs you can review at www.dol.gov/ofccp/regs/compliance/aaps/aaps.htm.

2. Writing the perfect job ad can be tough. Roy Maurer posted valuable tips in the article "Crafting the Perfect Job Ad" on the SHRM website.

3. Speaking of job ads, an increasing amount of research shows that gender-neutral ads yield more candidates. For the ZipRecruiter blog, Matt Krumrie wrote a piece titled "Are You Limiting Candidates with Biased Job Ads?" and Jeanne Anderson posted some tips to remember in "Data Doesn't Lie: Removing These Gendered Keywords Gets You More Applicants."

4. SHRM offers an excellent resource for recruiting workers with disabilities. "Where Can Employers Find Qualified Applicants with Disabilities?" can be found under the Resources & Tools section of the SHRM website (www.shrm.org/resourcesandtools/tools-and-samples/hr-qa/pages/applicantswithdisabilities.aspx).

5. Mark Fogel's *HumanCapital3* blog (humancapital3.wordpress.com) focuses on high-performance human resources and helping organizations grow talent strategically.

SECTION V
Selecting the Best Candidate

In Section V

You'll probably notice that Sections IV and V are pretty similar in length; that's because organizations need to spend just as much time selecting the right candidate as they do sourcing one. I've seen many organizations put tremendous resources behind sourcing and then spend very little time on selecting the right person.

This section is important because it addresses one of the first times that a candidate comes into face-to-face contact with the company—during the interview.

CHAPTER 8:
Interview Experience

CASE STUDY
Candidate Nightmares!

I'm a big fan of the blog *Lifehacker*. The blog focuses on a little bit of everything—careers, technology, food, lifestyle, etc. A couple of years ago, it ran a piece asking readers to share their worst job interview experiences. There were hundreds of replies. Here are a few excerpts (which I edited for brevity and clarity):

> I was greeted in a surly manner and given forms to complete (the kind that were copies-of-copies-of-copies-of-copies), all of the information being requested was easily and clearly available on the online forms required for the interview process. I finished the forms with about 10 minutes left until my appointment. I was not seen until 45 minutes after my appointment was scheduled. Neither explanations nor apologies were provided.

> I meet with the CEO, and we're chatting. He was nice and friendly, and things were going great. He asks me to tell him about myself. So, I did. Suddenly, his demeanor and attitude changed. He became condescending and aggressive in his questions, not giving me enough time to answer. The whole experience left me in shock (and I had another interview somewhere else nearby). It turns out he's a bit of an elitist. I graduated from a top-ranking computer science university. My grades were good. I was vice president of a tech-related club on campus. I was working two programming jobs for professors and did well during a rigorous interview process. None of that mattered because I was a transfer student from a community college. The fact that I did my general education at a community college seemed to deem me unworthy to work there.

> During the interview, the manager asked all of the normal questions and then asked if I was ok with pranking and making fun of my coworkers. I said not really unless it was in good humor and no one's feelings would be hurt. She stopped for a moment thinking about this and said that everyone at their location has a great sense of humor and they're always joking around or playing tricks on each other, so it's important to not let it get to you. A few days later I get a call from her, and she told me that unfortunately I didn't get the job and thanked me for applying. A few days later, I get a call, and the manager asks when I can come in for an interview. I was a little confused but told her my availability and then reminded her that I had previously interviewed the week prior. She paused for a moment and apologized because she said she didn't remember me or my interview then asked what our previous phone conversation had been about and if she had already offered me the job. I said that during the previous conversation she had told me that I hadn't been offered the job. Another long pause, then she said, "I'm sorry I called you twice, but I think I will stick with my previous decision and not offer you the job."

Before we talk about the interview experience, I think it's important to share my definition of what an interview is: It's a conversation about a job and a person's interest in and qualifications for the job. Emphasis on the word *conversation*. I believe there are times when both companies and candidates forget the interview is supposed to be a two-way conversation. I also believe it's the recruiter's responsibility to create an environment in which interviews can be the two-way conversation I defined. If a conversation doesn't happen, several things can occur:

- The company may not elicit the information—or enough information—it needs to decide about the candidate. The result is a potential loss of talent.

The candidate doesn't obtain the information he or she needs to decide about the company. Yes, the candidate is interviewing the company too. As a result, the candidate walks away with a negative experience. Don't forget Chapter 4 and what a negative candidate experience means for the organization. The interview experience is a subset of the overall candidate experience, and it's one of the most visible parts. If you consider the hiring process up to this point, most of it has been very impersonal. Candidates see marketing, websites, job postings, and the like. Now they are going to meet people. Once that happens, the experience changes. Expectations change as well.

The Screening Interview

I hesitate to classify a screening interview as a "mini-interview" even though it is a shorter type of interview. I like to think of it as more of a qualifier. By definition, a screening interview is a brief conversation (again—conversation) that allows the organization and candidate to decide if the other meets the minimum qualifications for a job. To me, the screening interview focuses on the deal breakers.

If the organization says that candidates must have communication, organization, math skills, and experience, then the screening should make sure the candidate has those qualities. Candidates shouldn't progress in the process if they don't meet the minimum criteria.

Likewise, if the candidate has an absolute "must have" for a job, the organization needs to confirm it can deliver. Honestly, no one wants to go through three to four interviews to hear that a candidate's salary requirements, for example, do not match the employer's salary range. It's time to put old-school thinking aside about when it's acceptable to talk salary. Companies should ask candidates about their requirements during the screening call.

The more interviews that take place, the more the candidate and company want to feel positive about the experience and that they will be able to negotiate what they are looking for.

TIPS
How to Handle a Bad Screening Interview

During the 2017 TAtech Spring Congress, Kevin Gaither, senior vice president of sales at ZipRecruiter, shared a great way to handle the bad interview. As much as we try to set the right tone, sometimes candidates just don't open up. Or candidates don't have the qualifications. Or the company can't give candidates what they're looking for.

Gaither suggests that if you (as the recruiter or hiring manager) see the initial screen isn't going well, flip the conversation, and let the candidates ask the questions.

Every single piece of interview advice to candidates is that they need to come to an interview prepared with questions. So let them ask their questions. Maybe it will change the conversation. Give candidates an opportunity to demonstrate their ability to ask good questions, and you'll find out where their head is at.

More importantly, this approach also allows candidates to leave with a good impression of the organization, regardless of whether they get the job.

Applications versus Resumes

Applications and resumes are not the same thing. Resumes are a summary of a candidate's professional experience. Applications contain legal wording about full disclosure and about lying being a terminable offense. You get my point. Even if candidates give you a resume, they need to fully complete an application—none of this "please see resume" stuff. I learned this lesson the hard way.

Years ago, I was hiring for a manager position. The director of the department sourced the candidate whom the staff members wanted to hire. They had worked with the person before. Seems perfect, right? The candidate came in for an interview, everyone loved the person, and an offer was extended. I told the director that the candidate needed to complete an application. The director responded, "I know this person. I've worked with them before. It's completely unnecessary." So, I tried to be cool and said okay.

Fast forward a couple of months. I was at home one morning before work and read the newspaper. There was an article about former workers in the juvenile justice system who were now being accused of violating the rights of teenagers. And of course, one of the people featured in the article was the manager I just hired. Needless to say, I broke a personal record getting into the office that morning.

How did the story turn out? Well, the director met the manager in the parking lot and came to my office. I asked if the manager had read the morning's newspaper. The manager said, "I should probably resign." This scenario could have been ugly. I know there are times when we want to be cool with hiring managers and let them cut corners. Find ways to do it without exposing the company to liability.

Applicant Tracking Systems

In Chapter 7, we talked about applicant tracking system (ATS) technology from the recruiter perspective; now I want to talk about it from the job seeker's point of view. If your organization uses an applicant tracking system, your technology provider likely can easily explain how its solution works for recruiters. But, the real value in applicant tracking software is when *job seekers* use it.

The thing recruiters have to remember is the job seeker's user experience, or UX in tech speak. If the company has a great ATS, but applicants become frustrated with it and don't complete the process, the ATS isn't helping your efforts.

POV
Job Seeker Frustrations with ATS

Years ago, I spoke with Jessica Miller-Merrell, chief innovation officer at Workology, about why organizations use ATS software. We realized that there are probably plenty of job applicants who are frustrated with applying for jobs online. They feel that their resume is shipped off to some sort of *black hole* never to be heard from again. And HR professionals feel that they are being labeled as lazy for not responding to online applications. Here are a few key excerpts from that interview:

Lots of companies have transitioned to having people apply for positions online. Why do companies accept online applications (versus walk-in applicants)?
Accepting applications online helps HR to organize and sort through the application process. Online allows for keyword search, data storage, and aids in compliance for companies who have government contracts and those that have hiring managers and employees who manage and hire teams in different places.

We've both heard that the downside of applying online is applicants feel the process lacks the human touch which can, in turn, come across as "lazy HR." Is there a plus for candidates to apply online (that might make up for the lack of human interaction up front)?
The application process is built to store and sort resume databases. Sometimes HR is lazy, but most often HR is responsible for so much within the organization, they are working to balance hiring, firing, training, advisement, and employee investigations in addition to the recruiting process. Companies are flooded with calls and emails by employees who are checking in on their application. Applying online ensures that your resume is stored and searchable within the database. It's important to aid in making your resume and application more searchable by including key words increasing the chances that the hiring manager will review your resume.

It certainly helps to have a personal connection inside the organization. This is where personal relationships can come into play to aid or elevate your application. Having a personal relationship or referral inside the company whether it's a business contact, family member, or someone you've recently connected online, can make a difference.

Last question. Let's talk about hiring managers. In your experience, what do hiring managers want from HR in the recruitment process?
Hiring managers want HR to get it right and send them the best-qualified candidates for the position. The problem is that HR doesn't often understand what the hiring manager wants or needs. They haven't walked a mile in their shoes or even truly understand the industry or the organization. Sometimes that is due to the process, and sometimes the hiring manager doesn't really understand. It's important for HR to ask lots of questions not only to the hiring manager but employees who currently hold the same position that you are hiring for. I've had success taking a more consultative approach to recruiting using a checklist and a position review form to get as much information about the position as possible.

Hiring managers don't always want to hear this or take the time in which to do it, but the time upfront spent makes the recruiting process more enjoyable and the process quicker and more efficient.

The In-Depth Interview Experience

There are three basic types of interview questions. They are all valuable. The key is using the right question at the right time. Here's an example:

Closed-ended questions have yes or no answers. An example of a closed-ended interview question is, "Do you have good customer service skills?" Let me add, while this is an example of a closed-ended question, it's a poor one because who is really going to say, "I have absolutely horrible customer service skills; the last thing you want to do is put me in front of your customer"? Ideally, closed-ended questions should be ones that confirm information (such as "Would you be able to occasionally work third-shift?") or questions that involve a specific answer (such as "How many direct reports did you have in your last manager role?").

Open-ended questions give candidates an opportunity to display their knowledge and provide information. Using the customer service example above, an open-ended question would be "How would you calm an angry customer?" This question is obviously better than the closed-ended one, but it's still not perfect. Candidates can give you a textbook response for dealing with difficult customers, but that doesn't mean they will do it when presented with the situation. Use open-ended questions when you're trying to understand more about the candidate but not necessarily his or her experience. For instance, "If I were to talk with your co-workers, what would they tell me about you?" or "Where would you like to be in your professional career in the next five years?"

Behavioral interviewing questions allow candidates to share their experience. They typically start with the phrase "Tell me about a time." For example, a customer service interview question would be "Tell me about a time when you had to calm an unhappy customer. What was the situation, and how did you handle it?" The candidates' answer to this question not only indicates that they know how to handle an angry customer but that they've done it.

Panel Interviews and Collaborative Hiring

I once worked for a company in which every single candidate interviewed with five to six people, including the founders. It was a small company that prided itself on having a family-like work environment. Hiring took a long time, and it could be frustrating for candidates.

Over the course of time, I realized that having a long process in which a candidate met lots of people was a good thing. Because the organization was small, we had many "unwritten rules" that weren't in a handbook or policy manual. And truth be told, sometimes the founders changed the rules. New hires needed a way to figure out what was going on—often without asking their boss or HR. So having a collaborative hiring process allowed candidates to meet people. It was a benefit to the new hires. But the real success in this approach happened when we started telling candidates the process and why we were doing it.

If you're considering panel or team interviews, think strategically about the individuals who participate on the panel. These individuals are buying into the new hire (and the new hire's success). Recruiting teams should be composed of a diverse group of people. We're not just talking about diversity in race, gender, and age. It's important to include employees with long and short company histories, as well as people from different departments.

Video Interviews

Organizations can save both time and money by considering video interviews, especially for virtual positions. Candidates don't have to fly in for interviews, saving them time as well. And interviews can be recorded, providing efficiency for the recruiting team.

According to Thomas Boyle, principal talent acquisition consultant for Cornerstone OnDemand, video interviewing technology could provide strategic benefits as well. "With most video interviewing providers offering live and pre-recorded interview options, companies are able to extend their candidate reach, while elevating their brand to a broader audience. By being able to record and share interviews companies will also see an immediate increase in collaboration, resulting in better quality of hire."

If the idea of video interviews makes you shiver from a legal perspective, have a conversation with your friendly neighborhood employment attorney. Boyle mentioned that, in the past, the Equal Employment Opportunity Commission (EEOC) has stated that the video interview and in-person interview are viewed as equivalent. "I have worked with many companies who see it as a way to ensure they are following consistent and transparent interview practices. It helps HR sleep a little better knowing that at least all the interview team members are asking the same questions."

Boyle shared five best practices for organizations considering the addition of a video interview component in their hiring process:

- Video interviewing is not one-size-fits-all. Leverage both live video and on-demand recorded interviews based on each unique position type. If you're hiring at the director or executive level, start with a live interview. If you're filling entry-level professional positions, send candidates an on-demand interview to complete. If your position is hourly or call center-related, perhaps start with an on-demand phone interview, and skip the video altogether.
- Video interviewing should never be considered a one-way conversation. Leverage technology to engage candidates with authentic video content before, during, and after interviews.

- Candidate experience is paramount when it comes to video interviewing. If your candidates don't complete the process or have a poor experience, it can be detrimental to your brand. Skype or Google Hangouts might be okay at first, but ultimately these tools were not built for the complexities of HR and talent acquisition.
- If you're leveraging on-demand interviewing technology, allow your candidates to introduce themselves. It will make them more comfortable with the camera and provide them an opportunity to sell themselves outside the position-specific interview questions you might be asking.
- It's extremely important that, if you're asking candidates to complete an on-demand or prerecorded interview, you provide them some level of flexibility when responding to your questions. One of the big benefits of this technology is the ability to determine if and when candidates can re-record their answers. Think about starting by allowing them to re-record their answers; then as they invest more time in the process, remove the re-record option from later questions.

Preparing Hiring Managers for Interviews

One of the organizations I worked for offered interview training for managers. I'm sure a lot of companies do. But let me suggest that you consider including a conversation about cost-per-hire in your interview training. We're going to talk about cost-per-hire and how to calculate it in Chapter 16, but I want to plant the idea here about a way to use it in interview skills training.

At my organization, we started interview skills training with a discussion about the process of bringing a person into the organization. What does it involve? Interviews, paperwork, training, etc. Then we discussed the cost of doing those things, specifically, the time—an hour to do an interview, four hours for orientation, and so on. I then shared the latest profit and loss statement so managers could see how much those activities cost. We calculated an approximate cost-per-hire.

Afterward, I distributed to every manager a list of their terminations for the past year and let them calculate how much they've spent hiring people. This was an eye-opening exercise for hiring managers. They realized that they could buy equipment, fund employee incentive programs, and allocate resources in other ways with the money they were spending.

This conversation allowed us to reach an agreement about hiring and terminating employees:

- Like most businesses, our organization will require documentation to make decisions that involve thousands of dollars. If departments want to create a new program or buy equipment, they have to write a proposal, with backup, and a plan. When it costs thousands of dollars to hire and terminate employees, managers should expect to provide documentation for their decisions.

- Like most businesses, we will not make decisions that involve thousands of dollars on a moment's notice, meaning that thousand-dollar decisions are discussed, debated, and planned. When it costs thousands to hire and terminate employees, managers cannot come to HR about terminating an employee and expect the conversation to last 15 minutes. They should expect more conversation and even investing some coaching time or other alternatives.

The other thing to consider with interview skills training is refresher training. Some managers go months without hiring someone, and then the need arises, and they don't want to go through the full training program again. They also may not want to admit that they've forgotten a few things along the way. Create a folder on your company intranet or in a cloud file storage system like Box or Dropbox so that managers can access information at their convenience—no need to clog up e-mail sending out files. Here are a few ideas to consider for refresher training content:

- A list of behavioral-based interview questions that align with the organization's values. No matter who managers are interviewing or for what position, they will need these.
- A couple of videos (three to five minutes max!) that explain common interview activities such as how to take good interview notes or how to properly wrap up the interview.
- A list of the top 10 tips for managers to remember. These can be the top takeaways from the interview skills program. Here's a top 10 list I put together for *HR Bartender* that I've had people tell me they're using in their training programs. If you like it, feel free to adapt it to suit your needs.

Top 10 Things New Managers Need to Know about Recruiting

1. **Tell HR when an employee resigns.** According to the Society for Human Resource Management (SHRM), the average time to fill a position is 42 days. The typical notice period is two weeks. If you tell HR about a resignation when it happens, then you're only potentially without an employee for 28 days (assuming the employee gave a two-week notice). If you tell HR on the employee's last day, that increases to 42 days. Allow HR to help you—tell them as soon as you know.

2. **Review the job description.** This is the perfect opportunity to make sure that what's written on paper about the job is what the employee actually does. Responsibilities change regularly—and that's okay. Just make sure the job description reflects what the employee is going to do. And make any necessary updates.

3. **Discuss contingent staffing.** In #1, we talked about how long it takes to fill a job. If you already know you can't live a month without an employee, talk with your manager and HR about what can be done. Maybe overtime can be authorized, or a freelancer can be brought in to help.

4. **Hiring managers are allowed to source candidates.** When job openings occur, remind people that the employee referral program exists (the company does have one, right?). Encourage them to tell the opening to their friends. Send out info about the opening to your social media network. Sit down with HR and tell them where you have connections. Work with them to source applicant flow.

5. **Don't assume you know how to interview.** I know on the surface that interviewing sounds very easy. But it's not. There are questions that are ill-advised to ask, such as "How old are you?," and some states ban asking "How much money do you make?" There's an art to interviewing. Ask HR if there's an opportunity to attend interview training.

6. **Take good interview notes.** Don't try to remember everything! After interviewing 3-4 people, it will be tough to distinguish between candidates. Find out how to take good (and legal) interview notes. Tell candidates during the interview that you will be taking notes.

7. **Collaborate!** Identify a couple of people who the employee will work with regularly and get them involved in the recruiting process. It helps to create buy-in, and it allows a new hire to know more than one person when they start. Every organization has unwritten rules, and new hires will want to find answers—but maybe not from their boss.

8. **Keep the candidate informed.** At the end of an interview, tell the candidate how the recruiting process works, the timetable to make a decision, and who they should contact once they leave. But first, make sure you and HR are on the same page about this information. Even if the candidate doesn't specifically ask, let them know anyway.

9. **Always send a TBNT (Thanks But No Thanks).** The people who interview with your company have the opportunity to also buy your product/service. You don't want to lose a candidate and customer at the same time. If a candidate isn't being considered any longer, let them know. They will respect you and the company. Coordinate response letters with human resources.

10. **Look for talent, even when there's not an opening.** In #4, we talked about managers helping to source candidates. That doesn't have to take place only when there's an opening. Managers should always be looking for talent. For example, I've never worked with sales directors who weren't always on the search for good sales talent. And when they found them, they presented the candidate to the company. It didn't matter if we had an open requisition or not.

FYI
Asking Candidates about Salary History

In my top 10 list above, I mentioned ill-advised interview questions. An increasing number of states are enacting legislation that would prohibit organizations from asking about a candidate's salary history during the interview process. Advocates for this legislation say it will improve pay equity in the workplace. On the other hand, limiting conversation about salary history could be a waste of time for both candidates and employers. Think about a scenario in which a candidate goes through a lengthy interviewing process only to discover that the company can't meet his or her salary requirements.

Organizations should watch this legislation for two reasons. First, to make sure they stay in compliance with the law. Next, to form an opinion about it. A workplace with several locations around the nation might opt to not discuss pay with any candidate (versus trying to remember which locations can and which ones can't.)

Interviewing Your Future Boss

We've talked about interview structure and questions. One special scenario worth addressing is if recruiters are presented with the opportunity to interview their future boss.

This scenario could happen for a few different reasons: A recruiter or hiring manager may be new to the organization and not have enough experience to be the boss. The recruiter or hiring manager may not want the boss's job. You may be asked to interview someone you would report to indirectly, such as the president of the division or region. My point being, it's not out of the realm of possibilities to interview someone you will report to.

Tom Darrow, SHRM-SCP, SPHR, has some experience with interviewing a future boss. He's founder and principal of Talent Connections, LLC and Career Spa, LLC in Atlanta, Ga. I met him when he was chair of the SHRM Foundation Board of Directors. I asked him if recruiters should be nervous or apprehensive about interviewing someone they might report to. He said recruiters should be thrilled to be interviewing someone they might report to or someone they might serve (for example, a hiring manager): "When the recruiter is involved in the assessment process, they not only have input into who gets chosen but they also lay the foundation for a strong relationship with the incoming leader."

Darrow added that interviewing is all about assessing the candidate's fit with the role, so this type of interviewing really shouldn't differ from other interviews. "When a recruiter is interviewing someone who would be their supervisor, they should focus more on the candidate's leadership style and their thoughts on recruitment strategy and process." Darrow provided some questions to consider:

- Give me some examples of how you've developed recruiters in the past.
- If I went to a recruiter who has reported to you in the past, what three words would they use to describe what it's like to work for you?
- Share some thoughts on your philosophies on recruitment strategy and process.
- Give me an example of a time when your recruitment team needed approval from above for a technology or another headcount. How did you develop the business case to upper management?
- Do you support recruiters attending conferences to stay abreast on latest best practices?
- How do you reward and recognize recruiting results?

Another part of the interview to be prepared for is candidate questions. Remember, this is a *conversation*. The candidate—your possible future boss—is interviewing you. Darrow shared questions a recruiter expects this candidate to ask:

- How do you measure the success of your recruiting results?
- Describe a difficult search that you've conducted.
- Describe a situation where you had a difficult hiring manager you've had to serve.
- Describe the respect level that talent acquisition currently has within the company.
- What have been the barriers to success?
- How is the morale of the employee base?
- As you're recruiting candidates, how do the compensation and benefits packages of the company compare to the market you're competing in?

After the interview, it's possible the candidate will want to connect with you on social media. You're in the same industry, so it makes sense. Darrow is an advocate of the practice. "Frankly, recruiters (and recruiting leaders) who have any hesitation about connecting on social media is a RED flag. After the employee referral program, social media is the primary source of top candidates."

One more thing. The scenario that Darrow and I've talked about so far is one with an external candidate. It's possible a recruiter might interview an internal candidate who is looking for a promotion, which can be tricky if the internal candidates doesn't get the job. Darrow recommended being prepared to share job-related examples of why the internal candidate isn't the right fit for the role. "Be truthful. Offer to work with them on a career development plan to help them advance so that maybe they are qualified for a similar role down the road."

The Realistic Job Preview

One of the best ways to explain a job to candidates is by giving them a real-life look at the job. I'm a believer that, if you want to know what it's like inside a company, just look at how it conducts meetings. Unfortunately, we don't always get to attend a company meeting before accepting a job offer. However, employers may want to consider sharing videos of their meetings. Google offers a sneak peek into what it's like to work there in its YouTube video "Search Quality Meeting: Spelling for Long Queries." It videotaped a meeting for the whole world to see.

Another common way to provide a realistic job preview is by using an inbox activity, described below. This is very helpful in work environments that rely heavily on e-mail as a form of communication. The goal of the activity is twofold: candidates get to see a sampling of the types of e-mail they should expect during a normal workday. And the company gets to see how candidates would react to the e-mails.

I would strongly suggest that, if you decide to incorporate an inbox activity into the interviewing process, be deliberate in its design and implementation.

TIPS
Conducting an Inbox Activity

The University of Kent in the United Kingdom put together a great overview of how an inbox activity works and said I could share it with you. Inbox exercises are usually conducted individually but can be run as a group exercise.

Activity Overview: This is a business simulation, where you play a member of staff who must deal with the tasks of a busy day. You will be given a selection of letters, emails, and reports in either paper or electronic format, which somebody who is doing the job might find in their inbox first thing in the morning.

Instructions: You should read each item, decide on the action to be taken, the priority to be allocated to it, and complete related tasks such as summarizing a report or drafting a reply to an email. Each item will start by describing the background scenario. The subject matter is usually related to the job you are applying for. Obviously, there is a lot of work to get through caused by your return from vacation or having to cover the work of an absent colleague.

There is a tight time constraint. You will be given one to two hours to complete the tasks which will consist of many items (perhaps 20 or more) to see how well you can handle several complex tasks in a short period.

Some tasks may just require a yes or no answer. Other items may need a longer response, such as drafting a reply to a customer complaint, writing a report, delegating tasks to colleagues or recommending action to superiors. You may need to analyze information for some items (i.e., calculating budgets or sales figures, using information provided). New items may be added while the exercise is in progress.

As part of the exercise, it's possible you might be asked to make a phone call to a "customer," a role played by one of the members of the hiring team.

In the end, you may be debriefed by a member of the hiring team and asked to discuss the decisions you made, and the reasons for these or you might be asked to prepare a memo outlining your priorities for action, or make a short presentation.

In some industries, a realistic job preview involves something like "mystery shopping." The candidate may be asked to have a meal or visit a location to observe service or use the product. I've seen hotels and restaurants require this type of exercise. The reason behind it is for candidates to experience what customers see—because once candidates become employees (and the staff knows who they are), they lose that anonymity. Their experience changes.

Like the job preview, organizations might give new employees a chance to experience the product when first hired (if they haven't already). For instance, hotels may have new front desk agents spend a night in the hotel so that they are knowledgeable about the product. Likewise, restaurants make sure servers eat the food so that they are in a position to recommend dishes to customers.

The job preview provides a look into the job that candidates (or new employees) cannot experience any other way.

The Interview Experience Is Worth an Investment

I know recruiters and hiring managers are busy, but the time spent during interviews is worth it. What happens during an interview determines who gets hired. It starts the process of building positive work relationships.

But I will confess that not everything can be discovered during an interview. The good news is that organizations have additional resources at their disposal to help them select the best candidate. Let's explore those options in the next chapter.

TIPS
3 Tips for Taking Your Interview Experience to the Next Level

In Chapter 4 we talked about the candidate experience and how it's changing. As the candidate experience changes, the interview experience must change along with it. I asked three professionals from different vantage points in the human resource space to share their thoughts.

1. **Barb Buckner** *is a seasoned HR professional with over 20 years of experience working in startups, family-owned businesses, small and midsize corporations, and nonprofit volunteer organizations. As a consultant for Timeless HR Solutions, she serves as a trainer and coach for supervisors, office managers, and HR practitioners wanting to better understand and manage employee relations, recruiting, and human resources as a strategic partner in today's organizations.*

While many recruiters have the interview process nailed, some still aren't finding "the right candidates" because they don't own the process before it gets to the interview stage. We talk about how the market has changed, how the candidates are harder to find, how employees are hard to keep ... but most of this is because we (on the whole) are still trying to approach recruiting the same way we always have. I'm not talking about networking or job boards, but more so getting down to the core of not only what the company wants in their next employee but what is realistic to expect in looking for that candidate. Hiring managers will just pull old job descriptions and say, "Find me a star to do this!" They put a list of requirements and "must haves" together based on their desires or experience and then hand it over to the recruiter to fill. Today's recruiters need to be more proactive and educate their clients or hiring managers as to what kind of candidate they should be looking for and what is realistic of their expectations with today's market.

- How many years of experience does your ideal candidate need?
- Is a degree or certification really a "must have"?
- What are the skills that the position, as it stands today, really requires to hit the ground running?

Those job descriptions are a great starting point for discussion, but most haven't been updated in years ... or ever! A recruiting professional isn't just looking to fill a position but to find the right "fit" for the company, so they gain a long-term employee and not a short-term replacement. Help them see past their immediate need to just "fill a position. " When you talk about other options in candidates that might be a better fit for what they are hoping for before you start the interview process, you set the stage for your client or hiring manager to honestly consider the final candidates you put in front of them. Be their true partner in this process and don't be afraid to have that discussion for fear of upsetting them or losing them as a client. Some may not listen or think you are wrong, but that is part of the stigma that we have to change these days about recruiting. Want to set yourself apart from that? Own the process ... from the first step.

2. *As employer communications manager at Glassdoor,* **Lisa Holden** *has spent the last decade helping companies brand themselves effectively to different audiences, including customers, employees, and prospective talent. At Glassdoor, she helps employers brand themselves to prospective talent in order to recruit informed candidates.*

Having a difficult interview process is a strategic approach that more employers should take. In fact, recent Glassdoor Economic Research finds that more difficult job interviews are statistically linked to higher employee satisfaction. Overall, a 10 percent more difficult job interview process is associated with 2.6 percent higher employee satisfaction later on, suggesting that if the interview process is tough, employers are doing what they should be to give candidates an accurate picture of what the role will be like.

However, there is a limit to how tough is too tough. On a five-point scale, the optimal or "best" interview difficulty that leads to the highest employee satisfaction is 4 out of 5. (Interview difficulty ratings based on a five-point scale: 1.0 = very easy, 3.0 = average, 5.0 = very difficult.) This results in an interview experience that is difficult but not overwhelmingly so for candidates.

3. **Ramona Taylor,** *owner of Abundant Professional Services in Virginia, has been a recruiter and human resource professional for 17 years. Her company provides human resource training, staffing, and consulting to small to medium businesses, nonprofits, and government agencies.*

The job market is still slowly recovering, and many applicants have been out of work or underpaid since the recession, increasing the pool of candidates tremendously. Obtaining a well-rounded quality employee is always a priority; however, those employees often get tossed to the side due to their frustration over the job market. Have the conversation. Administering a "Pre-screening Professional Behavioral Mindset Conversation" before the interview is a win-win every time.

During this conversation, the recruiter will simply engage the candidate in a variety of behavioral questions, but explore the scenario in detail, such as what is ethically and morally correct in their eyes. A few examples include:

1. While working for company XYZ, how have you become a better employee?
2. What type of professional development did you receive while employed with XYZ? How did the training help you to meet the company's expectations?
3. Name a company goal and how did you meet that specific goal?
4. How did you manage inner office or department competition, personally and professionally?

Ask follow-up questions, such as how was this scenario played out in your previous job. How did it effect you? What's your ideal job? And more. This is the time to see if candidates are still dragging workforce baggage from previous employment. If so, they will take it to the next job and will not last long, hence creating a costly revolving door. The conversation environment is relaxing, professional, and informative enough to make a decision whether the candidate should be formally interviewed or not. This formula is successful among both, the employer and candidate.

CHAPTER 9:
Selection

 CASE STUDY
Kronos Provides Interns More Than an Opportunity

Interns are a great source for new hires. They know the company, and the company knows them. Even if an intern isn't currently interested in a position, he or she may have friends who are looking for a new opportunity.

As employers are faced with a candidate-driven job market, building and maintaining a positive working relationship with interns will be an important part of their recruiting strategy. But how do you do that? Send postcards or regular e-mails? Both of those are possible, but the real way to stay connected is by holding an event that bonds the interns and the company. Something everyone will talk about. Something interns might want to attend post-internship.

Kronos Incorporated keeps interns engaged by holding its own Intern Kronolympics and by partnering with five fellow Greater Boston technology companies to hold a Battle of the Interns. Aron Ain, chief executive officer at Kronos, shared the company's philosophy for the events:

> Parents, families, teachers, and schools all play a critical role in shaping the workforce of the future—but I believe employers should also play a major part by offering resources, mentors, and events that inspire and motivate young minds. I'm so proud of how our own growing internship and co-op programs are helping build the leaders of tomorrow, and we have gained just as much value from our college and high school colleagues than they have from Kronos.
>
> While the goal of these events is to give interns an event they'll never forget—and I think Kronos was very successful in doing that— they also accomplished a couple of other things.
>
> Industry Connections: The Mass Technology Leadership Council

(MassTLC), the region's leading technology association which hosted the Battle of the Interns, offered volunteers to help with the event. This provided interns with the opportunity to connect with a professional association that can help to advance their career.

Networking: After the events, the interns and company employees were able to celebrate and network. Just think—next year's networking event is a perfect opportunity to invite former interns. They can share stories and stay connected with the industry.

The goal of an internship program is to provide young professionals with an opportunity to experience the industry they've chosen. It's to give them a chance to gain some work experience. That doesn't mean you can't have a little fun along the way. In fact, maybe one of the best things you can teach interns is the importance of working hard and playing hard.

Internship programs, like the one at Kronos, give organizations and employees the opportunity to "select" each other. Back in Chapter 5 (Workforce Planning), Andrea Paris shared with us some legal considerations regarding internship programs. But I want to address internship programs here because they offer a valuable purpose for both organizations and individuals.

For companies, it gives them an opportunity to work with young professionals and gain insight about what's being taught in today's colleges and universities. It allows them to work with someone who they might want to hire someday. And it gives them the chance to help students start their professional careers with relevant work experience.

For students, internships provide a glimpse into the real working world. It's an opportunity to see how the theories and models they've learned in school apply in a real-life work setting. They get to show a potential employer what they're made of.

10 Components of a Successful Internship Program

If your organization has been toying with idea of creating internships, some great resources are available. For both companies and students to gain the full benefit, an internship program should be formally created to support the effort. Here are some things to consider:

1. **Determine the company point of view about internships.** Top-down support is essential for the success of any program. Make sure the senior manage-

ment team believes in the program and its purpose. Internships are not about free labor. For the internship program to be successful, it needs resources.

2. **Create meaningful work.** An internship program is not a substitute for a filing and copying clerk. It's also not corporate servitude. Smart companies are using internship programs as a "test drive" for talent, hoping that the students will want to return after they graduate.

3. **Confront the pay issue.** The U.S. Department of Labor (DOL) offers guidelines on internship programs. Just because you call someone an intern doesn't mean he or she passes the test to be an "unpaid" intern. Make sure your program is compliant with the law.

4. **Give managers the tools and resources to effectively manage interns.** Since the goals for interns are different than for regular new hires, supervisors need to be given proper training and guidance. Hopefully, they're already receiving training for employee coaching and performance reviews.

5. **Provide interns with the tools to be successful.** Just because interns are working with you only a few months doesn't mean you should avoid giving them work space, training, and other things they need. If you want interns to be effective, give them the tools they need.

6. **Set goals and hold interns accountable.** It's true that internship programs are providing a learning opportunity, but companies should still hold interns accountable. Whether you pay interns or not, the goal is for them to learn certain things during the time they spend with you. Set goals for interns, and hold them accountable for achieving those goals.

7. **Document the program.** There are three reasons to document your program. The first has to do with the DOL (see #3). The second is for recruiting. Interns want to know what they will be doing during their internship. Companies need to sell their program by sharing what happens. The third reason is to keep track of what took place from year to year.

8. **Elicit feedback and update the program.** Think of this step as an exit interview for interns. To keep your internship program fresh, ask interns for feedback. Find out what they enjoyed and ask for suggestions for future programs. Their feedback can be used to update the program and as information for future interns.

9. **Measure results.** Graduates today don't get jobs without internship experience. Being able to share data on how many interns land jobs is valuable information. Obviously, the company wants to know how many interns started and finished the program. It also wants to know how many are hired. Depending on your goals, it might also be helpful to measure program satisfaction from both the manager and intern perspective.

10. **Stay in touch with interns.** Create a mechanism to keep in touch with interns. This not only gives interns a mentor who will help them be successful, but it also gives the company opportunities to share open positions the intern might be interested in.

10 Top Selection Techniques for All Positions

The company selects the candidate, and the candidate selects the company. In Chapter 7 (Sourcing), I mentioned the top 10 sources according to the *2017 Talent Acquisition Benchmarking Report* from the Society for Human Resource Management (SHRM). In the same report, SHRM shared the top selection techniques:

1. Structured interview (75 percent).
2. References (74 percent).
3. One-on-one interview (64 percent).
4. Phone screening (58 percent).
5. Panel interview (53 percent).
6. Behavioral interview (45 percent).
7. In-person screening (45 percent).
8. Group interview (42 percent)
9. Unstructured interview (30 percent).
10. Behavioral/personality assessment (28 percent).

The good news is we have dedicated an entire chapter of this book (Chapter 8) to the most used selection technique—interviews. It reinforces the importance of having a focus on the interview experience and training everyone involved in the hiring process on how to conduct an excellent interview.

However, selection and interviewing aren't the same thing. Interviewing is the technique used to acquire the information about the candidate that will be used in selection. So if organizations don't conduct good interviews, they won't receive good information, and they may not make good hiring decisions.

I'm not prepared to say that poor interviews lead to bad hires. It's possible organizations will get lucky—it's happened before. But given how much hiring someone costs, do you really want to take the chance?

Establishing Selection Criteria

Organizations should decide how they will determine the best candidate for the job. Selection criteria shouldn't change every time a company is recruiting. All employees in an organization should know the criteria and refer back to them throughout the entire hiring process. Moreover, the company's selection criteria should be evident in all job postings, interviews, and other steps in the hiring process.

Typically employers use two ways to decide who to hire:
- Skills.
- Culture fit.

Ideally, companies should want to hire employees who have the desired skills and fit with the organizational culture. But often, we're faced with a dilemma: hire the candidates with rock-star skills and hope they get along with everyone *or* hire the person who gets along with everyone but is missing a few critical skills. So how do we make the decision? That's the crux of selection criteria. When we must decide what's more important (skills or culture fit), which one do we choose?

Skills-Based Selection

Selecting employees based on their skills makes sense. We want people who can do the job. In fact, organizations often want people who can do more than the job. You know what I'm talking about. It reminds me of hiring sales people. I've worked with directors of sales and marketing who would identify fantastic sales candidates. They had an impressive record of crushing their sales goals.

In many cases, those candidates also had a history of being arrogant or even abusive to co-workers. This is a perfect example of hiring people for their skills and ignoring their ability to fit with the culture. And if you've never been in this situation, let me tell you how the story ends. At some point, the company has to decide if these high performers are so valuable that it will allow them to operate outside the culture and to be held to a different standard from everyone else, if they're held to a standard at all. It's a tough decision.

The moment that skills trump being a part of the culture, the company loses its culture. The workplace becomes the "wild west," and all the effort that was put into developing an employment brand is lost. (I could write another book on the impact of this decision. I think you realize that it would be bad, so I'll just leave it at that.)

Culture-Fit-Based Selection

At this point, you might be saying to yourself, "Well, if hiring for skills puts culture at risk, then obviously the answer is to hire for culture fit." And it's true, putting culture first preserves the company culture, which in turn helps with employment brand, candidate experience, etc.

But organizations that focus solely on hiring for culture fit can fall into a "similar to me" bias, meaning that people equate being a good culture fit to being the same. This can lead to issues like candidates trying to become something they're not simply to get the job. From an organizational perspective, it could lead to groupthink, which stifles creativity and innovation in the organization. (Again, we could write another book on the value of organizational diversity. I don't have to tell you it's important.)

Organizations and individuals must understand where culture ends and individual thought begins. Candidates and employees can express unique thoughts and still align with company culture. This might sound counter-intuitive, but the secret to diversity is creating the ability to express differences in company culture. It's also the ability for individuals to be different and still be successful within the culture.

So there's the dilemma. Too much focus on skills can hurt culture, and too much focus on culture can hinder diversity. That being said, there's one other option that could be the answer: that's using values and competencies.

Values and Competency Match

Before we discuss using values and competencies in selection, let's make sure we're on the same page about what those terms mean.

Values are the standards that guide organizational culture and beliefs. Common values include integrity, accountability, honesty, respect, and courage. These are words that every organization wants to guide their activities. From a department meeting to a customer interaction, companies want employees to share and follow their values.

While values are a part of organizational culture, they can offer some flexibility. How employees hold themselves or co-workers accountable may differ. The way a person shows respect varies based on the person and the situation.

Competencies are defined sets of behaviors that demonstrate a person's ability to do the job. They are broader in scope than skills. In fact, skills—along with knowledge and abilities—make up a competency.

An example of a competency is managing change, which includes being able to process change personally, developing new processes or procedures as a result of change, and helping others through the change process.

Some people may argue that it is easier to teach an employee a skill than a competency. For example, let's say the organization is looking for a training manager in the human resource department. The individual in the role will have to conduct new-hire orientation, so a skill for the position would be presentation skills. A competency for the position would be effective communication because you won't be a great presenter if you lack communication skills, and developing effective communication competencies can be hard. But if the organization hires only for skill, it may not select a qualified candidate. So candidates who have proven they both embrace the company's values and exhibit the job's competencies may be the best to select. But this assumption is predicated on one very important thing:

The organization's values and the job's competencies must be accurate.

I've worked with organizations whose values and competencies were for show. The organizations selected edgy and cool values and competencies to look good on business cards, win them awards, and attract customers. For example, I have a client whose values include "scrappy." You know what? It's a scrappy company. This is a case in which the value fits. Not every company is scrappy or can pull it off.

Companies that are going to use their values and job competencies to hire need to have ones that align with who they are. Their values need to be clear and understandable. They need to be identifiable. Using my scrappy example, both the company and the hiring managers need to know what scrappy looks like. Candidates may not know what scrappy means to the organization, but that's okay. At some point, they'll find out. But when candidates talk about themselves in interviews, the company should conclude, "Yeah, they're scrappy" or "Nope, not scrappy enough."

FYI
Recruiting Moderators

At the 2017 Great Place to Work Conference, Arden Hoffman, vice president and global head of people at Dropbox, shared a really cool idea for making sure that her organization stays on track when it comes to selecting candidates. Dropbox has recruiting "moderators." These are people who are skilled in facilitation and help the recruiting team by being an impartial piece in the process. The moderators evaluate recruiting team notes, point out inconsistencies and bias, and facilitate conversations within the team (things the team members might have missed or need to clarify).

Assessments

One of the tools that organizations can use in the selection process is assessments. There are many different types of assessments, but pre-employment tests generally fall into three categories:

1. **Aptitude:** These assessments measure qualities every employer is looking for. Examples include critical thinking, problem-solving, and learning ability. Research has routinely affirmed that cognitive aptitude is one of the most predictive factors of job performance and long-term success.

2. **Personality:** These assessments are designed to uncover whether the candidates will be content and comfortable doing the job. Because they assess "job fit," personality tests can be helpful for increasing retention. For example, personality assessments include (such as the Big Five Inventory) include dimensions of agreeableness, conscientiousness, extraversion, openness to experience, and stress tolerance.

3. **Skills:** These assessments measure acquired knowledge and job readiness. Examples are verbal, math, and computer skills. They are generally predictive of short-term success, meaning that the candidate can do the basic everyday tasks required in the job.

Regardless of the category of assessment, all assessments should be valid and reliable. Validity means the assessment measures what it's supposed to and is predictive of job performance. Reliability indicates that the assessment produces consistent results.

 POV
Technology Transformed Assessments

In today's high-tech world, many assessments are available online. I spoke with Josh Millet, Ph.D. He's the founder and CEO of Criteria Corp., a leading provider of web-based pre-employment testing services.

Josh, how has technology impacted assessments?
Technology has transformed assessments. Technology-based assessments offer dramatic possibilities for enabling advances in test security, increasing the efficiency and accuracy with which applicants can be assessed, and much more. Web-based testing has made it much easier to gather data quickly and efficiently and has allowed for easier applications of things like item response theory and other analyses that help make tests more accurate, more objective and less biased.

Compared to pencil and paper tests, web-based tests allow for dynamic item delivery that yields much more secure tests, creating a near-infinite number of test forms, and ensuring that no two candidates will get the same test. With dynamic tests, deriving an "answer key" is virtually impossible. Technology-based assessments also generally are shorter and more efficient than paper and pencil tests, because they can utilize formats that gather information more rapidly and efficiently: Computerized Adaptive Testing (CAT), through which algorithms dynamically react to a test-taker's response patterns and adjust item difficulty, are an example of this. Finally, technology-based tests greatly reduce if not eliminate human error in the grading process, and allow for easier remote testing than is practical with paper and pencil testing.

Obviously, for organizations with a global workforce, web-based assessments provide tremendous flexibility. But what do global companies need to consider when it comes to assessments (i.e., languages, culture, etc.)?
For organizations with a global presence, it is important to remember that not all tests can be translated easily, and much will often be "lost in translation." Certain types of skills tests generally translate very well, as do certain types of cognitive items such as those that measure numerical problem-solving or spatial reasoning. However, verbal ability tests do not translate well, and personality tests do not translate universally across languages and cultures, so often it will be necessary to revalidate assessments or use assessments originally designed and published in foreign languages when testing globally.

Another staffing dynamic that's increasing is the gig economy or contingent workforce. While contingent workers don't come into the office every day, they are an extension of the organization. Should organizations with a large contingent workforce consider assessments for part-timers or freelancers?

Organizations who have a large contingent workforce should absolutely consider using assessments. For workers who will often be working remotely or in minimally supervised environments, assessments can be a very efficient way to ensure minimal standards are met and to predict performance without large time investments that HR departments typically commit to evaluating permanent staff.

References

The final activity that organizations use to select candidates is to check references. Job references are provided by the candidate. They are typically the names of individuals who can attest to the candidate's abilities.

And this is where I struggle with references.

I've always felt that, if the candidate is giving you the names of people who can attest to their abilities, the references will say the candidate is wonderful. Think about it. Have you ever agreed to be someone's reference and then told a company the person is interviewing with that he or she has no skills and is a terrible person?! You get my point.

I'm apprehensive to tell companies that references are a great way to select candidates. That being said, references can provide insight about candidates that you didn't know. For example, references might share a story that you didn't hear during the interview process. I've worked for organizations that required reference checking, and I discovered things about candidates that confirmed we were making the right decision, which can definitely be a good thing.

Whether or not your organization checks references is entirely up to you. If you are checking references, it's important to have a policy in place. On a side note: when your organization is making the decision about reference checking, it also needs to decide about providing references. These policies should align and need to be run by legal counsel. Training should be provided to anyone who is responsible for providing references. Enough said.

Selection Is More Than a Decision; It's a Step in the Process

Selecting the right candidate should be considered more than simply a decision. It should have a methodology that has been carefully thought out and is regularly followed.

It should also not be an impulse decision. The organization has collected a tremendous amount of information from candidates and their references. They've taken assessments. The selection process is about bringing all that information together and asking the question, "Based on what we know, will the candidate bring value to the organization?" and "Do we feel the candidate will be happy here?"

TIPS
3 Tips for Taking Your Selection Process to the Next Level

Many of the processes we've talked about so far, like workforce planning and recruiting strategy, are dynamic. They need to be evaluated and updated regularly. You may find that the selection process doesn't change quite as much even though it's still critical. Here are three things to remember when it comes to establishing your selection process.

*1. **Suzanne Crest,** SHRM-CP, PHR, is the director of human resources at the Longmont Humane Society in Longmont, Colo., a nonprofit animal shelter where she has been working for nearly six years. She has over 12 years of human resource experience.*

> Recruiters need to get to know the culture of the business they are hiring for; only making matches based on the job description doesn't work. It seems like most recruiters want to stay inside the box, finding people quickly in a database using a checklist of skills. I've had recruiters tell me they've found someone who has great experience in virtually everything I'm looking for, but then when I meet the candidate in person, I'm disappointed. To be able to find candidates who not only have an excellent skill set but unique qualities that would make them a great fit, recruiters need to take the initiative to learn what it's like to work for their client's company. Instead of asking the client to describe their culture and/or doing research online, when possible, recruiters should physically go to the place of business and observe some behaviors—it can take less than 5 minutes to identify a few key cultural characteristics. For example, I was waiting to be interviewed once, and the employees were talking non-stop about their company-wide Weight Watchers challenge. The last thing I wanted to do was to get on a scale on my first day! (I was polite and stayed for the interview anyway.)

*2. **Taylor Dumouchel** is an executive recruiter for Peak Sales Recruiting. Her early years in the recruiting business were spent helping employers find top-performing sales executives. She then worked her way up through the ranks, becoming a specialist in recruiting and marketing and an expert in B2B sales and hiring matters. She is a graduate of the University of Ottawa, and she regularly contributes to The Peak Sales Blog.*

One trend that is on the rise in recruiting is embracing data science. Many studies show that making hiring decisions based on scientific evidence is proven to increase hiring accuracy and decrease turnover rates.

One of the ways companies can start introducing science into their recruiting process is including a psychometric assessment. It's important to better understand a candidate's communication style so you can identify how that will fit into the culture of your team and/or be received by the customer's they are selling into. Using a behavioral assessment is key to understanding if an individual is naturally "wired" to handle rejection, ask difficult and challenging questions, and be persistent enough to get the job done.

In sales roles, individuals are compensated based on revenue generating activities so identifying candidates that are motivated by money and ROI (return on investment) is key. This is where the motivators aspect of the assessment we use comes into play. You may have someone with a hunter personality, but if they're not motivated to push the bar forward or achieve their goals, they may not be successful in a sales role. In addition, if you have a candidate with a strong sales track record, but highly values helping others/altruism, you can mitigate risks around them becoming too much of an advocate for the customer by placing parameters around samples, trial periods, and margins.

It's important to note assessments should be used as part of a complete and structured interview, and candidate assessment processes are not valued at more than 20 percent of your hiring decision.

3. **Libby Sartain** *is an active business advisor, board member, and volunteer. She is well-known for leading business transformation initiatives as the head of HR for both Yahoo and Southwest Airlines. She served as board chair for SHRM and currently serves on the board of AARP.*

My response to that question [What should readers do to take their selection process to the next level?] is to "Think Like a Marketer." I have five suggestions that might help:

1. **Discover the Important Connection between People and Brand**
   I learned during my time at Southwest Airlines that our key differentiator versus other air carriers was customer service. So, we marketed our service, and thus, our people strategy became critical.

Recruiting and retaining the right employees, a reinforcing culture, and strongly aligned leadership were essential to the delivery of our brand promise. Our simple philosophy took hold; employees are our most important customers. Our CEO, Herb Kelleher, famously coined a controversial phrase: "Employees first, Customers second." That defined desired leadership behavior and culture.

2. **Concentrate on Alignment between Employer Brand and Customer Brand**

An employer brand articulates the experience the company committed to create for employees so they, in turn, would commit to delivering the brand promises made to customers.

Instead of delivering HR programs, brand the employee experience just as marketing would brand the customer experience. Each stage of the experience should have its own look, feel and personality aligned with the messaging used to market the company brand. Recruiters should focus on aligning the candidate experience with the customer experienced.

When recruiters think and act more like a marketer, we begin with the end customer in mind. For example, when thinking about strategic workforce planning, the conversation starts with "how the customers will be served?" versus "how many heads will we need by segment?" Insights can also be analyzed to tie employee behavior to the customer experience. Measuring employee engagement against customer loyalty will reveal a correlation between the variables.

3. **Use Marketing Tools and Techniques**

Marketing tools can also add value to strategic workforce planning and talent management. Just as customer analytics related to consumer behavior can inform business decisions around products, services, marketing messages, and customer relationship management (CRM), employee analytics can provide insights to strengthen the employee value proposition (EVP) and the promotion of the EVP inside and outside of the organization. Employee segmentation can be as powerful as customer segmentation in determining offerings to the employee audience.

4. **Use Social Media for Listening versus Selling**

Social media can also be used for "candidate listening." Online consumer discussions boards, as well as product rankings, ratings and reviews posted online have revolutionized the world of market research, offering businesses a massive source of data on what customers think about their products and company. Tools are being developed to enable marketers to listen to the "voice of the customer." Web-scraping tools or apps can be used to find out what employees and candidates are saying online as well. Sites like Glassdoor, LinkedIn, and Vault provide such insights.

5. **Measure Brand Value and Effectiveness**

Marketers have tools and rankings to measure the value of their Consumer Brands. The Net Promoter Scores (NPS) is used to measure the customer's experience and quality of the brand. NPS asks customers if they would recommend a brand or product to a friend. Use similar tools to measure the candidate experience.

When HR thinks and acts like marketers our work and programming related to recruiting, rewarding, and developing talent resonates throughout the organization. And, the entire organization understands their role as brand deliverers and will join in that work. The people agenda aligns with the organization's strategy around customers, and the work is simplified. The employer brand becomes essential to the strategy of the business, just like the corporate/consumer brand. END

SECTION V: 3 Key Takeaways

- Interviewing is harder than it looks. Individuals on the hiring team should be given interview skills training, so they do it effectively and legally.
- The questions a candidate is asked during the interview will determine how much information the organization receives to make a hiring decision. Bottom line: Ask good questions. It's probably worth planning questions in advance.
- Developing selection criteria is one of the most important things organizations can do. There's more involved than "hiring the best candidate." The decision has a far-reaching impact on culture.

5 Resources to Make Your Job Easier

1. The Workforce Institute at Kronos is "a think tank that helps organizations drive performance by addressing human capital management issues that affect hourly and salaried employees." The institute has published three books, including *Creating the Workforce and Results You Seek* and *Elements of Successful Organizations*. You can easily read these books on an airplane trip.

2. *HR on Purpose: Developing Deliberate People Passion* encourages human resources professionals to drop the preconceptions of what HR should be and "to focus on what HR could be." Authored by SHRM board member and *Everyday People* blogger Steve Browne, SHRM-SCP.

3. If you're trying to learn more about assessments, Criteria Corp has developed *The Definitive Guide to Pre-Employment Testing*. It's a quick but comprehensive read about assessments. You can download a copy at http://resources.criteriacorp.com/definitive-guide-whitepaper.

4. Libby Sartain is the author of several books, including *HR from the Heart: Inspiring Stories and Strategies for Building the People Side of Great Business*, *Brand from the Inside: Eight Essentials to Connect Your Employees to Your Business* and co-author of *View from the Top*.

5. re:Work (rework.withgoogle.com) is an open-source site used to share information from Google and other organizations about the employee experience. It covers "unbiasing," hiring, goal setting, management, and people analytics. For each topic, the site shares case studies, guides, blog posts, and guides.

SECTION VI
Extending the Offer

In Section VI

While the actual time it takes to call a candidate and extend the job offer is small, the behind-the-scenes time it takes to prepare a job offer is huge! That's why this section is longer than you might expect.

Job offers are about details. If organizations get a job offer wrong, it can lead to misunderstandings, and that's no way to start out your relationship with a new hire.

Job offers are also very sensitive. The company is about to learn highly confidential information about its soon-to-be employee. The process needs to be handled respectfully.

CHAPTER 10:
Background Checks

 CASE STUDY
Gonzaga University Integrates Background Checks with ATS

With more than 1,200 employees and more than 300 new hires each year, Gonzaga University is a dynamic, fast-growing institution offering a wide range of undergraduate and graduate programs in Spokane, Wash. Its growth was being hampered, however, by a manual background check process that significantly slowed time-to-hire.

Effective background checks are a critical security step for ensuring campus safety for students, staff, faculty, and facilities, but slow background screening services and unwieldy procedures were time-consuming and difficult. Gonzaga staff were taking more than 30 minutes per candidate to manually enter an individual's data into a background check form. Then, the actual screening process took five days or more to complete. In fact, screening was often not completed until after the individual's start date, which created an awkward situation if the check uncovered something that precluded hiring.

Gonzaga University found that by integrating its applicant tracking system (ATS) and background screening process, it could offer a seamless experience to stakeholders. Background check reports are now completed in an average of 2.5 days, a 50 percent reduction over the previous process. In addition, the manual data entry step was eliminated because integration enabled the data candidates provide from the ATS to pre-populate into the background check form directly from the job application with just the touch of a button. If additional data are required from applicants, the background check company contacts them directly by text, phone or e-mail via the candidate portal through which candidates can answer questions or directly submit required information.

The integration also improved the hiring process for HR staff and enhanced the recruitment experience for candidates, while helping the university increase security.

I don't know of a single company that lacks some form of background checking. The question isn't whether to conduct background checks. It's more of what kind of background checks employers should conduct.

Some industries have legal requirements concerning background checks. When I worked in the airline industry, we had strict rules we needed to follow to give employees security clearance. In other industries, we didn't have those same legal requirements. Those industries were still concerned about security; they simply used different protocols.

Speaking of protocols, one of the great things about background checks is that companies exist that specialize in screening. They are completely current on all the legal requirements. As the Gonzaga University case study shows us, we can find very capable partners and excellent technology solutions to help us with this step in the hiring process.

Therefore, I don't want to spend a lot of time talking about the legal piece of background screening. I'd like to think that everyone knows background screening protects the organization. The aspect of background screening I do want to talk about is the candidate experience. Being legally compliant and providing a hassle-free experience are not mutually exclusive.

Back in Chapter 4, we talked about how the candidate experience includes employment branding, career portals, and offer letters. It even encompasses other steps in the overall hiring process, like background screening, in which organizations may leverage third-party service providers.

We know the value background screening creates in more consistent organizational safety, improved compliance, and (most importantly) better quality of hire. However, new staffing strategies require a new approach to the background screening process. For example, the 2017 *HireRight Employment Screening Benchmark Report* found that 86 percent of contingent, contract, or temporary workers are screened (up from 41 percent five years ago). As organizations tap into contingent workers as part of their recruiting strategy, they also need to evaluate how they hire, train, engage, and retain contingent workers—and if and how employers check their backgrounds.

While the percentage of background screenings being conducted for contingent workers seem to be increasing with the popularity of the gig economy, one area that has seen a decrease in background screening is global workers. As the HireRight report noted, "only 15 percent of respondents indicated they verify the international background of U.S.-based employees, and merely 13 percent of U.S. employers screen employees based outside of the U.S.—a decrease of 6 percent since last year."

Our organizations are filled with global workers. Today's employees are truly borderless. They have obtained a global education, worked for global employers, and managed global assignments. This means a vast majority of background checks have a global component. We want those global candidates to become our employees because their experience and expertise bring value. And yet, according to the report, 85 percent of respondents do not conduct global verifications.

Organizations understand that a positive candidate experience yields the best talent. They also understand that the term "candidate experience" extends beyond interviewing to all aspects of the recruiting cycle, including background screening.

Contingent and global staffing are just two examples of how rapidly changing employment processes are impacting background screening. As talent acquisition professionals, we need to stay on top of these trends. We can't afford to have ineffective and inefficient processes negatively affecting the candidate experience.

Types of Background Screening

We've already covered hiring ex-offenders (Chapter 7—Sourcing) and checking professional references (Chapter 9—Selection). You may be familiar with a few other background screening categories:

- **Education verification.** Some industries require it. For instance, you wouldn't expect to obtain a position as a professor or teacher without an education verification, right?
- **Motor vehicle check.** This type of background screen verifies a valid driver's license and uncovers any traffic infractions. Employers typically run this check when a position requires driving or when an employee might use a company vehicle.

In both of these situations, the decision to run a background check is based on the requirements of the job. If the employee isn't using a company car or driving as part of the job, then the company may not need the information. Same with education. If the employee's educational background is not a factor in selection, then conducting a background screening in this area may not make sense.

While background screening is important, organizations have to balance compliance obligations, information received, and cost. Obviously, legally required screenings must be budgeted for and completed. But there are some screenings that, while they would be nice to have, don't necessarily change the selection process, and organizations might choose not to conduct them. Then, there are some background screenings, like drug screening, that are advantageous for businesses because they receive preferred insurance rates. But not every business conducts drug screening.

Marijuana 101

While marijuana isn't legal in every state, public opinion about marijuana is changing. And for businesses and employers, this means you need to stay on top of what's happening regardless of what your organization does regarding drug screening. Your organization could be one election cycle away from having to address marijuana laws.

POV
Medical Marijuana Policies

I had the opportunity to interview Dr. Todd Simo, chief medical review officer with HireRight, for the *HR Bartender* blog last year, and I wanted to share his comments with you.

Dr. Simo, I've heard the title medical review officer (MRO) for years, and I'm sure that I don't know everything the role entails. Tell us a little bit about what an MRO is responsible for.

MROs are licensed physicians responsible for receiving and reviewing laboratory results generated by an employer's drug testing program and evaluating medical explanations for certain drug test results. MROs must ensure the accuracy and integrity of the drug testing process, provide quality assurance reviews, and determine if there is a legitimate explanation for any positive, substituted, adulterated or invalid test results. They must also ensure that test results are reported in a timely manner to employers while protecting the confidentiality of the drug testing information and ensuring compliance with all federal, state and local laws.

MROs enhance the validity and reliability of the employer's overall workplace drug testing program. Their review helps ensure fairness to the donor and offers more protection to the employer in case of later litigation due to a "positive" drug test where the employee has been suspended or fired or an applicant not hired.

It seems like public opinion is shifting where the use of marijuana is concerned. What trends do you see with regard to marijuana?

We're certainly seeing wider acceptance of medical marijuana across the country. This acceptance is based on the true intent of medical marijuana, compassionate care for profoundly ill or terminal patient[s] where no other treatment is available. However, in the real world, medical marijuana is causing new challenges for employers since younger and younger people are being approved for medical marijuana with less severe medical problems.

With this in mind, employers who conduct drug testing are realizing they need a more explicit screening policy for medical marijuana use, although many aren't quite sure what to do. In the 2016 HireRight Employment Screening Benchmark Report, we found:

- Only 5 percent of employers say they accommodate medical marijuana use, and over half say they don't have a policy either way.
- The number of those who do not accommodate nor have a plan to in the next year dropped almost 15 percentage points in the last year, signaling more employers may be considering this in the next year.

With disparate state laws, developing a coherent and sustainable policy can be a challenge. But it's still a DEA [Drug Enforcement Administration] Schedule 1 drug and going without any rule could be asking for trouble. It's important for employers to have a policy in place—for hiring, risk mitigation and more—that reflects and balances company culture, responsibilities, and state regulations.

Okay, so there's "medical" marijuana and "recreational" marijuana. What's the difference?

Medical marijuana and recreational marijuana serve different purposes and have separate legal classifications. Those using medical marijuana are doing so for health reasons and have been recommended by a physician. Recreational marijuana is just that, recreational. Marijuana has gained more acceptance for medical use than for recreational use, an increasing number of states are considering legalization measures, so these numbers are sure to change soon. ...

Still, medical marijuana is a controlled substance. But if it were legal everywhere, why should employers be concerned?

Employers should be concerned for a few reasons. First, employers in more safety-conscious industries like transportation, health care, and manufacturing must consider the nature of the job and what's necessary for risk mitigation. Widespread marijuana use among employees who have the ability to affect public safety could pose serious problems.

Even in more white-collar, less safety-conscious industries, marijuana use can have an impact on productivity. There are numerous statistics out there around how drug use can lead to increased workers' compensation claims, higher medical costs, and inefficiencies in productivity, proving that drug use is not just a matter of safety, but can affect employers and employees in a variety of ways.

It's up to the employer to set the standards for what's acceptable and what's not, considering job responsibilities and corporate culture, since marijuana use, even if legal, can affect a company's reputation, work output and the well-being of all stakeholders involved.

The legalization of marijuana would present a very tactical issue—identification of impairment. Urine drug screening identifies a metabolite of marijuana in a repository; therefore, you cannot extrapolate a level of impairment (like you can with breath/blood alcohol testing). Oral fluid testing may be able to give you a rough estimate of time of use and impairment, but there is no industry standard that can be referenced. Functionally, the legalization of marijuana will cause employers and society as a whole a great deal of issues.

Simo shared with me a link to the e-book *Employer's Guide to Medical Marijuana*. I've included the address in the resources section of this book. You can download it to learn more about medical marijuana and how it could impact recruiting.

Previously we had to remember only one thing about marijuana—it was illegal. Now, it's a bit more complicated. Organizations need to stay current. And even if your organization doesn't operate in a state that permits medical marijuana use, candidates and employees may still have exposure to it. Clear communication is essential, especially regarding how organizations will implement drug screenings.

POV
Social Media Background Checks

The other type of background screening that's new and evolving is social media. We've all read the horror stories about a candidate who was turned down for a job because of a picture on his or her Facebook page. I'm not weighing the justification of rescinding the offer. But what organizations need to decide is whether they're going to conduct social media background checks.

Heather Bussing is an employment lawyer and regular contributor at HRExaminer. We've collaborated on several posts on *HR Bartender*. We had a recent conversation about this very topic, and she graciously agreed to share her research.

For the recruiters out there who are asking themselves, "Should I or shouldn't I Google a candidate?" What do they need to consider?

I think all recruiters Google candidates these days.

It used to be that the attorneys wanted the people involved in hiring to know as little as possible about a candidate's demographics, especially the ones that relate to any protected class. That way, if there was any claim of discrimination, the organization could claim they did not know the person was Asian or pregnant, or blind. This never really worked, even way back then (a few years ago) because you learn most of that information in an interview anyway. Also, people who never even made it to the interview stage almost never sue for discrimination because there is usually no way to know why they were rejected.

Now, it's common to see photos of candidates, especially on LinkedIn, and people have a lot of information available about them publicly. So instead of pretending we could not have possibly discriminated, we must not discriminate. This is a good thing.

There are three main things to worry about when looking for information about candidates: 1) the reliability of the information; 2) whether the FCRA [Fair Credit Reporting Act] or a state privacy law applies; 3) whether it's creepy.

1. Reliability

Be careful relying on information you find online because it may not be accurate, may be out of context, may be old, and may not even relate to the person you are considering to hire.

Check your source, consider the context, and don't make decisions based on something you find online without verifying it. Really.

If this seems like a lot of work, it is. So, it may not be worth it based on the value of the information alone.

2. FCRA and Privacy Laws

The Fair Credit Reporting Act (FCRA) potentially applies whenever you do a background check on someone during the employment process—not just hiring. When the FCRA applies, you must give the candidate or employee notice and get their permission to gather information on them. Then, if you decide not to hire or promote someone because of something you found, you have to let the person know what you relied on and give them an opportunity to correct the information. (This does not mean you have to hire them, even if they correct the information).

The key to whether the FCRA applies is whether the information you are collecting constitutes a background check and whether the person collecting is a consumer reporting agency.

A background check or consumer report can include almost any information, including social media and other public information online. So just because you aren't checking how much they owe on their mortgage on Lexis, that doesn't mean that your digging around is not a background check.

But the FCRA only applies to "consumer reporting agencies."

A company is a "consumer reporting agency" under the law if it assembles and evaluates consumer report information to provide those reports to third parties.

So, an organization can generally Google a candidate and look at publicly-available information without triggering the FCRA because they are doing it internally for their own use and not relying on apps or third-party services for the information. However, the minute you order that Intelius report, or use any app or third-party vendor for the information, it is likely that the FCRA applies.

A good test is that if you have to pay for the information, the report, the app, the service, the subscription, then the FCRA applies. Although, this is not the test under the law. The FCRA does not address payment at all; it simply says the law applies to anyone *providing* the information to a third party. Still, most people don't do that kind of work for free, so payment is still a key factor to determine when the FCRA is triggered.

In addition, some states have privacy laws and other restrictions on how information can be obtained. So, check with an employment or privacy attorney in your state to make sure you understand the entire legal landscape on obtaining and using information about candidates.

3. Brand and Creepiness

My other advice is: Don't be a weasel. Don't be creepy. If you find personal or private information, don't save it or use it. Don't look for back doors into private social media accounts (which is often illegal) or make friends with their friends to see people's private posts.

Be careful about the messaging you send to candidates about the culture and the organization in doing background checks. To the candidate, it feels like the relationship is starting off with distrust and unfair scrutiny. Then, if the first thing you do when they are hired is make them read a bunch of policies that tell them how to act, what to put in their Twitter bio, what to wear, and grounds for termination, you are going to quickly lose that excitement and delight of starting a new job. Job changes are a stressful time for people; don't make it worse.

Figure out what level of scrutiny is important for the position based on responsibilities, the level of authority, access to confidential information and money, and whether the position affects public safety. Don't stalk people online just because you can.

So, it is generally okay to Google someone and see the publicly-available information. It's okay to look someone up on LinkedIn or Twitter, which are both public. And it's okay to decide not to hire someone if you find information that contradicts what is on their resume if it indicates they don't have the experience they claim to have or shows a lack of integrity.

If you do check out candidates online, it's a good idea to take screenshots of what you viewed, so there's a record if there are any concerns. And if there is no issue, then don't pass that along to the hiring manager. Just say you reviewed LinkedIn, Twitter, and did a general Google search that showed no issues.

If a recruiter suspects that a hiring manager is acting on information he or she found while checking out a candidate on social media, what can the recruiter do?
Make sure the information is accurate, don't discriminate, and determine whether the FCRA applies. If it looks like it does, then let the manager know that they need to check with legal about how to handle it.

Reliability and taking care that hiring decisions are not discriminatory are the most important issues though because the FCRA will rarely apply to hiring managers.

If a recruiter is concerned about a hiring manager using sketchy information, then he should tell the manager that he needs screenshots of everything she looked at for the files in case there are ever any questions about discrimination or privacy issues. If the manager says, it's not a problem, then the recruiter should ask her what she looked at so he can get screen shots. If that doesn't work, then the recruiter needs to decide whether it's important enough to take to his manager or legal. It might be if it looks like the manager is likely to rely on information that could result in a discriminatory or other illegal hiring decision. It's not if the likelihood of a problem is low and it is just about a power struggle.

If a company decides it wants to conduct social media background checks, does it make sense to consider an external provider? Why or why not?
Most external providers are aware of FCRA requirements and can help the organization hiring them comply with the notice, permission, and all follow-up requirements. There are also varying levels of reports available. Sometimes, the employer just wants to know whether the candidate acts like a lunatic or not in public. This is a reasonable thing to wonder, especially if the job involves dealing with customers a lot. If you outsource the information gathering and checking, then you can just get an answer to your concern without also finding out the person's politics, vacation photos, or food preferences. Although it is perfectly legal to discriminate against someone who loves dark chocolate, you would be making a huge mistake because chocolate lovers are the best!

So, outsourcing is good for compliance with the FCRA and allows you to just get the information you need, and not information that would influence your decision, but shouldn't.

Doing your own social media check is probably not subject to the FCRA, which means you don't have to get permission from the candidate. But you will learn information both good and bad about the candidate that will influence your decision. Bias is a hard thing to see and even harder to overcome. So, before you decide to check on people, think through what information really matters.

Personally, I believe the four points that Bussing shared above are applicable when looking for any type of background screening firm. They need to understand the law, provide adequate reporting, comply with all privacy and security requirements, and act with credibility.

Create a Background Screening Partnership

Your organization's background screening partner will have access to highly sensitive data and information about your candidates and employees. It's one of the first "tests" that candidates are exposed to during the hiring process. Candidates get to find out if the company treats their private information confidentially and with respect.

Only your organization, with the help of legal counsel, can decide which background screenings to run. But recruiters have the ability to make sure the process enhances the candidate experience.

 TIPS

4 Tips for Evaluating an External Social Media Background Check Company

1. Ensure it knows how to comply with the FCRA and will make sure everything it does complies.
2. Ensure it offers varying levels of reports and information allowing you to find out if someone seems okay, but does not provide the details unless it's important to do so.
3. Ensure it complies with all applicable privacy and data use and storage laws. These can be state, federal, or international. The penalties for improperly transferring personal data about people can be severe. And many countries, including those in the EU, have strict laws about transferring data. If you are a global organization, are interviewing people all over the country or the world, or do business with people in other countries, these laws probably apply to you, and it's important to understand them.
4. Ensure they aren't weasels, won't misuse the information, and have integrity.

 TIPS

3 Tips for Taking Your Background Screening to the Next Level

Background screening is serious business, and the way organizations handle this part of the hiring process speaks volumes about the way they will handle other aspects of an employee's career. While a significant responsibility falls with the company that completes the background screening, recruiters also have a few considerations.

1. *Jonathan A. Segal is a partner at Duane Morris LLP in the employment, labor, benefits, and immigration practice group. He is also the managing principal of the Duane Morris Institute. The Duane Morris Institute "provides training for human resource professionals, in-house counsel, benefits administrators, and managers at Duane Morris, at client sites, and by way of webinar on myriad employment, labor, benefits, and immigration matters."*

Cybersecurity continues to be a significant concern for businesses, and it is only going to get bigger. Much of the media focus is on cyber attacks from outsiders, such as ransomware. Sometimes less discussed is that the cyber attacks are inside jobs. Of course, not all inside jobs are deliberate. Sometimes they are due to human error. That is why robust employee education is so important. But there are cases where the breaches are deliberate. The question becomes how do we mitigate this risk?

One possible way to mitigate the risk is more robust background checks. Of course, there are complex federal, state, and local laws that must be considered in developing a criminal background or credit check program. But the first question that almost always is asked is who should be subject to such checks. HR often makes that determination and sometimes excludes itself.

Well, sometimes HR is the culprit. Think of all the information to which HR has access. For example, only social security numbers, protected health information (PHI), and personally identifiable information (PII). Yes, HR needs to revisit the degree to which it subjects itself to the background checks to which it subjects others. This is critical for two reasons:

First, it increases HR's credibility. We recognize the risk and do what we can to mitigate the risk in our own group.

Second, it may just avoid hiring an HR professional who can deliberately cause a breach, potentially causing irreparable harm to your employer and its employees.

2. **Kelly Max** *is CEO of Haufe US, a provider of employee-centered enterprise transformation solutions and programs. The company provides Success as a Service (SXaaS) HR solutions that transform company culture and enhance businesses' ability to attract and retain top talent.*

Recruiting as a standalone function is dying. Winning companies around the world are transforming themselves into *people-first organizations* to attract, engage, and retain the talent they need to stay on top. As part of that transformation, the biggest trend in recruiting is to realize that "recruiting" is not a discrete and separate function, but an integral part of a networked, people-first *organizational operating system* that creates a perpetually self-reinforcing, multi-dimensional virtuous cycles across entire organizations.

This networked "PeopleOS" provides a holistic, real-time, socially interactive view of the company for everyone who works there, which in turn makes everyone a potential recruiter. A company with 5,000 employees networked into a PeopleOS has 5,000 recruiters on the payroll.

The goal of network-driven workplace transformation is to evolve from a situation where people are forced to conform to a rigid organizational structure to one where an agile, flexible organizational structure continuously rearranges itself to empower people. The very existence of a networked, people-first organization creates recruiting magnetism—the best candidates are naturally drawn to the energy, excitement, innovation, and trust emanating from an employee-centric organization.

3. **Jim Stroud** *is the global head of sourcing and recruiting strategy at Randstad Sourceright U.S. He likes to describe his role as "alleviating the sourcing headaches of my clients with data and imagination." He's also the author of three books including* Resume Forensics *and* Content Is the New Sourcing.

To stay ahead of the current trends in background checks, one must first know what the currently emerging trends are. To do that, I suggest searching Google for "trends in background checks" and limiting the results to the last year. Do you see anything in the search results that you are unaware of? If so, research it further and decide if the practice cited is right for your company. To take it a step further, create a Google Alert on the topic so that as new content enters Google's database, you are made aware of it.

Moreover, to track trends in background check policy, I would suggest monitoring trends in privacy and big data. Google things like: "big data and privacy issues," "privacy and social media" and "big data civil rights. " Why? All of those topics, in some way, intersect with background checks. I suspect that with so much happening with technology, new privacy laws might hinder today's background checking policies.

So, to sum it all up, my advice is this: research, react and review. Research new and emerging trends. (Automate that with Google alerts.) React to what you learn by implementing the processes as you see fit but, within ethical and legal standards. Finally, review the effectiveness of your procedures. Did the background check policy fail miserably, resulting in financial disaster (or a public relations nightmare)? Did your policy validate your hiring manager's decision to make that key hire? In either regard, staying ahead of the trends on background checks can produce a positive impact on your company.

CHAPTER 11:
Extending the Job Offer

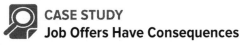

CASE STUDY
Job Offers Have Consequences

You might think that extending a job offer is a no-brainer: call the candidates and tell them they're hired. Surprisingly, mistakes and even fraud can occur if a job offer isn't extended the right way.

Donna Ballman, employment attorney and author of the book *Stand Up for Yourself Without Getting Fired: Resolve Workplace Crises Before You Quit, Get Axed or Sue the Bastards,* shared several common job offer flubs and mistakes that are a not only devastating for candidates and new hires but a potential liability for recruiters and companies. Here are a few real-life scenarios:

- A candidate is extended a job offer and told that her title will be vice president of something. On the new hire's first day, she discovers that her title is senior director. When she asks about it, the company informs her they she needs to "earn" the vice president title.
- The company tells a candidate that it has run the background check, all is good, and the job offer is extended. The candidate accepts the offer and gives his notice. Then the company calls and says "Whoops!," they missed something on the criminal background check and have to rescind the offer. The candidate isn't able to get his old job back.
- A candidate accepts the job offer, moves to a new city, and shows up on her first day of work to discover that the job doesn't exist. The organization says that the person who extended the offer didn't have the authority to do so.
- The company extends offers to several candidates. So, several

people show up on the first day to find out they're actually competing for one job.

- A sales person is extended an offer. On his first day, he signs a non-compete. During the first week, he is asked to upload his contacts to the company's CRM (customer relationship management software). Then he is asked to take a colleague with him on sales calls. Once that's done, the new sales person is released within the introductory period.

Ballman advised that organizations could open themselves up to liability in terms of fraud or fraudulent concealment if they knowingly misrepresent the job or conceal information—or negligent misrepresentation if they don't act intentionally. For example, a company is experiencing financial troubles but fails to disclose this information during the interview process. The candidate accepts the job offer, and a few weeks into his or her employment, the new hire is part of a reduction in force.

Another deceptive situation would be representing a position as being regular full time when it's really a temporary assignment.

In addition to company liability, recruiters can individually be held liable for their actions. And recruiters aren't able to claim ignorance. Ballman reminded us that negligent misrepresentation can be asserted (that is, you didn't know, but you should have known.) She advised, "Recruiters need to make sure they communicate accurately with candidates and stand up when they are aware of misinformation being passed along to candidates."

Recruiters need to build trust with candidates, so they know the job offer they're receiving is legitimate. Putting job offers in writing is a good place to start. Remember your reputation will follow you.

Extending a job offer is exciting, and in the excitement of the moment, it can be difficult to write down and remember all the details. The offer letter is your chance to document all these details, including base pay and information about when and how the candidate will learn benefits details and other aspects of the person's new role and the company.

Offer Letters and Employment Contracts

Speaking of offer letters, one of the decisions that organizations have to make is whether to extend job offers using an offer letter or employment contract. It's an important decision, and, as we learned from the case study, it can have consequences.

I asked Kate Bischoff, an employment attorney and HR consultant at tHRive Law & Consulting LLC, to explain the difference between an offer letter and an employment contract. Bischoff responded, "An offer letter proposes terms and conditions of employment—approximate salary, describes benefits, schedule, etc. An employment contract does some of these on steroids because it sets out the specific terms (e.g., exact salary) and imposes additional duties such as a non-competition, non-solicitation, and/or confidentiality provisions. These provisions then become enforceable in court whereas an offer letter may give approximations, but it is not typically enforceable in court."

Bischoff said that the decision of whether to use an offer letter or an employment contract comes down to guarantees and specifics: "When an employer or employee wants specific and enforceable provisions, a contract is the way to go. An employer may want the non-solicitation, non-competition, assignment of inventions provisions and an employee (particularly high-level employees) may want a termination for cause provision that includes a separation payment or permission to moonlight. When a party wants a guarantee, they should use an employment agreement."

If an organization is considering the use of an employment agreement, it makes good business sense to start with thinking about what's important and what needs protection. For example, a startup with newfangled technology might want confidentiality and assignment of invention provisions. A business in a highly competitive industry might need a sales person to agree to nonsolicitation and non-competition agreements. Either way, organizations should be upfront with candidates that these provisions are must-haves.

Also, Bischoff suggested that companies find out if candidates already have agreements with their current or former employers. If they do, it could hamper their ability to hire and put the candidates to work. Here are a few other points she mentioned when using employment contracts:

1. General Information. First, the general terms and conditions of employment, such as compensation, title, a brief outline of job duties, can be found in a contract.

2. Restrictions. A big portion of a contract is taken up by restrictions. These include confidentiality, assignment of inventions, noncompetition, non-solicitation, etc. These restrictions dictate what the employee can and cannot do while employed and sometimes even after the employment ends.

3. Termination. The contract usually includes a termination provision that governs how the relationship will end, such as if the employee must be terminated for cause and what that means or whether the employee will receive a separation payment if terminated without cause.

Finally, Bischoff reminded us that the contract will contain a bunch of legalese that is really important:

Even if written in legal mumbo-jumbo, employees should really read these provisions carefully and maybe even with the help of an attorney. These include things like "entire agreement" clauses that say there is no other agreement or side agreements. This means that if an incoming employee had a "gentleman's agreement" for additional bonuses but then signed an employment contract, the "gentleman's agreement" no longer exists. Another could be an arbitration provision, meaning that if the employee ever wanted to sue the employer for breach or discrimination, the employee would have to bring it in private arbitration.

The Essential Elements of an Offer Letter

While many organizations use employment contracts, offer letters are used just as much (if not more).

Organizations usually design a template for offer letters to ensure consistent structure and content. Then employers add pertinent information personalized for a candidate. Before using an offer letter, organizations should have it reviewed by legal counsel, who may want to insert specific language (for example, "at-will employment") about the employment relationship.

The Society for Human Resource Management (SHRM) website, under the Resources & Tools section, lists a how-to guide and other resources for drafting offer letters. Most offer letters have a few consistent elements:

- Basic information about the job such as job title, supervisor, base pay, and working hours.
- Effective date information like start date and orientation date.
- Company information such as benefits (and their effective dates) and a point of contact in human resources or administration, in case candidates have questions before they start.
- Any terms or conditions of employment like background checks, confidentiality or non-compete agreements, and compliance documents (U.S. Form I-9 is a common one).

The SHRM website also has a sample form and other resources for a conditional and unconditional job offer. We discussed background checks in the last chapter. Organizations anxious to have a new hire start may want to condition a job offer on a satisfactory background check. And most of the time it is satisfactory. But part of HR's role is to protect the company, so all job offers must be clear.

POV
Non-Compete Agreements

Bischoff mentioned non-compete agreements. On the surface, they might seem self-explanatory, but actually, they are a bit more complex than meets the eye. I spoke with Mark Neuberger from the firm Foley & Lardner LLP about the benefits and considerations in using non-compete agreements.

Mark, what is a non-compete agreement?

A non-compete is a commitment by one person or business entity not to engage in competitive business behavior for a defined period. In the employment context, employees are frequently asked to sign a covenant of non-competition where they agree that in exchange for their employment, they agree that when they leave that employment, they will not go to work for a competitor, or they themselves will not set up a competing business.

Non-competes are also used in the contract of buying and selling businesses. Often, the selling business or owners of that business or top executives, will agree not to compete with the buyer for a specified period.

A non-compete does not have to be a separate agreement but can be a covenant or part of some other agreement such as an employment contract or agreement to sell a business. Frequently, non-competes are joined with provisions that prohibit the solicitation of employees and of customers to leave the entity, as well as covenants of confidentiality.

Why should organizations consider using non-compete agreements?

The simple answer is to protect their investment in technology, their relationships with their employees, and the good will they have created. In this electronic age, it is incredibly easy for an employee to download a company's critical confidential information (the formula to Coca-Cola if you will), their entire customer list and other critical information which can be instantly used to set up a competing business.

The business that created that information likely invested a lot of time and money developing it and the good will that comes with it. It seems incredibly unfair that someone can reap all of the benefits of such information and relationships without similarly investing their time and money. When a non-compete, joined by covenants of nonsolicitation and confidentiality, are done right, they provide a type of "insurance" in the event someone does try to steal your information or customers.

What are the downsides for organizations if they use a non-compete agreement?

At their essence, non-competes are anti-competitive restraints of trade. Our free enterprise system generally makes restraints of trade illegal. In the words of a great American legal scholar, John C. Mellencamp, "Ain't that America ... home of the free." However, certain narrow exceptions have been applied by either legislation or court decisions to allow for non-competes in certain circumstances.

Many employees believe they are inherently unfair because they tell the employee that, just because they go to work for one company, they can't leave and go to work for another even if they don't take any of the first employer's information. If an employee has very industry specific skills and experiences, a non-compete could easily prevent them from earning a living. Because of this, insistence of a non-compete at the time of hire could cause a candidate to reject the offer and go to work elsewhere, especially if that candidate has highly marketable skills and experience.

If a company wants to start using non-compete agreements, where should they start?
Start by understanding that the law of non-competes is state-specific and the laws, hence an employer's ability to enforce them, vary widely. For example, as a matter of policy, non-competes are virtually unenforceable against people who live or work in California. By contrast, Florida has a state statute that holds non-competes in the employment context for two years or less are presumed to be reasonable.

An employer contemplating using non-competes for employees needs also to understand that the employer must give the employee something (the legal term is "consideration") in exchange for the non-compete. In some states, continued employment is sufficient consideration such as "You want your job tomorrow, sign this or else?" In other states, you must have the employee sign at the inception of employment or else give them some additional economic incentive like a bonus or stock options to have the non-compete to apply after they have already been employed for a while.

In addition, employers should understand it can be very expensive to legally seek enforcement in the courts. In such court cases, employers will have to demonstrate that they took all reasonable efforts to protect the confidentiality of their information and that they and the information are worthy of protection. The law of non-competes has many pitfalls. If an employer is serious about using them and being able to enforce them, they need the assistance of an attorney skilled in this area of the law.

Handling Rejection

I know we're talking about offer letters, but an equally important piece of extending an offer to the candidate you've selected is letting the other candidates know that the position is filled. Back in Chapter 4 (Candidate Experience), we discussed the importance of the candidate experience. One of the complaints I consistently hear about from job applicants is rejection. Not as much about the rejection itself—although I'm sure that's part of it—but more about how the rejection was handled.

I learned a long time ago that, not only is bringing closure to the employment process important, but the way you bring about that closure is equally important. My entire corporate career has been spent in workplaces where the job applicant was also a past, current, or future customer. So even if the company wasn't selecting an individual for a job, we still wanted the candidate to recommend the company as well as buy its product or service.

 FYI
At-Will Employment versus Right to Work

A couple of pages ago, in a section about the essential elements of offer letters, I mentioned the term "at-will employment." This is a term used in U.S. labor law that allows the employer or employee to end the employment relationship at any time and for any reason or no reason at all. For those of you who are wondering, yes—this is the law that allows companies to fire or dismiss employees without cause. But also keep in mind, it's the same law that allows employees to walk off the job without notice. I bring this up because sometimes employees don't realize that employment at will protects them too.

Often the concept of employment at will is confused with another term called "right to work," which means that an employee in an unionized workplace has the right to join or not join the union. As of this book being published, only 28 states have right-to-work provisions.

Organizations need to understand if they are subject to right-to-work laws and/or at-will employment and how being subject may affect the job offers they extend.

To illustrate how important this is, let me share a story. Years ago, I interviewed a candidate for a manager position. She was a great candidate, and, ultimately, we extended an offer for the job. She turned us down saying that she found another position. Was I disappointed? Sure—we had spent a lot of time and energy with her during the interview process. We ended up extending an offer to another candidate, and he was terrific in the position.

Meanwhile, I sent a note of congratulations to the original candidate. I told her I hoped her new position worked out well. Three weeks later, she called me and asked for an appointment. She hated her new job and wanted to know if we had any openings. While the position she initially applied for was taken, we had another opening, and she was a good fit.

I always enjoy sharing this story because I feel the way this rejection was handled (by everyone involved) ultimately created 1) a win for the original candidate, 2) a win for the candidate who was selected for the initial open position, and 3) a win for the company for ending up with two great managers. What more could you ask for?!

The same philosophy applies to other types of organizations. When I was a SHRM volunteer planning the HR Florida conference, hundreds of people sent in speaker proposals. Of course, we couldn't accommodate them all, but we took extra care and consideration in communicating speaker rejections because we realized those speakers could be future attendees, sponsors, and supporters of our event.

When it's time to "reject" a candidate, here are a few things to consider:

- **Do you have a formalized way to communicate closure?** Candidates want to know if they are no longer being considered. While it might not be the answer they want to hear, it's an answer that can help the candidate move on.
- **What's the message?** Look at the rejection messages you send to candidates. Consider if it's the kind of messaging that would make a candidate still support your company, product, or service.
- **When is the message being sent?** I've seen plenty of candidates find out they were rejected for a position when the new-hire announcement was distributed. This situation is especially prevalent when internal candidates are being considered. Folks, this is just wrong. I know there's an excitement to announcing a new hire, but when the new-hire announcement also serves as the rejection letter for others—nope, not right!

Whether it's for a job, board position, speaking gig, or whatever, candidates understand they have to go through a process. And sometimes that process ends in rejection. The way an organization communicates that rejection will speak volumes. The goal is not to alienate the potential customer or supporter.

Rescinding the Job Offer

No chapter about job offers would be complete without addressing rescinding job offers. When extending the job offer, it's important to tell candidates when the offer is conditional. In my experience, there are two different ways to think of conditional.

The first is "the company is extending you a job offer contingent on a satisfactory background check and drug screen." I've worked at places where the candidate accepted the job but never showed up for the drug screen or supplied the background check information. We interpreted it as a polite way of saying, "I can't pass the background check and drug screen." And we moved on.

That being said, I've also had candidates not pass the drug screen. I called them into my office and asked them about it. Their response: "Oh yeah, I smoked some weed last week. I figured I would see if I could sneak through." Hmm ... sorry, but no. And we both moved on.

The second kind of conditional is about the company and the job itself. I've mentioned previously that, years ago, I worked for an airline. We were constantly recruiting. One day, we experienced an accident that made the national news. We stopped all recruiting efforts, pulled all our recruitment advertising, and called every candidate. It wasn't the right time to be recruiting and onboarding new hires. While candidates were disappointed because they were out of a job, they understood our position and appreciated hearing it directly from us. When we were ready to start recruiting again, we contacted those candidates. Some had found jobs, but others came to work for us.

If you've extended a verbal offer and are rescinding it, I believe the candidate deserves a phone call. If a written offer letter has been sent, then follow up with a written letter.

Job Offers Are Promises the Company Intends to Keep

One of the most exciting things that happens to individuals is they get new jobs. It might be their first job or a big job or a job they've wanted their whole life. Candidates remember a job offer because it's a promise from the company. And they're excited about it.

After extending the job offer, organizations have a decision to make. Are they going to keep their promises?

TIPS
3 Tips for Taking Your Job Offers to the Next Level

I know what you're thinking. How can someone take a job offer to the next level? The real question is how can organizations ensure they're delivering on the statements they make during the interview process. The job offer represents the company and all the conversations that the candidate had with recruiters, hiring managers, and others. Here are some things to think about when it comes to the way you currently extend job offers.

1. *James Celentano, MBA, SPHR, is a managing director at EnterGain LLC, the business and talent advisory dedicated to enterprise growth. He helps companies gain talent, ability, scale, and employer brand. He is also on the adjunct faculty at New York University.*

> Today's emerging leaders seek work environments that have purpose and sustainability. The transition from recruiting to onboarding is critical. Whatever the employer brand promised prior to the job offer needs to come sharply into focus from the day the offer is accepted. Organizations need to deliver on the employer brand promise from the moment the offer is accepted.
>
> If work-life balance is one of your employer brand pillars, then provide pre-start materials that will resonate with the hire's entire family.

If "community" is one of your company's stated values, invite your new hire and their family to an activity where they can participate in the impact your company has on the community.

Be realistic about the fact that job interviews have limitations in enabling a boss and new hire to get to know one another well. Conduct professional references less for screening, and more as a way to mine valuable insight: structure the reference questions in a way that the manager gains insight on how to best coach, stretch, listen and let go so that this new hire can be uniquely successful. And make it a two-way street, encourage your new hire to conduct a mini 360 on the boss, so they quickly learn the manager's style and expectations.

2. **Pam Goncalves** *is chief of staff at GuideSpark, a leader in employee communication. The company's solutions combine content, technology, and extensive expert guidance to deliver employee campaigns that match the effectiveness of marketing initiatives.*

Rather than sit a new hire in a room with piles of paper to read as part of the onboarding process, companies can engage new hires by using personalized content in different formats to communicate and reinforce messages. An example would be using "campaigns" whereby relevant info is pulsed to the new hire via video and other mediums over a specific time period. It beats being locked in a conference room with the employee handbook.

Tip 1. Think Like a Marketer
The new trend in HR communications, including onboarding and new hire training is "marketing" campaigns. Content that inspires, informs, and reinforces is the way to catch new hires before day 1 and throughout their first 90 days vs. the traditional "one and done" approach. This content delivered over time helps the absorption rate for new employees who are typically saturated within the first couple of days.

Tip 2. Communicate in Multiple Formats
Today's employee expects a consumer-grade experience even from their employers. So, offering on-demand resources that they can access digitally at any time from any device is the new norm. Deliver your content in different formats—including text, video, and other multimedia experiences.

Tip 3. Simplify and Snackify

Employees are on information overload so you should invest some time in simplifying your HR program communications in a way that everyone understands, including those playing along at home (spouses, domestic partners, adult children). In addition, let's be honest about the amount of time people have to read your content. Break up your information into "snackable" pieces, so new hires can digest it quickly as they have time.

3. **Franny Oxford** *is vice president of human resources for a manufacturing operation located in Houston. She is known for building HR functions and aligning them to emerging company needs at midsize companies. Also, she's used to handling corporate recruiting with almost no brand and no budget.*

The most important thing a recruiter can do at the offer stage is to personalize it as a thoughtful surprise. Find a way to marry what you've learned about the potential new hire to the company's culture, future, or strategy. I don't mean a gimme cap with the company logo—I mean sending a thoughtful gift with the offer, or adding a perk to the offer, that shows a meaningful connection between the potential new hire and the company. For example, if the applicant loves to kayak and the company is an outdoor gear company, send a kayak paddle with the offer. If the applicant regularly volunteers with Meals on Wheels, see if you can get the applicant regular time off once a week to deliver food, or even buy a table at the next Meals on Wheels benefit in the applicant's name. Show, in the offer, that the new company "sees" the whole person, and that they want that whole person at work.

SECTION VI: 3 Key Takeaways

- Background screening is an essential component of selection. It's also a component that many companies outsource. Choose the right partner.
- Educate hiring managers on how to responsibly handle the urge to search online about candidates. It's a win for everyone involved.
- Offer letters are like promises. Getting a job offer is one of the greatest days for employees. Give it the respect it deserves. Have a little fun at the same time.

5 Resources to Make Your Job Easier

1. If you're wondering how to set up Google Alerts, there's a tutorial on the Google Support pages. And it's not narcissistic to set up a Google Alert for yourself. It will let you know when your name is mentioned in the news. In today's tech-savvy world, that's a good thing.

2. Check out Donna Ballman's book, *Stand Up for Yourself Without Getting Fired: Resolve Workplace Crises Before You Quit, Get Axed, or Sue the Bastards.* Ballman typically represents the employee side in disputes. It's great to get a different perspective.

3. SHRM offers lots of HR forms related to employment contracts and offers. You can find them on the SHRM website under the Resources & Tools section. This information is worth the cost of membership alone!

4. Want to stay on top of legal issues? Kate Bischoff has a blog at tHRive Law & Consulting (www.thrivelawconsulting.com). Also, check out the Foley & Lardner Labor & Employment Perspectives blog (www.laboremploymentperspectives. com); Mark Neuberger works there.

5. The *HireRight Employment Screening Benchmark Report* is a must-read in my opinion. The report is produced annually (www.hireright.com/benchmarking).

SECTION VII
Onboarding

In Section VII

I believe this section is so important because onboarding is where organizations see the results of their hiring process. Yes, the metrics are important, and we'll discuss those in the next section. But onboarding is where all of the strategy, sourcing, selection, and screening comes together. The new hire is starting work.

While some recruiting professionals may not be formally involved in the onboarding process, I believe recruiters need to know what happens. At some point, you might be asked your opinion about onboarding, and you would appear uninformed if you failed to offer any ideas. Trust me; I'm saying this because I've been there.

CHAPTER 12:
Before a New Hire's First Day

 CASE STUDY
McLeod Health Improves the New-Hire Experience and Saves Money

McLeod Health is a South Carolina-based health care organization with almost 5,000 employees. At one point, the company averaged over 1,000 requisitions annually and, through analysis, discovered it was taking nearly 268 minutes to "touch" a new hire (4.5 hours—ouch!). Needless to say, its existing onboarding process was negatively impacting employee engagement and productivity.

To streamline the onboarding process, the company implemented an onboarding technology solution that included the use of blogs, videos, events, and interactive pages—all designed to reinforce the organization's core message and brand. The onboarding portal gave new hires the information they were looking for in terms of company background, organizational culture, employee benefits, and even a "day in the life" at the company.

That's not all. The onboarding solution allowed the organization to send new hires a welcome video from the CEO as well as initiate activities like new-hire paperwork.

According to Heather Grier at McLeod Health, the new process benefited the company: "It's definitely saving us paper, and it is definitely saving us time and since time is money and paper is money—it is saving us money." Remember, before implementing the technology solution, it took McLeod 268 minutes to "touch" a new hire. After implementation, it took 30 minutes. The cost savings was the equivalent of two full-time employees.

In addition, the new onboarding process improved the employee experience. McLeod was able to reduce the number of times new hires had to sign something on their first day of work from 33 to 0. Now employees can focus on getting up to speed in their jobs instead of signing a lot of paperwork.

> McLeod was also able to reduce the amount of time spent in orientation by 20 percent. This outcome sent employees to their departments sooner and freed up the human resource team for other projects.

Hearing the McLeod Health case study reminded me of the purpose of onboarding, which is to welcome employees into the organization and get them up to speed as quickly as possible. It also reminded me of what I always look for in a technology solution—efficiency and cost savings while improving the user experience. And when I refer to the user experience, I'm not just talking about new hires. Any time HR can eliminate killing a bunch of trees, signing a pile of papers or having to file a bunch of stuff—I would say that solution is worth it!

McLeod Health was able to improve its onboarding process by adding a pre-boarding step. Pre-boarding is defined as laying the groundwork for an employee's first day on the job. It is the step in the onboarding process that creates success for the employee and the manager. Once the groundwork is finished, the manager and employee can dedicate their focus to the job and to building a good working relationship.

The Society for Human Resource Management (SHRM) defines onboarding as "the process by which new hires get adjusted to the social and performance aspects of their jobs quickly and smoothly, and learn the attitudes, knowledge, skills, and behaviors required to function effectively within an organization." Organizational culture defines when the onboarding process starts and ends.

Regardless of when our company's onboarding begins and concludes, one thing is consistent—there are three primary stakeholders in the process:

1. **New-hire employees** are excited about their new role with the company. They want to make a great first impression. They want to do awesome work. And they also want information like when they're going to be paid and how to sign up for benefits.

2. **Hiring managers** invest a lot of time finding new employees. Maybe they've been running the department short staffed and can't wait for the new hire to start. Maybe this is a new position, and the employee will help the department achieve its stretch goals. Hiring managers want to get their new employees trained and working ASAP.

3. **Human resources** is responsible for making sure that new employees are welcomed into the organization and effectively brought onto the payroll. HR professionals need to make sure all the i's are dotted and the t's are crossed.

However, if number three (the human resource part) doesn't happen, then employees and managers will not be positioned for success. The employees will be distracted because they don't have answers to their questions about pay, benefits, and so on. And their managers won't be able to spend time building a relationship with their employees because they are waiting on HR to finalize the administrative part of the process.

At some point, organizations have to make sure that the onboarding process covers both the paperwork and the social and performance piece. And recruiters need to play a part in this process. I know sometimes onboarding is the time when recruiting hands over the new hire to the learning and development function. But I contend that the transition isn't always smooth. The candidate has only interacted with recruiting, so recruiting needs to stay involved until the new hire connects with more people within the company.

Pre-Boarding: Bring High-Tech and High-Touch Together

In his 1982 book *Megatrends*, John Naisbitt coined the phrase "high tech, high touch." The idea is that the more technology we are exposed to, the more of a personal touch we want in our interactions. There's never been a better case study for this idea than onboarding.

Employees and organizations want a high-touch experience. It helps with engagement. But both employees and companies want efficiency. To get that high-tech, high-touch balance, many organizations are finding that onboarding technology solutions are the answer. The key is making sure that the solution sets human resources, employees, and managers up for success during the crucial pre-boarding process.

An effective onboarding process contains the following elements:

- **Capable.** Onboarding solutions should be able to handle batch processing of documents. In my past corporate roles, we often hired several interns or seasonal employees at the same time. The solution gave me the ability to send multiple offers at the same time. The faster I could bring employees into the organization, the happier everyone would be.

- **Configurable.** Every organization has at least one unique form. It might be for an employee benefit or emergency contacts. A technology solution should let you create your own forms and distribute them accordingly. That allows the company to have a consistent employment brand. Candidates see the same brand as employees.

- **Compatible.** Today's technology solutions should be compatible with your existing software. I'm impressed that many of the HR solutions on the market have the ability to work with Microsoft Office. Let's face it: we still get resumes and inquiries via e-mail. And Microsoft Office is used by 80 percent of the *Fortune* 500. With an HR onboarding solution, I'm able to immediately move those documents. No separate sign in, just a click of a mouse.

Some of you might be saying, "That's great, but we do not have the resources to implement a technology solution." And that's okay. The challenges with onboarding administration still exist, and it's possible to create an onboarding process that is capable, configurable, and compatible.

Pre-Boarding Checklists

Creating a checklist can accomplish the three goals above of being capable, configurable, and compatible. It provides a consistent means of pre-boarding new hires and keeping track of the process, and it can be designed to fit your organization's unique needs. The form can be stored on a company intranet or file storage platform like Box or Dropbox, where employees can access it at remote locations. And it can be updated and distributed easily.

If you're looking for a pre-boarding checklist, here are a few things to consider (you could turn this into your own pre-boarding checklist):

Have ready for a new employee's first day:

- **Equipment.** I know this sounds basic, but I've worked for companies that didn't have office space ready for new hires. So make sure that new employees have a desk and a chair. Even if the space is temporary, you want new hires to feel that their arrival wasn't an afterthought.
- **Technology.** Work with the IT department to supply new employees with a computer, e-mail address, phone, and any other technology they'll need. I know of organizations with open-office concepts that give employees headphones. If your organization embraces bring your own device (BYOD), have a plan in place for new hires to get required software and security so they can work.
- **Marketing.** Business cards are a marketing tool. Same with name badges (if you use them). Employees are super excited on their first day of work. Make their position official with cards and badges. Neither of these items is expensive, so there is absolutely no reason to wait until new hires successfully complete their introductory period to order them.

Send new employees:

- **A warm welcome.** It always amazes me how communication drops off between the time when employees accept the offer letter and their first day. The opposite seems more logical. Send a video welcome to a new hire. Have some of the current employees who met the candidate send a text welcome or voice mail. Let employees know you're looking forward to their arrival.
- **Greetings from the team.** Organizations need to recognize that employees want to feel that they're part of a team. Building that team culture begins with new hires having the same "stuff" as current employees, including T-shirts, water bottles,

travel mugs, notebooks, and pens. Welcomed with items like these makes new hires feel not only that they are marketing the company but that they're part of the community.

Tell new employees:

- **Attire.** Let employees know what they should wear on their first day. Is it casual Friday or Denim Day? Encourage employees to wear the T-shirt you sent them. Employees will feel welcome if they feel comfortable. I don't mean comfortable clothing. I mean that they will feel they are dressed appropriately compared to everyone else.
- **Parking.** What do employees need to know about getting to work on the first few days? Even if they later take public transportation or carpool, tell them about parking in case they drive themselves.
- **Food.** Share information with employees about the food situation. Planning to bring in breakfast or doughnuts for new hires on their first day? Tell them. What do employees do for lunch? Does the company offer beverages? Tell them which kinds: for example, coffee, tea, water, and soda. Also, if your organization lets employees do a tequila shot to celebrate a big account, let new hires know. And let them opt out if it's not their thing.
- **Orientation.** We've talked about sending employees new-hire paperwork before their first day. Some documents may need to be signed and witnessed onsite. Let employees know when to expect orientation. Some companies hold it on day one, others on day four or five. Keep employees from being distracted about orientation topics and focus on work by letting them know when and what to expect with orientation.
- **Hashtag.** In today's social media age, it makes sense to share with employees the company guidelines regarding social media. I have friends who tweet and post about their first days at work. Why not leverage the enthusiasm and create a hashtag that employees can use? First, you can monitor the hashtag stream. Second, other prospective candidates might see it—and like what they see.

Recruiters have a great opportunity to contribute to a new hire's success by covering a few of these topics during the hiring process. While some of them (like getting a T-shirt or lunch on a new hire's first day) probably aren't going to sway a candidate to come work for the company, they do tell a story about the company. The little things let candidates know the company cares and is in their corner.

Pre-Boarding Sets Employees Up for Success

Pre-boarding—whether it's done via a technology solution or a pen and paper checklist—

is designed to get administration out of the way so the company and new employee can focus on the fun stuff—yes, that means the work. But it's not all about the paper.

Pre-boarding also serves to welcome new hires to the organization and make them feel like they're part of the team. Sometimes when we're consumed with dotting the i's and crossing the t's, we forget that we need to be building relationships with employees.

But pre-boarding isn't the only step in the process of getting new hires up to speed. In the next chapter, we'll talk about the next step: orientation.

 TIPS
3 Tips for Taking Your Pre-Boarding Process to the Next Level

I believe one of the unique things about hiring is that candidates get two "first impressions" of the organization. The first one happens when candidates initially apply. The second one is when they receive the job offer. The pre-boarding experience tells candidates, "I made the right decision." For organizations looking to keep their pre-boarding process fresh, here are a few things to consider.

1. *Joe Britto is a psychological coach, writer, and interactive management consultant at Innate Leaders. His passion lies in helping clients develop the mindset and behaviors of leadership and leveraging that mindset to lead their business and themselves.*

> Getting ahead of future trends means predicting the future. That's tough, but in my work with forward-thinking companies, I see the future of recruiting being a focus on helping new hires develop a growth mindset. Why? We all know Millennials are looking for more than a good job, good benefits, and a challenging work environment. Educated and switched on, this is a generation looking to bring their ideas and their passion for their jobs. They're looking for companies that are receptive to those ideas. That's what a growth mindset is all about. It's about seeing ways of doing things differently and challenging the status quo. And of course, it's about working for a company that shares those values.
>
> If you're looking to attract employees either looking to develop a growth mindset or who already have one, it begins with making your cultural values clear in your recruiting process: your ads, the way you interact with candidates, and the way you introduce them to your business. And that's before, during and after they're hired.
>
> The ideal would be hiring people with a growth mindset, so in that

case, a pre-boarding process that helps identify high growth mindset potential would be ideal. An alternative would be an introduction to the concept during orientation and ongoing exposure during the onboarding process.

2. **Jenna Filipkowski,** *Ph.D., is the head of research at the Human Capital Institute, a thought leader in the new discipline of strategic talent management. Her research program educates human resources, talent acquisition, and learning and development professionals on the important trends and topics that cover the entire talent lifecycle.*

In our 2016 research, we profiled successful onboarding practices, budgets, stakeholders, challenges, and outcomes from a survey of over 400 HR practitioners. We found:

- Organizations that invest in onboarding accomplish four things: emphasize people and performance over paperwork; make it a partnership among HR, the manager, and the employee; establish onboarding as a continuous process; and measure outcomes.
- Invested onboarders are twice as likely to reduce new hire time to proficiency.
- Two-thirds report that onboarding practices have been underutilized. Only 40 percent say onboarding is effective at retaining new hires, which is most likely because it has been focused on paperwork and processes rather than people and performance.
- In most organizations, onboarding activities stop after the first week in the new role; this is not nearly enough time to orient, prepare, and develop a new hire to be successful in their new position.
- Most respondents believe that "re-boarding" an internal hire is just as important as onboarding an external hire, but only 27 percent report that they effectively re-board employees after they take on a new role.
- One-quarter of respondents' organizations will invest in onboarding programs in 2016 and 65 percent report that their budget will stay the same.

A full copy of the research can be found at www.hci.org/ hr-research/onboarding-outcomes-fulfill-new-hire-expectations.

3. ***Amber Hyatt*** *is the vice president of product marketing at SilkRoad, "the leading provider of talent activation solutions." In her role, she evangelizes how employers of choice attract, develop, and retain top talent. She oversees solution positioning, packaging, and the go-to-market process for SilkRoad.*

We recommend to clients that they use the interview process to connect candidates to organizational goals. This provides a realistic preview for how organizational success is measured and forces the potential hire to think about how they can personally contribute towards achieving these goals. Once an offer is made, a strong emphasis must be placed on the pre-boarding process. Continuous communication during this time is critical. Pre-boarding needs to go far beyond new hire paperwork and should encourage cultural indoctrination with the company and team.

To expedite time to contribution, I would encourage companies to spell out in the pre-boarding process how the organization will nurture their personal talent journey and deliver on the commitments made in the recruiting process. Highlight the enablement tools and learning plans that will aid the new hire to quickly contribute towards achieving the organizational goals discussed previously.

CHAPTER 13:
Orientation

 CASE STUDY
Savvis Uses Orientation to Accelerate New-Hire Productivity

Back in 2010, Savvis Inc. was experiencing double-digit growth, along with a change in senior management that brought a renewed commitment to talent as a competitive advantage. With a new management vision and company business objectives, the global learning and development team in charge of implementing a new-employee onboarding program needed to be at the top of the company's priority list.

At the time, Savvis had no formal onboarding process, which created inconsistencies in the employee experience and a high time-to-productivity metric. New hires learned their jobs based on tribal knowledge and shoulder surfing. After working with a consultant, the company launched the initial version of the program, which included:

- New-employee orientation workshop (named "immersion").
- A 90-day onboarding experience roadmap for each employee.
- An employee online portal that provided on-demand information.
- A "peer coach" program.
- A manager training program on how to best use the process.

The effort paid off. Some 68 percent of new employees reported feeling that Savvis has a defined and formal process for onboarding (up from 14.4 percent), and 88 percent felt well informed about the senior management team and its vision for the company (up from 56 percent).

Managers reported that employee time to productivity was reduced by 58 percent. While at the same time, employee satisfaction with the onboarding experience increased 14.5 percent.

Savvis also tracked additional metrics about employee interactions to gauge learning and engagement: average number per new-employee calls to the IT help desk and to HR for benefits-related and policy questions. Lastly, the firm monitored the average number of employee referrals per new employee.

Savvis Inc. used Novita Training to help it design its program. Founder Robert Bilotti made an interesting statement in the full case study: "Onboarding is probably one of the most custom programs a company can create." It's so true.

This is probably a good time to talk about the difference between orientation and onboarding. I know many of us use the terms interchangeably—I've been guilty of it as well. But we need to understand the difference:

> **Orientation** is a program that new hires attend to begin their employee experience with the company. It provides the foundation for future learning and development. It also serves a role in administration and compliance.
>
> **Onboarding** is a process of organizational socialization and productivity. New hires need to be welcomed into the organization. They need to become part of the team. And they need to become productive and start bringing value to the organization.

To me, orientation is a part of onboarding. There's absolutely no way that new hires will be fully productive after orientation. There's too much to learn. Even when employees have lots of experience in their field, they have much to learn about the company. Although orientation may take days, some of what new hires need to learn isn't in a handbook or documented anywhere.

So orientation provides new hires with a start to their career with the company. Then onboarding takes over. For many talent acquisition professionals, this is when the new hire is handed off to the learning and development function. The recruiting function sources, selects, and extends the offer. Recruiters do the background checks and send welcome information. Now, learning and development designs and delivers orientation. These professionals work with managers on the onboarding process.

However, I'd like to suggest that recruiters need to understand what happens during orientation and onboarding. It's one of the reasons we've included both processes in this book.

Recruiters Should Learn Talent Development

A couple of years ago, I attended a conference in London. During the event, one of the speakers asked the audience of about 100 human resource professionals, "Who has a kickass talent acquisition function?" The answer was a surprise. Not one person raised his or her hand.

I get it. Recruiting is tough. I could understand if half of the audience didn't raise a hand, but not one. It was an eye-opening moment for sure.

Then the speaker turned the conversation toward the reasons that the recruiting function is struggling to meet the needs of the organization. Whether it's candidate quality, time-to-fill, cost-per-hire—or any combination of—there's a disconnect.

But it occurred to me as the discussion was taking place that part of the solution lies in the organization's talent development efforts. I know it's tempting to think of talent development as simply the newfangled word for training, but it is more than that. Talent development also includes career management and development, organizational development, and activities like succession planning.

All things employees want.

I happen to believe that, to become good at talent development activities like succession planning, you must understand recruiting. Think about it. How can you create a plan to develop talent within the company if you don't understand where and how to attract the best talent? How can you manage a plan to develop talent within the organization if you don't understand what talent needs to be developed (versus hired from the outside)?

Conversely, recruiters need to understand talent development. They need to know that the candidates being hired will fit into the organization's succession and/or replacement plans. They also need to understand how the company's programs will elevate each candidate's skills to fit the future needs of the organization.

I completely understand the need for specialization. Some people argue that the human resource generalist role is outdated. But this doesn't mean that we are absolved of our responsibility to understand how the pieces of the HR function fit together.

For example, both talent acquisition and development professionals need to use the same talent terms. I heard a couple of new ones during this conference:

> **Ready Now—Short** referring to employees who can assume new roles during the next one to two years.
> **Ready Now—Long** meaning employees who can assume new roles during the next three to five years.

This example raises a point: in addition to thinking about the talent pipeline, it's necessary to think about where the business will be short term (one to two years) and long term (three to five years). Both talent development and acquisition professionals must be able to identify and develop skills that the company doesn't even need yet. It only makes sense that they learn about each other's roles and collaborate to deliver—and develop—the best talent.

Perceptions of Time Are Important

I once heard an executive say, "Silicon Valley doesn't think in terms of years. They think in terms of days/weeks/months." While I understand Silicon Valley doesn't rule the world, it does produce much of the technology that drives business today. Which means its perception of time is important because it drives the way it designs the technology we use.

We may not like the idea that our phones and computers don't last forever, but we do have to figure out how to deal with the impermanence. Same with software. For example, we may not like it when Facebook and Google tweak their algorithm, but if we want to continue using their software, then we have to know how to manage it. But my point isn't about Apple or LinkedIn or Microsoft—or any of those technology companies.

My point is about taking their concepts about time and applying it to our workforces.
- What do your employees think "short term" and "long term" mean?
- What does senior management think "short term" and "long term" mean?
- Is everyone on the same page?

We talk with employees on a regular basis about time. Short-term goals. Long-term career plans. Does that mean weeks, months, or years? I can see employees getting really frustrated if they were asked to take on a responsibility "short term" and it ends up being years. Or being asked to commit to a "long-term" project only to have it abandoned after a few months.

The senior management team also talks in terms of time. Long-term results. Short-term objectives. Sometimes it even talks about medium-range goals. When management communicates, is it clear the results will take 1 year, 5 years, and 10 years?

Finally, do all those time frames align? Ideally, the company should set short-, medium-, and long-term goals. Talent management strategies should align so that the organization has the right people at the right moment with the right skills to accomplish those goals. Employees should be engaged throughout each respective time period, working toward being ready for those opportunities when they come available.

I don't see how that can happen if senior management thinks long term is 10 years and employees think it's 5 years. Timing is a critical ingredient to our business success. Organizations must define it and make it a part of their culture—because not only should everyone be working toward the same goals, but they should be working at the same pace.

Recruiting professionals should understand what happens during orientation, onboarding, and the employee life cycle. Frankly, they should be a part of conversations in which decisions are made regarding these topics. I can honestly say one of the most frustrating things I've seen happen is when I spent a huge amount of time sourcing, interviewing, selecting, and hiring a candidate only to have the new hire leave after 100 days because of a decision I didn't know about. If only I could have explained to the rest of the company that if it makes this change, candidates will choose not to consider our jobs.

On the other side, I totally believe the rest of the organization needs to understand recruiting—for the same reason. That's part of the reason I'm writing this book. (Please feel free to give a copy to your colleagues!)

Seriously, recruiters and talent acquisition professionals can start this conversation. Learn what happens in other departments and functions. Make sure everyone is in agreement regarding hiring talent. Set consistent expectations with candidates so when they become employees, they aren't surprised by something the company did (or didn't do).

That's why, in this chapter, I want to talk about what it takes to design an orientation program. I understand that someone in recruiting or talent acquisition may never design an orientation program. But you should know the basics of how a training program is designed. That way, you can insert your two cents as appropriate. No instructional designer will be able to shoo you away from the conversation.

5 Steps to Creating a New-Hire Orientation Program

Creating an orientation program doesn't have to be difficult. There are several proven instructional design models. Personally, I like the ADDIE model, which focuses on five key steps—assessment/analysis, design, development, implementation, and evaluation. Florida State University created the model for use in designing military training. It's a proven model; the other reason I like it is because, once you learn it, you'll find it to be very flexible in designing any program.

FIGURE 13.1: ADDIE Model

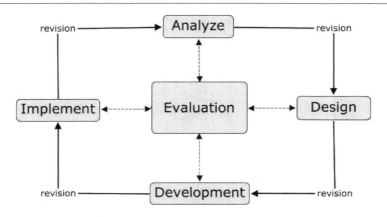

IMAGE SOURCE: https://en.wikipedia.org/wiki/ADDIE_Model

1. **Assessment/Analysis.** In this step, the organization conducts an assessment to establish where it is today and where it wants to be in the future. We're not designing the program yet. This step is about understanding the issues. To understand what's currently happening in the organization regarding employee orientation, you can look at orientation program evaluations, employee survey results, and exit interviews. Ideas for gathering valuable data include interviewing managers about their expectations for the program and conducting focus groups with employees about their first 90 days or six months. After you collect the data and complete a gap assessment, senior management should reach consensus on the goals for the program.

2. **Design.** Even though this step is called "design," we're still not creating yet. This step could include benchmarking what other organizations are doing successfully, brainstorming program options, and researching feasibility. Keep in mind, some of the options to improve orientation and increase employee productivity could include changing existing practices in recruiting or compensation and benefits. Any proposed changes should align with program goals. Before moving forward, get buy-in from senior management and secure budget resources. This isn't about creating something "cool." It's about the program being effective. The sooner employees feel they are bringing value, the sooner they become engaged with the organization.

3. **Development.** Now it's time to create the program! This is where the individual components of the program are finalized, including the decision of what elements will be created internally and which will be purchased from external sources. For example, in the hotel industry, bartenders and servers are given responsible vendor training, so employees learn the laws and practices about serving alcoholic beverages to guests. Organizations can create this training in-house, they can purchase an off-the-shelf program, they can hire a third party to come in and deliver the training, or they can send employees to an offsite workshop. Lots of options! Organizations should evaluate which one works best for them and then build it into their program.

4. **Implementation.** This is the most visible step in the process. Make sure all program materials reflect the company branding. It's so important to have a communication plan for sharing the contents of the program with managers and supervisors because they will be responsible for supporting what new hires learn during training. And they have additional training to deliver with onboarding. Before the formal launch, consider implementing a new program in phases. Not everything has to be done at once. Organizations can also roll out parts of a program to a single department before going companywide. Think of it as a pilot program.

5. **Evaluation.** Once the program is implemented, the work isn't over. Regularly analyze program results and adjust as necessary. Also, think about how existing employees will learn additions to orientation. Often, we remember to train new employees and forget about current ones (or vice versa). Any metrics being calculated and reported should align with program goals. Only measure what is valuable and can be controlled. Also, find opportunities to solicit feedback directly from managers and employees about the program. They might have ideas that would increase program value.

You can see how the comment at the beginning of this chapter about onboarding being one of the most customized programs in the organization is true. I wish I could tell you exactly what you need to have in your orientation program. Sure, there are traditional topics like ethics and anti-harassment and activities like a welcome lunch and tour of the building. But you have to decide where the other stuff fits in. Choosing topics for your orientation program could be driven by your industry or the frequency with which you hire.

However, I believe that *all* organizations need to discuss one area—social media.

Social Recruiting Creates an Expectation for Social Training

According to an article on *The Muse* website, 92 percent of companies are using social media for hiring. Now call me crazy, but it seems only logical that if companies are using social media as part of the hiring process, then employees will expect to see it once they are hired.

It makes no sense to hire people using LinkedIn or Facebook and then tell them in company orientation that using social media is banned. It sends the wrong message on day one of employment.

Employees who are hired using social media tools will expect to see social media in training. Companies building a brand presence on social media should want their employees to connect with the brand via social platforms—it enhances employee engagement. The question becomes how to create effective activities in orientation and onboarding that support the learning objective.

Here's an activity that involves the use of photos (that is, smartphones with camera and video capability, camera and video editing apps, and social sites that support sharing images) to learn and engage.

What if during orientation, you asked new hires to take a photo that validates your company culture? They all likely have those smartphones—right? In fact, instead of begging and pleading with employees to put their phones away, send them out on an activity with their devices. Ask them to upload their photo to a site you specify and debrief the photo collection as a group.

Also, we can use our phones to lead the learning effort. Obviously, one of the ways we learn is by visuals. We can create powerful learning experiences by using the right images at the right moment. This applies not only to technical training, in which we can take photos of actual equipment or shoot a quick video of how to do something, but it also applies to soft skills like the previous activity of validating the company culture.

As individuals and organizations do more with social media, the expectation will increase that social tools will be incorporated into all aspects of an employee's career.

Initially, it might seem like a challenge to introduce social tools into the learning experience, especially when you consider the pace at which social tools are changing. But this is where recruiting's expertise in social can bring value. Don't hesitate to share new platforms and learning with colleagues. Remember that, chances are, the social tools you're recommending are ones that employees already use, so there's a built-in adoption factor. Now that you understand the ADDIE model, make suggestions about how the tool can be incorporated into training design.

Telling Isn't Training. It's Not Orientation, Either.

I bring up the topic of training because orientation should be considered training. There's a real trend with orientation programs to have short sessions and leave more focus on the onboarding process, which is fine, and we'll talk about onboarding in the next chapter. But I've seen the trend have an impact on orientation in that orientation loses its interactive component and becomes more of a lecture on how to find information.

Training is the act of teaching employees a particular skill or knowledge for them to use in their current role or job. It's different from development, which is teaching someone knowledge or a skill for a future job. But it's also different from communicating a policy or procedure. I think it's easy to create a disconnect here, especially for new employees.

If the company develops a policy on a new procedure for answering the telephone and then holds a meeting to communicate the policy, that's not training. Don't get me wrong; new policies need to be communicated. That's a good thing. But again, it's not training.

If the company adds discussion and activities, giving employees the opportunity to see a demonstration of the new policy in action and practice the policy in a safe environment—that's *training*. But holding a meeting in which one person communicates a new policy or procedure, everyone else listens, and we all sign a form saying we will adhere to the new procedure doesn't mean training occurred.

Training also tends to imply that the subject being conveyed needs to be learned. For example, if the company developed a new policy on expense reports, it might hold a meeting to explain the changes but not a training session because everyone knows how to complete expense reports. However, if the company starts using a new software program to process expense reports, it might conduct a training session because no one knows how to use the software.

Orientation should be considered training. Orientation involves knowledge that employees need to digest and activities they need to learn. Even if most of the learning that happens during onboarding and orientation has become an exercise in how to look up your own answers, employees need to learn how to do that using the company systems. Orientation could include a scavenger hunt so that employees can practice finding information.

I talk to people on a regular basis who are frustrated with employees. They say, "We conducted training," when the reality is that the organization held a meeting and told employees the policy. At the end of the meeting, the company has no idea what employees learned, if anything. And management gets really frustrated when employees don't follow the new policy or procedure. Meanwhile, the employees say, "I never got any training!" when they're confronted with a performance issue.

This same thing can and does happen with orientation. New employees need knowledge and skills. That means they need training. I admit, the vast amount of that training will take place in onboarding, but some of it needs to happen in orientation.

The training we're talking about doesn't have to be long or complex. It does need to give new hires a chance to actively review the knowledge or skill topic as well as an opportunity to practice. When making decisions about orientation content, organizations must decide if the content will be simply "communicated" or trained. It makes a difference not only in the way information is shared but in how it is received. More importantly, how it is retained and accounted for.

Recruiting and Training Are Responsible for a Smooth Transition

New-hire employees deserve a smooth transition into the organization. If you're a solo practitioner, it's easy; you do it all. But at some point, even HR departments of one should help transition new employees over to their department.

The key is each function understanding what the other function does. Recruiters should build a relationship with training like the relationship they build with their hiring managers. It will make orientation and onboarding stronger, which benefits the employee and the company.

 TIPS
3 Tips for Taking Your Orientation Process to the Next Level
The key to a successful employee orientation is making the event about the employee, not about the company and paperwork. Here are suggestions on how to make that happen.

1. *Dave Ryan, SHRM-SCP, SPHR, is director of human resources at Mel-O-Cream Donuts and currently serves as director of the Illinois State Council, a Society for Human Resource Management (SHRM) affiliate.*

> When onboarding an employee these days, to be efficient, and save valuable time and dollars we want to get any possible document to the employee before arriving on-site. Then, we wish for them to complete these documents electronically and return them to us so we can get on to the matters at hand when they do arrive. In doing so, you are missing some valuable relationship building time with your newest employee. Chat with them as they complete the forms, answer questions they may have, find out about their interest, make them feel welcome and comfortable and get to know them. Seize the opportunity! You may have cost the organizer 60 minutes, but don't you want to invest in this person? We do want them to stay and feel engaged.

2. *Joel Passen has been at the intersection of talent and technology for his entire professional career. Before co-founding Newton, a Paycor company and developer of cloud- and mobile-based hiring technology for emerging and midmarket companies, he co-founded Gravity Technologies, a management consulting company for recruiting.*

> Prior to starting Newton, I started and ran a recruiting consultancy. Our clients were high growth technology companies mainly in Silicon Valley. One of the program areas that I created was aimed at increasing time to productivity and increasing overall retention rates of new employees. I took many of the same ideas and applied them as we were scaling Newton. We still use many of these best practices today.
>
> 1. **Share people's experiences.** Send a message to the entire company introducing your newest team members. Include something fun about each person, and share their experience and skills.
> 2. **Every new hire needs an ambassador.** Pair your new hires with someone from another department who can take them to lunch and expose them to a team they wouldn't necessarily work with right away. This is also a good retention practice as ambassadors take on a new level of ownerships while acculturating newbies.
> 3. **Eat together.** Bring in a catered lunch or go to lunch (especially if there is a group). Go out of your way to make it somewhat unique if possible so that you can have a new experience together.

4. **Bring in the brass.** Have a member of the executive team sit in on some of the general sessions. Ideally, have them lead a discussion on values or culture—the content that defines the company.

5. **Start an "exchange program."** Build a checklist and have new hires sit in on a meeting in every business unit during their first two weeks. Sales people should know the development team. Marketers should know the IT team, etc.

3. *Lauryn Sargent is co-founder and a partner at Stories Incorporated, a digital agency focused on uncovering powerful stories and creating engaging digital content to help its clients build connections with candidates, team members, and customers. Before starting Stories Incorporated, Sargent spent over seven years recruiting for entrepreneurial organizations and Fortune 500 companies.*

One great way to bring the candidate/new hire experience to the next level is to incorporate storytelling into your communications. By using real stories and experiences to communicate what it means to be a part of your organization, not general language, these individuals have a concrete understanding of what to expect and how to be successful in their role and the organization as a whole. In the application process, the result of this understanding is candidates realizing whether or not they are a good fit (and if they're not, self-selecting themselves out of the process and improving your overall quality of candidates!). In the onboarding process, this heightened understanding of culture will help lower the learning curve and result in the individual adjusting to the new position more quickly and effectively than they may have otherwise. Here are a couple of examples of how stories can be used in the candidate and onboarding process:

- At The Motley Fool, they use a two-minute video explaining one of their "Fool Rules," called the "Fool's Errand."' The video is part of a 45-page interactive onboarding site centered around company stories.
- Dell has a series of videos capturing the intern experience, including one about their open-door policy. The videos are also used in recruiting, which encourages newly-hired interns to take advantage of the company's open-door policy and network with individuals all around the organization.

CHAPTER 14:
Onboarding

CASE STUDY
AMRESCO Improves Employee Retention with Better Onboarding

AMRESCO is a manufacturer and supplier of biochemicals located in Ohio. A few years ago, it faced high turnover and poor retention rates, particularly in two critical departments. Realizing that it could not grow the business under these conditions, AMRESCO created a long-term plan to improve its onboarding to better retain talent.

As part of the plan, the company surveyed new hires for feedback on how it could improve the hiring and onboarding processes. AMRESCO used this information to create a three-part onboarding program:

1. **Orientation Plan.** New hires receive a roadmap for navigating their first 90 days. The roadmap describes their training and orientation, details the new hire's goals and objectives, and features practical information like the cafeteria location. The goal is for new hires to have clear expectations and deliverables during their first few months of employment.

2. **New Employee Orientation.** Orientation consists of a two-part class designed by senior management. The program introduces new hires to the business, organizational initiatives, the company's strategic plan, and the outlook of AMRESCO. It also goes one step deeper and shares each department's role and purpose along with how departments interact with each other.

3. **Buddy/Mentor.** New hires are matched with a top-performing buddy or mentor whose role is to help them acclimate to the company culture and answer general questions during their first 90 days.

> AMRESCO's onboarding program helped to reduce turnover and improve the new-hire experience. The orientation plan provided new hires with a clear and comprehensive plan that allows them to integrate into the company culture faster with the help of the new buddy/mentor. And, after attending the orientation program, new hires have a strong understanding of the organization and their future.
>
> AMRESCO's onboarding program was recognized for its results by NorthCoast 99, an annual program that honors 99 great workplaces for top talent in Northeast Ohio.

In Chapter 12, we talked about using technology strategically so new hires will not be inundated with papers to sign on their first day. In Chapter 13 (Orientation), we discussed the transition between recruiting and learning as well as how effective orientation programs are designed. For this chapter, I want to focus on why new hires need onboarding.

The Purpose of Onboarding

The primary goal of onboarding is to make employees productive. The better the onboarding process, the faster an employee can engage with the organization. If employees don't engage with the organization, they will leave. And turnover is expensive. Neither recruiters nor hiring managers want to continuously recruit for the same openings.

An article on the website for the Society for Human Resource Management (SHRM) cites an Aberdeen Group study that found that 86 percent of respondents felt a new hire's decision to stay with the company is made within the first six months of employment. For many companies, that aligns with their onboarding process (aka the time it takes for an employee to become productive).

According to the *2012 Allied Workforce Mobility Survey*, the reason that companies lose new employees within the first year is *ineffective onboarding*. Here are a few findings from the survey:

- Almost 30 percent of companies reported that it takes a year or longer for a new employee to reach full productivity.
- Twenty-five percent of companies said their onboarding program did not include any training.
- Sixty percent of companies indicated they don't set any milestones or goals for new hires.

There's an old cliché about never having a second chance to make a first impression. These survey results would indicate that it's true. New hires are excited to join the organization. They want to show the company that they are the right candidate. Not providing new hires with the tools and information to be successful makes them wonder why the company hired them.

The other aspect of the survey that might factor into these findings was the amount of money dedicated to onboarding. Or more accurately, the lack of it. Approximately 35 percent of companies spend $0 on onboarding. *That's not a typo.* They spend zero, zip, zilch. I understand that we have to manage the budget, but to spend thousands of dollars on hiring employees and $0 on making them productive sounds like stepping over dollars to pick up quarters.

If your organization is like AMRESCO and looking to breathe some new life into your onboarding process, here are a few places to start:

- Know how long it takes for an employee to become productive. The purpose of onboarding is to give employees the information they need when they need it.
- Find out why people are leaving the company via exit interviews—and not just why employees are leaving but what caused them to go looking in the first place. And don't just file away the information. *Use it* to create change!
- Ask employees what they like about working for the organization (that is, conduct stay interviews).

These are things you want to make sure new hires know about. We'll talk about stay interviews and exit interviews more in the next chapter.

It would be great to have an unlimited budget devoted to onboarding. But we all know that's not realistic. What could help increase the onboarding budget is being able to show the costs to hire an employee, the average length of employment for new hires, and the cost of an employee resignation. I've never met a CEO who lets money fly out the window—*show them the numbers.*

The First Rule of Onboarding: Always Explain the WIIFM

WIIFM: What's in it for me?

Elmer Wheeler, the "world's greatest salesman," put it best with his often-quoted "Don't sell the steak, sell the sizzle." The first rule of adult learning is telling participants what's in it for them. If you want people to buy into your idea, you have to tell them the reason on their terms. Customers will buy your product or service if it fixes one of their problems or makes their life easier.

I've had more than a few conversations with people who don't know what WIIFM is. They don't understand why they have to tailor their messaging to their audience. The mere fact that they've built a product or service means it must be valuable and everyone should buy it. Same with some recruiters. They've already sold the company during the hiring process, so they feel they don't need to sell it anymore. Sorry, that's incorrect.

We have to tell people what's in it for them because it isn't realistic to think that everyone will figure this out on their own. Or that *they'll even want to.* WIIFM isn't selfish. It's a legitimate question. It's your business case. What will I get for listening, participating, buying, etc.? Value must be present. Customers and employees will not give their time and money to something with no value.

If you're saying to yourself, I get it—communicate to others on their channel—but how? Honestly, it's not hard.

Ask them. Here are two ways to get people's attention:

- **Be authentic.** The best messaging is both authentic and geared to the audience. Today's audiences expect messaging to appeal to them. They don't want to search for the uniqueness that applies to them.

- **Make the connection.** There's a constant conversation about "noise" on the Internet—how there's so much information, it's hard to filter through all of it. People want information that helps them fix a problem, that educates them on a subject, or that just makes them laugh or smile. But it must create a connection in some way.

The Second Rule of Onboarding: Don't Overwhelm

I think the first rule of onboarding is about the quality of content. The second rule is about quantity.

One of the onboarding mistakes I see organizations make is that they give new hires too much information. Remember, successful onboarding is about employees getting the information they need at the moment they need it because that's also how people learn. If I attend a training session but don't get to use the information for six months, chances are, I'll forget it. But if I learn something and am immediately able to apply it in my job, chances are, I will remember it!

As a result, some companies have decided that instead of onboarding they will create information repositories that employees can use to find information at a moment's notice. The problem with this method is that they're basing it on the old phrase taken from the movie *Field of Dreams*, "If you build it, they will come." The truth is … they won't. It takes more than just creating or building something for people to use it. People must understand the WIIFM—what's in it for me—before they start using something.

So back to the repository example. A company builds a terrific repository of information for employees to use. It's great because all the information is online and accessible anytime. But employees don't use it. Why? Well, there could be several reasons:

- No one knew it existed.
- It's easier just to walk around the corner and ask someone.
- The system has a lot of information, but it's not updated regularly.
- Information located in one section of the system doesn't match information found in another section.

And the list goes on.

Onboarding needs to contain the right quality and quantity of information based on the questions we discussed at the beginning of the chapter: How long does it take for employees to become productive? What do they like about working for the company? And what do they need to know?

The Third Rule of Onboarding: Maintenance Matters

When we create something, part of the process needs to establish a clear understanding of how we will maintain it. I've heard plenty of quality ideas that fall to the wayside because no one stopped to consider what happens once we implement them.

Here's another way of looking at the topic that I'm sure you've seen before. A group meets to discuss an organizational challenge, like turnover. Someone says, "We should revamp our onboarding program." Everyone agrees. Then nothing happens. Because the person who came up with the idea to revamp the onboarding process thinks his or her part is done. Since the others weren't specifically told they were supposed to implement the idea, the new program never gets implemented.

Or maybe this has happened to you: A group meets and decides it will create a new onboarding process. And the members do. They design and build a terrific solution. Then they go back to their regular daily activities. After a few months, the group members realize no one is using the solution they created. They each thought communicating the new resource and maintaining it was someone else's job. They were just supposed to create it. Oh, and now the new onboarding program is outdated.

If your job is to build something, consider all the phases—not just design and creation but how to implement, communicate, and maintain. Otherwise, all your hard work is for nothing.

 FYI
Sample Onboarding Checklists for Creative Inspiration

When I'm starting a project, I sometimes find it helpful to research and see what's out there. Luckily some organizations are very kind and share their resources. Here are a couple of onboarding programs you can find with a quick Internet search.

Johns Hopkins University has a very comprehensive resource called *On-Boarding Toolkit: Guidance for the Hiring Manager*. The guide includes a "buddy" checklist, very helpful if you're considering a buddy program for new hires. It also has a template for check-in meetings between managers and new hires.

And don't forget about LinkedIn's *Onboarding in a Box*. It includes a "Best Boss Ever" checklist—a list of things managers can do to make sure the working relationship they are building with a new hire is positive.

I'm not suggesting copying these programs. Every culture is unique. Some of these suggestions will fit with your organization, and some won't. But you might look at them and gain some ideas that work for your onboarding program.

Use Talent Centers to Reinforce Onboarding

To fill the talent pipeline, recruiting and training functions must work together. Recruiters must be able to tell the organization which roles are better to develop in-house versus recruit from the outside. Trainers have to do the same thing. Let the organization know which jobs would be better to hire from the outside instead of developing from within.

In addition, training and recruiting have to work together to ensure that new hires are set up for success. Onboarding is the way to do that. It's the intersection between recruiting and training that creates employee success. According to TLNT.com, one-third of new hires quit their job in the first six months. And we all know turnover is costly.

When it comes to onboarding, I've started to hear more about a format called talent center. The idea is that talent centers are dashboards where employees, managers, recruiting, and training can monitor and measure onboarding progress. Within the talent center are resources and checklists that new hires and managers can use during the onboarding process.

Before you put down this book and declare checklists as evil, hear me out. On some basic level, we all work with checklists on a regular basis (that is, a to-do list). We need them to remind us because we're human and can't remember everything. Checklists can be used to:

- Outline what it takes to be successful in a new role (that is, competencies).
- Document compliance requirements.

A few pages ago, I mentioned information repositories. You might have thought from my comments that I'm opposed to them, but I'm not. They have a place in the learning process—just not as a substitute for onboarding programs.

The tricky thing about checklists is making sure they're used. That's the difference between a boring, outdated repository of information and an interactive, engaging talent center. It could make a lot of sense to include a talent center in the onboarding process and bring together recruiting, learning, and performance. If you start considering using a talent center, keep these in mind:

- **Train employees and managers on how to use the talent center.** Organizations should not assume that everyone knows how to effectively use a checklist. That's probably the number one reason that checklists fail—no one has ever received training in effectively using them. We're not talking about hours or days of training here. But do provide managers and employees with guidance on how to make the most of the resource.

- **Regularly survey managers and employees.** The other reason that checklists are not used effectively is because they can quickly become outdated. An outdated checklist is worthless. Survey managers and employees to make sure onboarding resources are current. (And on a side note: don't forget to put together a maintenance program for talent center materials.)

Remember the Three Rules on Onboarding

If employees receive good information in a timely fashion, they will become productive quickly and start contributing to the organization. This will help them become engaged with the company. And everyone will be happy.

Onboarding is an important step in the hiring process. If it's not done well, the employee will leave, and the hiring process must start all over again. The key is having an onboarding process that aligns with organizational culture and remaining patient. It can take weeks or months for employees to learn everything they need to know.

TIPS
3 Tips for Taking Your Onboarding Process to the Next Level

Even though onboarding is about training and bringing new hires up to full productivity, talent acquisition professionals should wear a generalist hat. Understanding the other aspects of talent management like learning, compensation, and benefits will only strengthen the recruiting function. Here are three things to consider when it comes to learning more about onboarding.

1. *John Fleischauer is the head of global talent acquisition for Saba Software, which delivers a cloud-based intelligent talent management solution. His personal mission is to become the best in the world at what he does. However, being the best is not what drives him. What gets him out of bed every morning is being surrounded by incredible people that are passionate about their craft.*

> Recruiters have a great opportunity to help build a team with the right people. After all, talent acquisition fits within a broader talent management strategy and the goal is to help people bring their best effort and passion to work so they can contribute in meaningful ways and continue to learn and grow so the business can thrive.
>
> For business performance to really take off, we need to have the right people working together in the right environment and guided by

the right leadership. We need to understand what success in a role looks like and how we can measure talent against that before we post for a job opening or write job descriptions. And this is a collaborative effort across talent acquisition, HR, hiring managers, and other employees who are part of that team.

We also need to look at bringing people on board and moving towards success quicker. Companies need to design and implement an effective onboarding program that engages new employees and sets them up for success—regardless of their physical location. Properly onboarding new employees can help boost retention for new hires, improve engagement, and reduce costs.

2. *Jennifer V. Miller* *is the founder of The People Equation, a consultancy focused on workplace dynamics. She is also the co-author of* The Character-Based Leader: Instigating a Leadership Revolution ... One Person at a Time.

One thing I find myself thinking about lately is how younger members of the workforce experience their jobs differently than we do. A young professional said to me the other day, "My dad kept telling me that in order to get a job, it's not about what I know, but who I know. Boy, I did not realize how true those words were." This young professional is talented, but he has underestimated the role that human interactions play in the workplace. Pairing that with some societal trends such as the fact that teens are gaining important workplace skills as teens (Check out the Talent Economy article, "Why Teens Aren't Working—And How It Influences the Workforce"), I think we might have an up and coming workforce that simply doesn't understand the value of human connections.

So, although this advice might seem old-fashioned, from my perspective one of the most important things a newly hired recruiter can do to "up" his or her game is to start making connections internally with the customers they will serve. Traditional orientations tend to focus on "here is the information you need to do your job" and indeed that's important. But once a recruiter understands the mechanics of the company's sourcing protocols, then the thing that will really make her stand out to her internal clients is her ability to find talent that matches the hiring manager's stated needs—AND the unstated ones as well. All hiring managers have biases (they're human, after all) so it's imperative that recruiters get to know their assigned managers.

I suggest that recently hired recruiters make a list of people they'd like to meet in their organization, then seek out the assistance of their team leader to facilitate those introductions. At the end of each meeting, the recruiter should ask, "Who else should I meet with?" Then listen for not only the name of the person but the reason WHY this person has been recommended. You'd be amazed at the information that can be gleaned by this one simple question.

3. *As senior director of global talent management at Kronos Incorporated,* **Kimberly Nugent** *is responsible for developing and executing the company's performance, succession planning, leadership development, culture, and engagement strategies for 5,200-plus employees around the world. She is also credited with building the global talent management function at Kronos. Prior to Kronos, she held similar roles at Liberty Mutual, including HR business partner, compensation, and analytics responsibilities, and earned her Master of Business Administration and Master of Social Work degrees at Boston College, with undergraduate work at Wheaton College in Massachusetts.*

Think like a marketer to take your onboarding game to the next level. The best marketing teams bucket prospective and current customers into different personas. These personas help companies understand what customers value so they can personalize the customer experience. Why can't we do that for our employees and create an onboarding (and other work experiences) that are meaningful to that individual?

Taking it a step further, let's turn the concept of customer journey mapping onto our people. If HR professionals take a more human-centered, design-thinking approach, we can zero in on "moments that matter" for our employees to create a more compelling experience. If you're lucky to work at a company with a talented marketing team, sit down with them, pick their brains, and start treating your candidates and employees like customers!

CHAPTER 15:
Post-Hire Activities

CASE STUDY
Cirrus Logic Lets Employees Tell It Why the Company Culture Is Great

One of the core topics in any orientation and onboarding program is company culture. We want candidates to see the company culture before they apply and during the hiring process, so they know they're a good fit. And we want them to fully immerse in the culture once they arrive.

I use the word "immerse" because some organizations are taking the challenge literally by creating cultural immersion programs. Cirrus Logic, based in Austin, Texas, has a culture camp it calls School of Cirrus Rocks. In an article for *Austin Woman* magazine, Chief Culture Officer Jo-Dee Benson explained the theme. "We make integrative circuits for audio applications, and a lot of our employees are musicians. It's a theme that has really evolved and resonated with our organization."

Think of culture camp as a mashup between Jack Black's *School of Rock* and Garrison Keillor's *Prairie Home Companion*. Here's how the program works.

Before the session, participants take pictures about what inspires them around Cirrus. On the day of the program, participants meet at a local bar. The first half of the day, participants learn about storytelling. Why? Because storytelling is how employees share the company values.

During the second half of the day, participants break into groups and are tasked with pulling their images together into a story. Then, with the help of local musicians, music is added. Basically, employees create a story in the form of a song about working at the company. The groups perform their song in the best place—a local bar with local musicians and their co-workers cheering them on.

While every company isn't going to create a *School of Rock*-themed culture camp, several takeaways can be applied to any company culture program:

- **Commitment.** It is obvious that Cirrus Logic is "all in" with this program when it comes to resources (that is, people and budget.) A lot of people and equipment are involved to produce the program, so it's only held three to four times a year. But when it happens, the company does it right. Organizations that are committed to a culture camp need to be fully committed.

- **Listening.** Cirrus Logic felt it was important for new hires to tell the company why Cirrus is a great place to work, versus the traditional other way around. Organizations need to listen to their employees and understand what employees love about the company. It will tell them what to keep and what to share with candidates.

- **Reinforcement.** The program itself reinforces Cirrus's organizational values like continuous improvement (accountability), innovation (investment to solve problems), integrity, communication, and job satisfaction. Any organizational program should align with company values, whatever those values are.

- **Recognition.** The Cirrus Logic program works hard to make participants feel special. First, they ask participants not to disclose what happens in the School of Cirrus Rocks to other employees. Yes, participants have some idea—but they want people to enjoy the surprise. And Cirrus also gives participants a very cool memento to remember their experience—a miniature guitar.

- **Communication.** I mentioned earlier that the first part of the session focuses on storytelling, the idea being that telling good stories helps your career. It's the "story" that gets you on the meeting agenda so you can sell your ideas to others. For example, organizations can create an activity for employees to tell their culture story in six words (like the Hemingway six-word story activity).

- **Teamwork.** Whenever you do something a little scary, something that takes you outside your comfort zone, like creating a song and singing it with your co-workers, you will remember it forever. This culture immersion camp helps bond people with each other and with the company. Trust me, participants will remember the people they went to camp with.

Again, what Cirrus Logic does in its culture camp works for the company, and it receives a return on investment that justifies the program. The point here isn't for other companies to duplicate the Cirrus Logic program. It's about making sure that employees understand your company culture so much that they can tell you about it (rather than being told).

By now, we all know that the concept of employee engagement is important. However, companies should start thinking about engagement early in the hiring process. If they wait until hiring someone to think about engagement, it's too late.

That's why organizations need to step up their game when it comes to developing onboarding programs. The program needs to not only satisfy the nature of onboarding but also build employee engagement, even after onboarding is complete. One way to build employee engagement is with a mentoring program.

Building a Successful Mentoring Program

We've talked about buddy programs in previous chapters, but I view mentoring as being a little different. My definition of "mentor" is a person who is a subject matter expert in the topic he or she is mentoring about. A mentor's method involves teaching and development. Mentors pass along their knowledge and skills. Mentoring is not superior to a buddy or coaching relationship; it's simply different and should be used in the right way.

Mentoring programs can be used as a part of onboarding. Typically, mentoring programs have three goals: a) to assist in career development, b) to increase staff retention and c) to improve employee engagement. These goals fit with what the organization is trying to accomplish during onboarding and beyond.

Organizations are facing some unique challenges when it comes to talent. With the Baby Boom generation in the process of leaving the workforce (or at least transitioning to part time or semi-retirement), companies want to make sure their organizational knowledge and history are passed along to new employees, who will lead the organization forward. Mentoring could be an ideal program to address this issue.

But mentoring isn't a short-term process, and it takes an organizational commitment. As much as we might like the term "Vulcan mind meld," it's not an effective way to pass along knowledge. Not *yet* at least. So, for now, organizations should pass along knowledge over time, give people the opportunity to process it, use it in the daily operation, and ask questions about it.

Once you have senior management support and the appropriate resources, you'll want to get your hands on specific resources to help you design the program. Here are a few of my favorites:

- For a high-level overview, the Kenan-Flagler Business School at the University of North Carolina (UNC) published a mentoring guide, *How to Build a Successful Mentoring Program*. It's a great overview and something you could distribute throughout the organization to gain support for building a mentoring program.
- A go-to resource for design ideas is the Infoline series from the Association for Talent Development (ATD). One book, titled *Tools for Effective Mentoring Programs*, includes a program outline, matching process suggestions, mentor position descriptions, and skills questionnaires.
- For more detail, ATD also offers the book *Creating a Mentoring Program* that includes how to conduct activities such as the launch meeting, celebrations, check-ins, and closures.

- If your organization isn't the mentoring program type, check out Randy Emelo's *Modern Mentoring*, which focuses on building a mentoring *culture* versus a mentoring program. I enjoyed the section on the advantages (and challenges) of using gaming techniques in mentoring.

The point here is that mentoring has value, and it's very flexible to your culture and business needs. The UNC guide is a great place to start the conversation, and the ATD resources can help you develop a program that works for your organization.

One last thing to consider is developing the metrics for evaluating the effectiveness of your mentoring program. These metrics should align directly with the program goals. Examples of measurements that can be developed include:

- Program quality such as the percentage of mentors and mentees that have met at least once per month and percentage of completion in the program.
- Participant experiences, including perceptions of value, match appropriateness, and levels of trust. This measurement applies to both the mentee and the mentor.
- Organizational impact, meaning the metrics that help organizations achieve their goals, including work performance, retention, and recognition.

Part of program design should encompass the metrics used to evaluate program effectiveness, the data gathered to create the metric, how often the data will be gathered, and the data points considered acceptable and unacceptable in evaluating the effectiveness of the program.

The beauty of mentoring programs is being able to leverage the organization's *current* talent to develop *future* talent.

Survey New Hires for Feedback

I simply cannot emphasize this enough: companies need to confirm that they are delivering on their recruiting promises.

New hires might be reticent about sharing their thoughts directly. If you're concerned about that, you have a few ways to elicit good feedback. First, let new hires know during orientation that they will be receiving a survey. If the survey is a normal part of the process, then new-hire employees will be comfortable with it. Also, consider making the survey anonymous. After all, the purpose of the survey isn't to know who said what. It's to improve the onboarding process.

The survey can ask new hires questions like:

- Did the interview process happen the way it was explained?
- Was there anything you were hoping to have covered in orientation that wasn't?
- During orientation, did you learn something about the job that would have been helpful to know before you were hired?

The hiring process is too important not to survey new hires regularly. There are also a couple of extra benefits to letting new hires know that the company does surveys. First, it lets employees know that their thoughts matter, which is terrific for engagement. Second, it sends the message that feedback is expected and employees can start to become comfortable delivering feedback directly (versus anonymously).

Tell Employees Why They Were Hired

Speaking of feedback, at some point post-onboarding, managers need to tell employees why they were hired.

It seems like such a simple question: Do you know why the organization hired you? But how many times does it actually happen?

One of my former bosses took me out to lunch one day to tell me why she hired me. She said, "Because you didn't come from the industry." She wanted an outsider who would ask questions and challenge the status quo. She felt that was what the company needed.

If organizations want employees to be engaged and successful in their roles, they should tell them why they were hired. Not what they were hired to do—but why *them* over anyone else. The new employee's hiring manager needs to have an intentional, planned conversation with an employee that explains:

- The previous experience that made the candidate's resume stand out.
- The knowledge, skills, and abilities that the company found impressive.
- The things the candidate said during the interview process that set him or her apart from everyone else.

This is part of setting a new hire up for success. New employees learn what the organization saw in them and their background and what the interviewers responded well to during the interview. Not only does this information give new hires confidence, but it also tells them something about how to communicate within the organization: it tells them which of their strengths to leverage.

This shouldn't be a one-sided conversation. New employees should communicate why they accepted the offer. When the hiring manager schedules this one-on-one session with the employees, let the manager know that this is the information the organization would like to learn:

- What was it about the company that made the candidate apply?
- What things were said during the interview process that really impressed the candidate?
- What aspects of company culture stood out during the hiring process?

Think of what this could tell organizations about their hiring process. You could discover what attracted candidates to the company's employment brand, how they perceived the interview process, and what closed the deal when they decided to accept the offer.

This conversation also helps build trust between the manager and the new employee. Positive working relationships start with an open and honest conversation about why the employee was hired and why the candidate accepted. I'd certainly like to think that this will not be a conversation that consists of a manager saying something like, "Well, we hired you because we could afford your salary." And the employee saying, "Well, I came to work here because you were the only company that called me back."

Managers can tell employees, "I want you to be successful with us. Let me share with you what impressed me during the hiring process." And employees can respond with, "I liked that the company offered flexible schedules. And I appreciated your comments about company leadership."

If having a formal conversation with employees about why they were hired isn't a part of your onboarding or post-onboarding plans, well, maybe it should be. It's the start of the feedback loop that's critical to workplace success.

Use Stay Interviews to Identify New-Hire Dissatisfaction

In the last chapter, we talked about the importance of soliciting feedback from employees on the things they like about the company. Stay interviews are structured interviews designed to learn the reasons that employees stay with a company or the conditions that might cause them to leave. As the talent wars continue, stay interviews can be a valuable way to engage and retain employees.

A couple of years ago, I had the chance to hear Dr. Beverly Kaye discuss her book *Hello Stay Interviews, Goodbye Talent Loss*, which talks about the dynamics of stay interviews. What I thought was interesting about the stay interview conversation was the idea of having recruiters conducting stay interviews.

Yep, that's right. Recruiters are doing stay interviews.

I asked Kaye about the role recruiters can play in stay interviews. She responded, "In my research, I'm finding that retention is the new measurement of recruiting success and different players have a role in the outcome. Clearly the employee's manager is the best bet to conduct a stay interview. But, the missing link is the recruiter who is often the first to really connect with the new hire. I believe that new recruits do bond with the person who gives them the interview and invites them to join the organization."

I asked her if she could share sample questions recruiters could use when they conduct stay interviews:

- What was something your last organization did well that we don't do?
- Is the job turning out to be what you thought it would be? How so? How not?
- What did your past job offer that you feel is missing in this one?

I totally get this. I've worked for companies that asked employees these questions during their first 30/60/90 days of employment. New hires have a fresh set of eyes, so getting their feedback is smart. And we've already talked about the challenges with first-year turnover. Making a connection with the company quickly is important, and the recruiter could be a key individual in the employee's success.

Objections to Stay Interviews

But I also want to bring a degree of realism to this conversation. I'm sure one of the biggest objections to doing stay interviews is having an employee suggest something that you know the company won't consider. Which leads me to my one note of caution when it comes to stay interviews: Please don't do them if you're not prepared to listen. The absolute worst thing you can do is ask people for their feedback and not do anything with the information. Kaye recommended a four-part approach for handling employee responses that cannot be accommodated:

1. Acknowledge—Listen to the employee and acknowledge what he or she is saying.
2. Truth—Tell the employee that his or her request isn't a viable option.
3. Care—Express a sincere concern to work with the employee.
4. Ask—Find out if there is another option that might be satisfactory.

Another objection to stay interviews may involve time. Some recruiters and managers may say they don't have time to do stay interviews—"I'm overworked, underpaid, and stressed out." To that I have a couple of responses:

- Don't forget that recruiters and managers are people too. If the company is serious about retaining talent, it should conduct stay interviews at every level of the organization. That includes the recruiting, human resource, and management teams.
- If you don't have time to conduct stay interviews, then chances are you don't have time to deal with employees resigning, hiring their replacement, and training them. Stay interviews will definitely take less time.

Objections behind us, it's important to find time to conduct a meaningful stay interview. (Translation: conducting the stay interview while multitasking isn't a good idea.) While conducting stay interviews in person is ideal, Dr. Kaye shared with me some strategies for conducting stay interviews with virtual teams: "I have seen managers with virtual teams use Skype to do their stay interviews. Being able to see the individual gives the manager the opportunity to pick up clues from gestures and facial expression. If this can be done for virtual employees, it can be as effective as face to face meetings."

Stay interviews have tremendous potential for the organization. Yes, it's possible the company may eventually lose employees even after conducting stay interviews because some offers are just too good to pass up. But the company will have learned something. And to quote the great bluesman B. B. King, "The beautiful thing about learning is nobody can take it away from you."

People Are "New Hires" for a Long Time

Once people attend orientation and go through the onboarding process, they don't immediately move from new hire to employee. There are still lots of things they need to know. I think it's fair to say that employees have to be with their companies at least a year before they aren't a new hire anymore. After a year, employees have been through an entire cycle with the company. They've seen the annual events and business cycles.

Organizations can use this frame of reference to their advantage. Treating people like new hires for a year allows companies to develop a pre-boarding, orientation, onboarding, post-onboarding cycle that truly welcomes employees and sets them up for success.

TIPS
3 Tips for Taking Your Post-Hire Activities to the Next Level

The good news is that organizations can make the post-hire experience whatever they want. That being said, the best way to create a post-hire experience that employees enjoy is by getting their feedback. Find out what employees want and incorporate their ideas into the employee experience. Here are some ideas to consider from fellow business professionals.

1. *Barb Sanfilippo, CSP, CPAE, is an award-winning motivational speaker, consultant, and coach. Her firm, High Definition People, inspires leaders and businesses to act on their highest aspirations, enrich employee and customer relationships and experience work and life at the highest level possible. She has received high marks for her mega and super sessions at several SHRM annual conferences, the SHRM Strategy Conference, and many Fortune 500 and leadership conferences.*

Onboarding new talent should be the beginning of a satisfying and rewarding long-term relationship with your organization. Unfortunately, often it's the end! Savvy HR executives recognize successful onboarding is not simply about what goes on before or during the actual onboarding. It's more about the overall experience and engaging each employee with your culture, their colleagues and especially their manager in the first critical six months! To extend the onboarding experience and take it to the next level, be sure to do the following:

Engage a new employee from the start by exposing them to your core business and the customer experience. One way to accomplish the first is to have them attend a staff meeting of a department they serve and report back what they learned. For the latter, have them go on a sales call, visit a customer's business and again report what they observed.

Once your new recruit leaves orientation, your managers need to step up and embrace their role like an Olympic Coach working hands on with their athlete. Give managers clear expectations and a checklist to ensure they provide coaching, connection and development opportunities for the first 6-12 months. Rather than just monitoring tasks, managers need to check in and demonstrate a genuine interest in developing their new team member.

2. **Mark Willaman** *is the founder of HRmarketer, a software product that helps social marketing teams make more people aware of and interested in their brand. The software also comes with an employee advocacy module that helps employer branding teams spread the word about their awesome company.*

Employee advocacy (EA) software is used by corporate employer branding teams to encourage and help employees to share positive information about their company on their social networks. Whether you have one hundred or one hundred thousand employees, everyone is a potential spokesperson to help spread the word about why your company is a great place to work.

Recruiters can adapt EA software for social recruiting purposes to generate more awareness and interest in their company (as a great place to work) and in open positions (to reach more candidates). Recruiters can also use social advocacy software as a non-intrusive way to nurture candidate relationships by sharing career information and other educational content with candidates.

3. **Brian Scudamore** *is the founder and CEO of O2E Brands, the banner company for 1-800-GOT-JUNK?, Wow 1 Day Painting, You Move Me, and Shack Shine. As a regular contributor to* Forbes *and* Inc. *magazines, he shares his insight from 30 years of entrepreneurship. When he's not launching a new brand, or coming up with a new, big idea, he's biking or hanging out with his family in Vancouver, British Columbia.*

Success doesn't happen when you're alone. Finding the right people to join your team can be a strategic asset and will be the foundation of your success. At 1-800-GOT-JUNK? we have been in business for 28 years, and when it comes to creating a successful business, it starts with finding the people. One of our main strategies for our People and culture team (HR) is hiring for fit and never compromising.

Once you have the team, you've got to spend time with them, care about them, understand what motivates them and show them how they fit into your company's vision. Building a company is a marathon, not a sprint and you need the right people with you to get to the finish line.

We are always looking to support and help our employees foster new leadership skills and provide an exceptional place to work. To ensure that we are helping our employees grow, we conduct annual employee engagement surveys. The survey has about 30 questions and covers a variety of topics. These surveys give us insight to our team's overall performance and if they feel supported, happy, and engaged with the company.

The survey results are first shared with every department head. They can compare their results from previous years and against the organization. Next, the individual team's results (if they have 4 or more people on their team) are reviewed with department managers. The department heads and managers come together to do a deep dive into what is working well and areas of opportunity. Then they pick areas of focus for improvement and create an action plan to improve workplace culture and team member engagement.

At an organization level, we also take the survey feedback to develop new programs that will further support our team members. For example, we changed our benefits program based on feedback from the survey to a flexible benefits program that our team was looking for. Our engagement survey is a big initiative across the organization. Managers touch base on how engagement is improving in their department in their team meetings. Team members are also held accountable to ensure our organization is a great place to work.

SECTION VII: 3 Key Takeaways

- Pre-boarding is about getting the administration out of the way so employees can focus on the job. Many organizations are looking to technology that will allow HR to focus on building a more welcoming onboarding experience.
- Orientation and onboarding need to give new hires the right information at the right moment in time. Recruiting and learning functions need to collaborate so that a smooth transition occurs.
- Even after onboarding, employees will still be "new" for a while. They need time to experience what happens at the organization.

5 Resources to Make Your Job Easier

1. The SHRM Foundation's Effective Practice Guidelines Series includes *Onboarding New Employees: Maximizing Success*. This free publication provides research and thought leadership on the topic of employee onboarding. Just search for the title online to find it.
2. Before her stay interview book, Dr. Beverly Kaye co-authored the international best seller *Love 'Em or Lose 'Em: Getting Good People to Stay*.
3. SHRM offers a seminar called Coaching & Mentoring: Building Effective Skills. The seminars are offered in-person and virtually.
4. SHRM offers the "New Employee Onboarding Guide" on its website (under the Resources & Tools section). It includes suggestions for a new employee's first day, first few months, and first year.
5. I would be remiss if I didn't mention my previous book, *Manager Onboarding: 5 Steps for Setting New Leaders Up for Success*. It's focused on giving new managers a dedicated onboarding process.

SECTION VIII
Evaluation

In Section VIII

It's time to bring all the pieces together. Part of that means formally measuring the success of your efforts. Recruiting is measurable, and recruiting professionals need to embrace the numbers.

That being said, you don't have to measure everything. In this section, I offer some classic metrics that everyone should calculate and a few to consider in the future.

CHAPTER 16:
Measuring the Effectiveness of Your Recruiting Program

 CASE STUDY
SmashFly Conducts an Experiment to Measure Advertising

SmashFly provides marketing automation software for recruiters. A few years ago, a client asked the company, "What's the best format for our job postings?" Basically, the client wanted to know how to get the most candidates for any given position. To come up with an answer, SmashFly designed an experiment using recruitment metrics and a modified version of A/B testing.

The experiment used the baseline job advertisements for two of the client's positions: a research nurse and a medical technologist. For each position, SmashFly created three additional variations of the same job ad to highlight different points of interest. Then, all four ads were run simultaneously on two different job boards in the same location. Here is a summary of the job ads:

Research Nurse (Job Title/Job Description Format)
1. Research Nurse/Job Description: Baseline ad
2. Are You a Research Nurse?/Job Description: FAQ
3. Immediate Opening for Research Nurse/Job Description: Department/Role/Company format
4. Research Nurse: Immediate Opening/Job Description: ASAP ad

Medical Technologist (Job Title, Job Description Format)
1. Medical Technologist/Job Description: Baseline ad
2. Are You a Medical Technologist?/Job Description: FAQ
3. Medical Technologist: Unique Opportunity/Job Description: Testimonial
4. Medical Technologist/Job Description: ASAP ad

> After measuring job ad views and apply clicks for two weeks, SmashFly came up with the results. The job titles that performed the best were number 4 (Research Nurse: Immediate Opening) and number 3 (Medical Technologist: Unique Opportunity). The job description that performed the best for both research nurse and medical technologist was the FAQ.
>
> Bottom line: Using A/B testing to determine optimal job titles and descriptions could lead to a significant increase in applicants per recruiting dollar.

Once organizations put a recruitment strategy in place, they have to start measuring results. My takeaway from the SmashFly case study isn't the results as much as the process. Every organization has to determine the right metrics for it and what results it will consider acceptable. But doing nothing isn't an option.

Auditing the Candidate Experience

I want to talk about metrics in the context of the recruiting process itself. One of the first components in recruiting is the candidate experience, so it only makes sense to occasionally step back and audit how candidates are receiving the experience.

We've spent plenty of time talking about the importance of eliciting feedback directly from candidates and new hires: you should go straight to the source. Here are a few other things that recruiters can do to take a pulse on the candidate experience:

- **Social recruitment.** Take a critical eye to your company's social recruitment efforts. Look at the social media where your organization has a presence (for example, LinkedIn, Twitter, and Facebook) and review its profile, posting history, responses, etc. Does the company profile accurately reflect the business? Does it contain links back to the company career site? Is the profile being maintained, or was the last post six months ago? Are candidate questions being answered? If you're too close to the social recruiting strategy, ask a manager to check it out and give you his or her honest opinion. Hiring managers have a personal stake in taking a few moments to do this. After all, they want good candidates for their job openings.

- **Career sites.** Ask friends or family members who don't look at your career site every day to visit your career portal and try to search for a job. Don't send them a link—have them find your site the way a candidate would. Then find out how easy (or difficult) the site was to navigate. Don't want to take work home and ask a family member? Ask a colleague and then offer to return the favor. Develop five quick questions for him or her to answer about the ease of navigating the site on a scale of 1 to 5.

- **Applications.** Staff members in the human resource department should time trying to fill out the company application online. See how long it takes. I've heard HR directors say they gave up trying to complete their own company application. If that's true, can you imagine how frustrated a candidate gets? Also, try to upload your LinkedIn profile to apply. And if you want to go one step further, try filling out your company's new-hire paperwork. Years ago, I taught at a university, and at some point it decided to convert us contractors to part-time employees. HR sent me a 31-page new-hire packet. That's not a typo—31 pages. For a part-time role with no benefits.

- **Mobile devices.** Speaking of applying for jobs, everyone today has some sort of mobile device. Check out your career site on a mobile device and try to apply for a job. Time how long the process takes both when you immediately know the job you're applying for and when you search for a job and then apply.

- **Candidate communications.** Probably the biggest complaint from candidates is that they never hear about the status of their application. Many companies are addressing this issue by creating response "rules." For example, at Enterprise Holdings, the standard for responding to candidates is five days. If your company has a response standard, it should be easy to confirm that the standard is being maintained. I've run into situations in which the HR department gets crazy busy, and standards get stretched. Regular monitoring makes sure candidate communications remain a priority.

None of these audit items are hard, though they do require planning and dedication to the effort. But it's exactly that dedication that ensures your organization will end up on the plus side of the candidate experience scale.

Gather Feedback from More Than Just New Hires

When it comes to programs like orientation, onboarding, and buddies/mentors, recruiters need to solicit feedback from people besides just new hires. For example, it makes sense to get feedback from the subject matter experts used during the onboarding design process, the instructional designers who wrote the orientation program, and the trainers or facilitators who delivered it.

Obtaining feedback from the hiring managers is also essential—find out their perceptions after their employees attended orientation. Did the employees come back excited and energized, or did they seem indifferent, bored or unenthusiastic?

You also need to acquire feedback about the orientation session itself. I know it might sound silly, but you do need to know about the logistics. I'm a firm believer that the mind can absorb only what the butt can endure. So if the chairs are hard, the seating is cramped, the lighting is poor, and the room is cold—guess what? It negatively impacts the session.

Also survey participants about the trainer or facilitator. There's a time and place for edutainment (education + entertainment), and there's not. I can't begin to tell you how many times I've asked participants about a facilitator and received the reply, "He's so funny!" I asked what the most important topic was and got the sound of crickets in reply. Having the right person deliver the content *in the right way* is essential.

 FYI
Kirkpatrick's Levels of Training Evaluation

Speaking of delivering content, let's talk about the goal we should have anytime we're passing along information: to have participants retain the material. We want a new hire who attends orientation to remember the information presented.

One of the most widely known models for evaluating training effectiveness is Kirkpatrick's model outlining four levels of training evaluation:

Level 1: Reaction evaluates the degree to which participants enjoyed the training.

Level 2: Learning assesses the extent to which participants acquired the knowledge or skills conveyed in training.

Level 3: Behavior measures the degree participants apply what they learned in training.

Level 4: Results determines the outcomes that occur because of the training.

There is a relationship between the levels. As the level of difficulty to calculate the measurement increases, the value of the measurement increases. Some might infer that, because a Level 1 measurement is the easiest to calculate, it is the least valuable (of the four.) However, Level 1 evaluations provide value if constructed properly. On the other hand, a Level 4 evaluation is the most valuable, but it's also very difficult to calculate, and some organizations might not have the resources to do so.

I'm sure some HR professionals might disagree with me, but the goal isn't always to measure training effectiveness at a Level 4—the important thing is to measure training, period. Even if your only measurement is a Level 1, you have a sense of how participants enjoyed the session. However, don't measure training by the number of hours alone. Simply understanding that participants spent a full day in training doesn't tell you how they viewed the program.

Find out about the actual training content. One way to do this is by giving an anonymous quiz at the start and again at the end of the session. The goal isn't to trick people. It's simply to understand what people know before the session and afterward. Needless to say, the number of questions answered correctly at the end should be higher than those answered correctly in the beginning. (P.S. This is a Kirkpatrick Level 2 evaluation).

Being able to solicit feedback about the orientation helps build good training programs. It gives companies valuable information to use before, during, and after sessions, allowing them to make adjustments that will enhance orientation sessions for future participants. All of these actions lead to one thing—more effective and impactful training that will deliver outcomes to benefit the organization.

5 Talent Metrics Every Recruiter Needs to Know

In one of my first HR jobs, I attended a weekly manager meeting. During the meeting, we went around the table and discussed the projects we were working on and the resources we needed from the organization. Every week, I watched other managers talk about their projects and get the resources they asked for. When it came to my turn, I would explain my project and the resources I needed. Sometimes I would get the support I was looking for, but most of the time I didn't. It was frustrating (to put it mildly.)

I decided that I needed to figure out what I was doing wrong. In thinking about what the other managers did, I realized that they talked about their projects in terms of bottom-line results. They used metrics and numbers and return on investment. When I talked about projects, I expressed results in terms of what would make the employees feel good.

Now, don't get me wrong. Senior management does care about employees and their engagement with the organization. But I found that, when I was able to talk about what the employees want in numerical form, I was able to get project and resources approved.

As the talent wars continue, it will become increasingly important to back up recruiting activity with numbers. What are the best metrics to show? It's easy to get caught up in pages of numbers only to find that no one is reading them. I've had that happen. Start small. Pick five. Calculate and distribute them regularly. Here are the five metrics I would start with.

1. Cost-per-hire

It's essential to understand the cost of hiring someone. Here are a couple of scenarios to illustrate the point.

You're the vice president of talent acquisition for a retail operation. Your company is getting ready to open a new location and will need to hire 100 employees. The senior management team is putting together the budget to build and open the new location. You will need to provide the team with the cost of hiring those 100 employees.

You're the director of human resources for a consulting firm that was just awarded a huge contract. In the proposal, the company indicated that it would need to hire three employees who would be dedicated to the project. The cost to hire those employees was included in the proposal.

The Society for Human Resource Management (SHRM) and the American National Standards Institute (ANSI) have partnered to develop a universally accepted calculation for cost-per-hire (CPH):

$$CPH = (EC + IC)/THP$$

- EC = external costs for all spending outside the organization, including staffing agencies, advertising, job fairs, travel, drug testing, background checks, and signing bonuses.
- IC = internal costs, including recruiting staff salary and benefits, time cost for the hiring manager, government compliance, referral bonuses, and fixed costs for infrastructure.
- THP = total number of hires for the time period being evaluated.

2. Source of hire

We talked back in Chapter 7 about sources. These data tell the company where their applicants, candidates, and new hires are coming from. Examples might include job boards, social media sites, and mobile platforms. Please note, there is a difference in where sources come from. It's possible that a source can provide a lot of applicants that don't turn into candidates, much less new hires. Companies need to spend their resources where they have the greatest positive impact.

Speaking of impact, employee referral programs continue to provide an effective cost- and quality-per-hire, which is why many companies offer a referral bonus. In essence, the employee is helping offset the cost of hiring and providing a quality candidate. Companies need to carefully consider the referral bonus amount, establishing it with cost-per-hire in mind.

As a reminder, employee referral bonuses should be given for doing just that—providing the referral. Referral bonuses are not retention bonuses. If an employee provides the referral and the candidate is hired, that's when the bonus should be paid—not three months or six months down the line. The company—not the employee giving the referral—needs to take responsibility for employee retention.

3. Turnover cost

Once you know the cost-per-hire (see number 1), you can use that amount to determine the turnover cost. This is a metric that should be shared with the management team. In the book *How to Measure Human Resource Management*, author Jac Fitz-enz used the following formula for calculating the turnover cost (TC):

$$TC = CPH + TRM + VC + LCL/THP$$

- TRM = termination costs. These are all the expenses associated with an employee leaving the company, including exit interviews, COBRA, unemployment, attorney's fees, and going-away parties.
- VC = vacancy costs. These include overtime, temporary staffing, and contractors that a company uses while a position is vacant.
- LCL = learning curve loss. This amount takes into account that new employees are not 100 percent effective on their first day of employment and the loss of productivity that occurs while a new hire is being onboarded.
- THP = total number of terminations for the time period being evaluated.

Once managers understand the cost of turnover, they may be more open to trying performance coaching before terminating employees. For example, let's say a manager decides that he or she wants to terminate an employee within the introductory period. The turnover cost number represents the investment that the company has already made and the expense associated with the decision to terminate. Knowing the turnover cost could change the manager's perspective about giving the employee additional performance coaching (versus letting the employee go).

In addition, turnover cost can change the way the organization makes decisions about employee terminations in general. For instance, if your organization has a three-step review process for any expenditure over $5,000, and the cost of turnover is over $5,000, doesn't it make sense to treat terminations with the same kind of rigor?

4. Turnover rate

The 2015 Deloitte *Global Human Capital Trends* study identified employee retention as one of the top issues in talent and human resources. Organizations should understand not only the cost of turnover but also the rate that employees are leaving the organization.

Turnover rate can be determined by dividing the number of separations by the average number of employees for a given time period.

Understanding how many employees have left the organization can provide insight into how much has been spent on turnover over a period of time. Companies can also use it to calculate turnover expense by department or job title.

To give the metric some frame of reference, compare the expense with something in the operation. Is the company turnover expense equal to a piece of equipment? The employee holiday party? The executive bonus budget? As you can see, turnover is a very real expense.

5. Yield ratios

When it comes to numbers, I believe yield ratios are underused. Yield ratios are particularly valuable because the hiring process has multiple steps, and this metric measures one step in the process to the next step. It can provide an overview of the effort necessary in recruiting. For example, take the earlier example of the retail location looking to hire 100 employees. Here are the yield ratios for 100 applications:

Sample Yield Ratios for 100 Applications

75	Screening Interviews	75%
40	Department Interviews	53%
30	Job Offers	75%
25	Acceptances	83%
10	Complete Introductory Period	40%

So let's say that the retail location is recruiting sales representatives. If the company receives 100 applications, it can expect to screen 75 percent (or 75 people). Of those 75 people, it expects 40 to receive department interviews (or 53 percent from those selected for screening). The call center will extend job offers to 30 people (or 75 percent of those receiving department interviews). Twenty-five people (or 83 percent of those receiving job offers) will accept the job offer, and 10 people (or 40 percent who accepted job offers) will complete their introductory period.

These yield ratios tell us that we need to generate a lot more applicant flow if the retail company is going to find the 100 employees it needs to open the new location. Yield ratios can identify possible weaknesses in the process or places where an increased focus is necessary. In this example, the company might want to examine the reason that 15 candidates accepted the job offer but did not complete their introductory period.

Some might say that these five metrics are pretty basic metrics. And that would be correct. The reality is that companies must get the basics right before moving to more complex calculations. These five metrics provide a lot of information. Use them to their fullest.

Measuring the Quality of Your Web Traffic

One of the most interesting conversations that took place during the 2017 TAtech Spring Congress was about web traffic. According to a report by software company DeviceAtlas, almost half of all web traffic (48 percent) is now generated by bots (aka web robots) and crawlers.

Bots and crawlers are software designed to visit your site and perform a function. For example, there are Google bots that crawl my blog, *HR Bartender*. The bot is helpful because it indexes information. That way, when someone does a search on Google for the "difference between knowledge, skills, and abilities," *HR Bartender* shows up high in the search.

Unfortunately, there are also not-so-good bots, and this is where recruiters and human resource professionals need to pay attention.

Many organizations use pay-per-click (PPC) or pay-per-applicant (PPA) recruitment advertising. It makes sense, right? Organizations pay for a recruiting source only when it delivers results. In this case, results are when a job seeker clicks through to see the job posting or actually applies.

Here's the problem. While today's technology has become very sophisticated, it's not good enough to distinguish humans from bots—meaning, when a click happens on your recruitment ad, the computer that's counting those clicks (the ones that you have to pay for) doesn't know if a person or bot did it. This impacts you two ways:

- You could be paying for clicks made by bots.
- You could have more bots than humans applying for jobs.

Either way, the situation is not good. And it keeps you from meeting your recruiting goals. But the answer isn't to eliminate recruitment advertising because let's face it: we need it.

In 2016, TAtech put together a workgroup to address this issue. During the congress, the workgroup shared its *Declaration on Traffic Quality*. The document is designed to protect advertisers from fake applicants and help organizations better understand web traffic. The TAtech community has taken this one step further. Recruitment advertising publishers that are committed to bringing accuracy and transparency to this issue are being recognized for their efforts. Think of it as the Good Housekeeping Seal of approval.

Recruiting advertising is a serious business. I think it's awesome that the community is creating higher standards for itself. As human resource professionals, we need to stay current with what's happening in this area. It can affect the success of our recruiting results and our budgets.

Earned Media Value

Tracking website visits and page views tells you quantity, but it's not enough to get quality. Back in the old days, there was one way to attract applicant flow—newspaper advertising. Today, recruiters can use a variety of media options—paid, earned, shared, and owned (PESO) to attract the right candidates.

Paid media is another term for traditional advertising. An example would be ads in industry journals to promote a career with your organization.

Earned media is publicity attained from other sources, such as an article written about your organization being a great place to work or offering a popular employee benefit.

Shared media happens when content receives recognition outside of the original source. For instance, that paid media ad in the industry journal being shared by employees via social media is an example of shared media. Or a blogger references content that was from a piece of earned media.

Owned media refers to communication channels within your control. Examples would be your website, blogs, and e-mails.

Word-of-mouth and word-of-mouse advertising are far more influential, and the decisions people make about their career are far more important than crowdsourcing which shampoo to buy. Successful organizations are reaching candidates wherever they are across PESO channels.

It's one thing to attract a lot of traffic to your career site. It's another to get applications. Recruiters need to understand what converts a job seeker into an applicant. Take that concept one step further: recruiters need to understand what makes an individual take notice of the company and its offerings.

Recruiting is about hiring the best candidate. Identifying the right sources and reducing administrative time and costs will give recruiters and hiring managers more time with the candidates. The additional time not only allows for a better selection, but it starts the process of building working relationships, which is essential for employee engagement.

Quality of Hires

According to SHRM, the Holy Grail of recruiting is measuring the quality of hire. And I agree that quality of hire is a great metric. But I will add that it's a difficult number to calculate. Let me explain.

Lou Adler, author of the best seller *Hire with Your Head*, defines quality of hire (QoH) as how well a new employee meets the performance standard of the job using a scale from 1 to 5 (1 = underperforms, 3 = meets performance requirements, 5 = exceeds performance requirements).

Using this definition, quality of hire can be assessed at three intervals:

Introductory period. Traditionally, employee performance is assessed at the end of the introductory period to see how the new hire is progressing during the onboarding process. Examining the quality of hire at this point can be a reflection of selection and also an indicator of the strengths and opportunities in the onboarding process.

Six-month anniversary. Once employees complete onboarding, they might be expected to exercise more independent judgment. Revisiting quality of hire can provide an opportunity to benchmark overall employee performance. It could also be a chance to evaluate specific skills that are success factors. For example, by the six-month mark, an employee should have mastered certain equipment, while he or she may be less proficient in other skills.

One-year anniversary. During an employee's annual performance evaluation, the employee's manager will discuss the employee's performance and evaluate specific job skills.

The organization can review an employee's performance at three points in his or her first year (introductory period, six-month mark, one-year mark) to ensure that the employee's progress is moving in a positive direction.

Employers can track these data by the individual, department, location, or company. Not only can organizations use quality-of-hire data to track the improvement in their quality-of-hire data, but they can use the information to examine their internal selection processes. For instance, if one department has a noticeable improvement in the quality of hire, the company can look for departmental best practices to share with others.

Unfortunately, sometimes the quality of hire is calculated via manager anecdotes. We have to resist the urge to do this. If you're going to measure the quality of hire, find a way to do it objectively.

3 Key Metrics in HR Predictive Analytics

The final set of metrics I want to share is predictive analytics. The term is tossed around a lot. So what exactly is predictive analytics? I like to think of it this way: HR metrics tell you what happened in the past, for example, time-to-fill. Or they're focused on cost-containment, such as cost-per-hire. Both metrics are valuable, but we might need more information to make business decisions.

Predictive analytics offers insights into the future. It's focused on probabilities and impact, so it provides flexibility to the organization's needs. There are times when today's business environment is moving so quickly that we cannot always be focused on what happened in the past. We have to give equal time (and some might argue *more* time) to what we think is going to happen in the future and plan accordingly.

That's where predictive analytics comes in because it involves what you do with the information you gather. Predictive analytics measures the three things business people talk about the most: efficiency, effectiveness, and outcomes.

- **Efficiency measurements** include some we already calculate, such as the average number of days to fill a requisition and cost-per-hire.
- **Effectiveness measurements** might contain new-hire performance ratings, engagement survey results, and exit interview data.
- **Outcomes** measure profitability, productivity, and retention.

Predictive analytics is about the connection between these three types of measurements. Here are a few examples:

- Number of open hires (efficiency)—Quality of hire (effectiveness)—Length of employment (outcome)
- Average cost-per-hire (efficiency)—Cultural fit (effectiveness)—Contribution to product quality (outcome)
- Amount of training attended (efficiency)—Hi/lo potential status (effectiveness)— Increased profit margin (outcome)

HR wants to be on the front end of predictive analytics because it's not going away anytime soon, if ever. An increasing number of HR departments are designing analytical roles. If you're looking to move up the career ladder, knowing something about predictive analytics will be important.

Recruiting Is Business; Business Is Numbers

There's a well-known business saying that "What gets measured gets managed." And it's never been truer. HR metrics, web traffic statistics, and predictive analytics aren't going away.

But that doesn't mean you should calculate all of them. Find out what your management team wants to see and report out on the numbers that make sense. Use the numbers that will help you get the head count you're looking for and the budget dollars you need to hire the best talent.

TIPS
3 Tips for Taking Your Evaluation Efforts to the Next Level

While measurement and evaluation are the last steps in the recruiting process, think of the process more as a loop, with the results being used to fine-tune future actions. Talent acquisition professionals can waste a lot of time and company resources without this step. Here are some ways to stay on top of the metrics:

1. **Kelly Marinelli**, *JD, SHRM-SCP, SPHR, is principal consultant with Solve HR. She is a member of the SHRM Talent Acquisition Special Expertise Panel and has proudly renewed her SHRM-SCP credential through 2021.*

> As recruiters and talent acquisition professionals, once we have the right metrics in place and are collecting data, we need to be mindful of ensuring that we put that data to good use to increase our effectiveness. Unfortunately, merely collecting and reporting data on everyday recruiting and hiring processes are sometimes seen as the end of the process, and unless the measures are wildly outside the norm, we may be tempted to settle for "good enough" and just keep collecting and reporting, without improving. In this situation, an executive leadership team may not even push hard for better results—this is a recipe for mediocrity.
>
> The more difficult (but rewarding) challenge is figuring out the causal relationship between our strategies and performance, and the variations in the data our metrics are delivering to us. Willingness to embrace creativity and fully utilize technology, measuring the effectiveness of new initiatives, and demonstrating return on investment to leadership will give our teams an edge.

2. **Kathy Rupar,** *SPHR, CCP, SHRM-SCP, is the director of recruiting for Progress Residential in Scottsdale, Ariz. She's a dedicated SHRM volunteer leader, holding key board roles as treasurer and membership director.*

> I want to make sure the data is supporting my strategy and not wait too long to change my strategy if the data *doesn't* support it. Too many times we think we know where our candidates are coming from, but the data isn't supporting it. Recruitment budgets are limited. I must plan to maximize where I am going to get the most bang for my buck. I am always challenging my recruiters to network in other places where transferable skill sets may come from. Once you get a couple of success stories under your belt, the word spreads throughout the organization quickly. Find the hiring managers who are open to change and then drive new candidates with transferable skills to them. With low unemployment, we must employ every tool in our toolbox to stay ahead of the trends.

3. **Jordan Wan** *is the founder/CEO of CloserIQ, the sales recruiting platform connecting top sales talent to tech companies. Previously, he was the head of analytics at PayPerks, sales manager at ZocDoc, and trading strategist at Bridgewater Associates.*

> In order to stay ahead of trends, our recruiting team holds a monthly "lunch and learn" session with industry leaders and experts.
>
> We invite to lunch a guest speaker who has interesting experiences and insights that our recruiters would enjoy meeting. It could be a startup founder, an HR leader, a customer, or someone who is an expert in our industry who can share their personal experiences. The team has lunch together, and we allocate time for Q&A at the end. A couple of key takeaways from our lunch and learns:
>
> 1. Every person has an interesting story to tell with their career. Our lunch and learn guests remind us who our customers are and the difficult journey that each of us goes through to get to where we are in our careers.
> 2. Lunch and learn guests can be a quick way to learn about a new vertical or profession. Having guests tell us about their daily routine and responsibilities is a great way for our recruiting team to retain their understanding of a new role they are recruiting for.

SECTION VIII: 3 Key Takeaways

- There is no good substitute for measurement than calculating the numbers. Enough said.
- Old-school formulas like time-to-fill and cost-per-hire still bring value.
- Ask members of senior management what they want to see. There's no sense in spending time calculating numbers that people won't read or take action on.

5 Resources to Make Your Job Easier

1. TAtech's *Declaration on Traffic Quality* is available free of charge in the TAtech bookstore (http://tatech.org/).
2. Jac Fitz-enz's book *How to Measure Human Resource Management* is my go-to book for HR metrics. He also co-authored a book on predictive analytics titled *Predictive Analytics for Human Resources*.
3. SHRM offers a seminar called Building HR Metrics to Guide Decisions.
4. To learn more about training evaluation, see *Kirkpatrick's Four Levels of Training Evaluation* by James D. and Wendy Kayser Kirkpatrick. It takes Donald L. Kirpatrick's work into the digital age.
5. SHRM offers an on-demand webcast series. The webcasts are available in a variety of topics, including talent acquisition and retention, technology and data, and employee law and regulation. You can search for programs under the Learning & Career tab on the SHRM website.

CHAPTER 17:
Next Steps in Recruiting

Well, we've done it. Together, we've walked through the entire recruiting process: from strategies to evaluation and everything in between.

Now that you've seen the process, it's time to take these concepts and apply them to your recruiting efforts. Whether you're an HR department of one and have total responsibility for talent acquisition or you're a hiring manager who wants to be better at finding the best talent for your department, the recruiting function is a work in progress. The business world continues to change, so people with some responsibility for hiring need to stay on top of their game.

That's what this book is for. It's a reminder of the classic models that people who hire need to keep top of mind. The trendy stuff you can read on blogs and in magazines because it changes. When the Society for Human Resource Management (SHRM) and I started discussing this project, our talks were always focused on giving professionals a single source of information that they would keep in their library. I hope we've accomplished that task.

You've heard from a lot of people in this book. Now that we're on the last chapter, I'd like to share my five big takeaways about recruiting.

TAKEAWAY 1. It's Cheaper to Train than to Recruit

Just because this book is about recruiting and recruiting is an important function, that doesn't mean "more recruiting" should always be the answer.

Here's an example: I learned a long time ago that in business it's cheaper to keep the customers you have than to continuously attract new ones. Sure, companies should always try to attract new customers, but companies should also focus on keeping the customers they have—for two reasons: first, they've already spent the cost to acquire those customers, and second, they've already won the customers over to their brand.

Businesses stay focused on keeping customers by knowing the cost of acquiring a customer and the customer's satisfaction with their product or service. In addition, they kno' the cost of *losing* a customer.

Occasionally, customers leave for all the right reasons, for example, when they outgrow the needs of a product or service. But they remain raving fans of the company—because that company helped them grow and succeed.

The same philosophy applies to employees. When a company hires an employee, it invests a lot of time, energy, and resources in sourcing, advertising, interviews, offers, and more. Then the new hire goes through orientation and onboarding and may participate in other kinds of company training. The new hire's supervisor spends time talking with the employee about performance expectations, departmental policies, and more.

My guess is that the company has thousands of dollars invested in this new employee. Think about the cost of hiring an employee, the impact of employee engagement, and the cost of losing an employee.

So, when the employee makes a mistake, instead of immediately thinking warnings, discipline, and possible termination, maybe we should consider coaching, mentoring, or additional training. After all, the company already has a lot of money invested in this employee.

I completely understand that it can be a huge challenge to fix employee situations and customer complaints. On the surface, finding another customer or hiring another employee may appear easier. But if we've already made the investment, it might make sense to look for alternatives to abandoning the relationship.

Talent acquisition professionals and recruiters need to be prepared to hold the organization accountable.

However, as with customers, sometimes allowing employees to leave the company is exactly the right thing to do. Maybe the company can't give them what they need. Letting employees pursue their professional goals, even if it means leaving the company, could turn them into raving fans for your business.

TAKEAWAY 2. Create a Process and Follow It

Consistency brings value to the recruiting process. Let's look at it like the first takeaway.

Customers like consistency. Think of your favorite restaurant. You probably go there because you know what to expect both in terms of food and service. The employees might even know your name. People want to know when they visit their favorite places that they will have an experience that was just as nice as the last time they were there. That's consistency. And that's why organizations have consumer brands.

Over the years, I've become a fan of Starbucks. But let me tell you the story that made ˙rence for me. My boss several years ago loved Starbucks and had a three-Venti-cof-ˇabit. My office was in the basement of the building, and he would walk by my ˙orning to get his Starbucks. When I came into the office early, he would stick ˙say, "Come grab a coffee with me." So, I did. It was my one-on-one time ˙eat.

Side note: As soon as my boss left, our employment attorney would show up, and I could also get some time with him. Usually unbillable. That was good too!

Anyhow, when I left that company, my new job had a Starbucks nearby. So I stopped there and realized that the baristas knew customers by name and had even memorized customers' favorite morning beverages. When customers walked in, they didn't have to order. The baristas immediately started making their drink, and the customers simply handed over some money.

I decided to conduct an experiment. I wanted to see how long it would take the baristas to know my name and my favorite drink. Keep in mind I have an unusual first name. And I made up a complex drink. Something like a Grande, nonfat, extra-hot chai latte. A tall drip was too easy to remember. It took a week for them to treat me like a regular. One week! I was impressed.

The reason I bring up this story is because candidates want to feel impressed too. They want a good experience with your organization. If they come in for an interview, candidates want to know what to expect in terms of the next step in the hiring process. If they're no longer being considered, they'd like to know.

In addition, consistency allows an organization to figure out what works. Using my Starbucks example, if customers tell the company that they love the "know my name and my drink" service, and baristas see that they get better tips when they provide that service, then it makes sense to continue the practice. It's a win for everyone.

Finally, consistency also helps the organization if it ever has to defend a hiring decision (or nondecision). Recruiters can explain the process, why the process works, and how that effected the decision they made.

TAKEAWAY 3. Test New Ideas and Then Incorporate Them into the Process

I just said that consistency is key, and it is, but that doesn't mean organizations should stop considering or making changes. There are two situations when testing new ideas makes sense.

The first is when things aren't working. Remember the definition of insanity that is often attributed to Einstein? It's "doing the same thing over and over again and expecting different results." The question becomes, when you know the current situation isn't working, what is the answer or solution?

A tried and true problem-solving process is the scientific method. Many of us haven't thought about the scientific method since our school days, but it provides a logical way of tackling business problems. As a reminder, here are the steps to the method:

1. **Identify the problem.** The first step in the scientific method is to identify and analyze a problem using data. We can collect data about the problem using a variety of methods. One we're all accustomed to is the classic who, what, where, when, how, and to what extent. The scientific method works best when you have

a problem that can be measured or quantified in some way.

2. **Form a hypothesis.** A hypothesis is a statement that provides an educated prediction or proposed solution. A good format for a hypothesis would be, "If we do x, then y will happen." Remember, the hypothesis should be measurable so it can help you solve the business problem identified in step one.

3. **Test the hypothesis by conducting an experiment.** This is when an activity is created to confirm (or not confirm) the hypothesis. Entire books have been written about conducting experiments. We won't go into that kind of depth, but keep in mind a few things when conducting your experiment:

   a. The experiment must be fair and objective. Otherwise, it will skew the result.

   b. It should include a significant number of participants, or it will not be statistically representative of the whole.

   c. Allow for ample time to collect the information.

4. **Analyze the data.** Once the experiment is complete, the results can be analyzed. The results should confirm the hypothesis as either true or false. Even if the experiment fails to confirm the results, it may still give you additional insight to form a new hypothesis. It reminds me of the famous Thomas Edison quote, "I have not failed. I've just found 10,000 ways that won't work."

5. **Communicate the results.** Whatever the result, communicate the outcomes from the experiment to the organization. This information will help stakeholders understand which challenges have been resolved and which need further investigation. In addition, transparent communication will create buy-in for future experiments. If needed, stakeholders might be able to help develop a more focused hypothesis.

Here's an example of using the scientific method in a recruiting-related context:

Step 1 (identification). Human resources has noticed an increase in resignations over the past six months. Operational managers have said that the company isn't paying employees enough. The company needs to figure out why employees are resigning.

Step 2 (hypothesis). If we increase employee pay, then fewer resignations will occur.

Step 3 (test). For the next three months, HR will have a third party conduct exit interviews to determine the reason employees are resigning.

Step 4 (analysis). The third party report shows that the primary reason employees are leaving is that health care premiums have increased and coverage has decreased. Employees have found new jobs with better benefits.

Step 5 (communication). After communicating the results, the company is examining its budget to determine if it should do either of the following:

- Increase employee pay to cover the health insurance premium expense.
- Reevaluate its health care benefits package.

The scientific method works best when a person or small group has a theory about how to solve a problem, but not everyone has completely accepted that theory. Offering the option to test the proposed solution, without a full commitment, tells the group that its suggestion is being heard and that the numbers will ultimately provide insight—after the full scientific method has been followed.

The second reason to test new ideas is because something different is available, and it might be worth investigating. I like to think of it as effective adoption. We've heard the term "early adopter," which represents people who start using a product or technology as soon as it becomes available. "Effective adoption" is about testing a product or technology before making a commitment to it and before falling behind on the adoption curve.

Some organizations are facing this situation right now. They didn't jump on the social media or mobile bandwagon, and now they're trying to figure out how to catch up. This situation is certainly not ideal, but companies can recover by updating their recruiting methods and technology.

Ultimately, businesses want to become effective adopters and be more open to trying out new things. To become an effective adopter, consider these five steps:

1. **Recognize the trend.** One way to see the next big thing is to notice what people are talking about, even if they're calling something a ridiculous idea. That could be a conversation worth investigating.

2. **Research the trend.** Once you have identified a potentially viable trend or idea, do your homework. It's perfectly okay to decide for yourself whether something is good for your business. Find out what others are doing and what they claim are the benefits and disadvantages.

3. **Make a commitment to try something new.** If the research indicates the possibility of a gain for the business, find a way to conduct your experiment. Define what you're planning to do and the resources you're prepared to commit. Also identify what result or outcome you are hoping to achieve.

4. **Participate at a high level.** It might be tempting at the first sign of difficulty to give up on the experiment and say, "I knew this was a waste of time!" Please, resist the urge. Give the experiment your full attention. The benefits may not be immediately realized, or an unanticipated benefit may emerge.

5. **Evaluate results.** Even if you decide not to move forward, my guess is you will learn a lot from the experiment. For one thing, you'll be knowledgeable about the topic and aware of trend changes.

For example, let's say a few years ago you heard about this "trend" called Twitter. On the surface, it looks weird—people talking about bacon 24/7/365—not worth your time.

But as time goes on, you hear more people talking about Twitter and even start to see television ads mentioning it. So you decide to investigate. You learn that up to 45 percent of Twitter's entire user base is under the age of 30 and that it's the most effective platform for hiring Millennials (ages 18 to 34). Based on that data, you decide to try it for 30 days to see what happens.

After a month, your verdict is you still don't understand how people have time for Twitter, and you close your account.

Later, you discover social media distribution tools like Buffer and TweetDeck. You remember your experiment challenges and decide to give Twitter another try—because the new tools address your initial objections. Now, you're getting the hang of it and seeing the results you were looking for.

Not everyone has to be an early adopter, but you certainly don't want to be so late to the party that you fail to catch up. When new trends start to emerge, think of using the effective adopter approach.

TAKEAWAY 4. Measure Results and Adjust Accordingly

I don't want to rehash the same information, but there are a few additional things to note whenever you measure something. The approaches I outlined in takeaway number three—scientific method and effective adoption—involve a measurement component.

It's important to understand that the words "data," "metrics," and "analytics" mean different things. I know they are sometimes used interchangeably, and I'm guilty of it myself. But here's a reminder of the definitions:

Metrics are focused on tracking past performance.

Analytics is about using past data to generate predictions or insights.

Data are statistics collected for use in analytics. The term "big data" refers to data sets that are too large and complex to manipulate with standard tools.

The discussion about metrics and data isn't focused solely on the calculation. It's about interpreting the findings. Don't think of it as a math issue—it's a critical thinking issue. When dealing with metrics, analytics, and data, keep in mind the following:

1. **Define the metrics of success.** Every organization has its numerical definition of success. For example, I've worked in industries in which triple-digit turnover was the norm. Therefore, getting turnover to 75 percent was a small miracle. In other industries, that number would be unacceptable.
2. **Establish targets, including acceptable ranges.** Speaking of defining success, it might make more sense to think of success "ranges" versus a single number.
3. **Understand capturing data versus using data.** There is a difference between capturing data and using it. Companies should focus on capturing data that will have an impact on the business. It makes no sense to capture data just for the fun of it.
4. **Realize that there will be exceptions.** As much as we should focus on the

analytics, there will be moments when someone says, "Forget the numbers. *This is what we're going to do.*" And you will have to figure out how to deal with the situation.

5. **Create a dashboard, including "at a glance" data with visual indicators.** If your department or organization is new to using metrics and analytics to make business decisions, having a dashboard can be very helpful. It provides people with one place to view information.

6. **Look for patterns, trends, and relationships in the data.** Sometimes a single number will tell you something. But more often, the *relationship* between numbers will tell you a lot. A metrics dashboard (above) can help individuals see the connections and make good decisions.

7. **Take action.** This is the most important thing to remember. There's no reason to spend time calculating and analyzing numbers if you're not going to do anything with them. Organizations need to commit to using the information they are gathering to benefit the business.

Numbers have always been a part of the business. Technology is pushing the conversation about metrics, analytics, and data down the organizational hierarchy. A conversation that once was reserved for the C-suite is now a skill that everyone needs to have.

TAKEAWAY 5. The Candidate Is Interviewing You

Never, ever forget that candidates are interviewing the company as much as it's interviewing them. Candidates are researching organizations before they apply. It's a candidate's job market, and organizations are reporting some significant challenges finding qualified talent.

Companies can have the best sources in the whole world. The recruiting process can look great on a piece of paper. Managers can be trained to conduct legally compliant interviews. HR can have the best talent acquisition system ever. But if the candidate doesn't have a good experience, your recruiting process isn't working.

I understand there's a lot of talk about bots and artificial intelligence, but the bottom line is that recruiting is about people. It's about having a conversation and seeing if there's a fit—and it takes lots of conversations to find the best talent. That's why recruiting is hard.

Hopefully, with this book, you're able to create strategies that elevate the candidate experience. You can streamline processes that allow you to spend more time getting to know candidates. And the company can provide solutions that reduce administration and increase engagement.

I wish you nothing but the best in finding the best talent for your organization.

References and Resources

Preface

"Simplifying Human Resources to Engage Employees," Sharlyn Lauby, *HR Bartender* (blog), August 26, 2014, https://www.hrbartender.com/2014/recruiting/simplifying-human-resources-engage-employees

"Reinventing the Employee Life Cycle," *SilkRoad* (blog), 2016, https://www.silkroad.com/blog/reinventing-the-employee-life-cycle

SHRM Policy Action Center, www.advocacy.shrm.org

SHRM Membership Communities, https://www.shrm.org/communities/volunteers/membership-councils/pages/default.aspx

Collins, Jim, "Good to Great," *Fast Company*, September 30, 2001, https://www.fastcompany.com/43811/good-great

Chapter 1

Recruiting Internally and Externally toolkit, *SHRM Online*, https://www.shrm.org/resourcesandtools/tools-and-samples/toolkits/pages/recruitinginternallyandexternally.aspx

SHRM Seminars: Creating a Talent Acquisition Strategy, https://store.shrm.org/training/learning-center/seminars/find-a-seminar.html

Chapter 2

Association for Talent Development Competency Model, www.td.org/Certification/Competency-Model

WorldatWork Total Reward Model, www.worldatwork.org/aboutus/html/aboutus-whatis.jsp

50 HR and Recruiting Stats for 2016, Glassdoor.com, https://b2b-assets.glassdoor.com/50-hr-and-recruiting-stats-for-2016.pdf

"9 Employee Retention Statistics That Will Make You Sit Up and Pay Attention," Maren Hogan, TLNT.com, November 30, 2015, www.eremedia.com/

tlnt/9-employee-retention-statistics-that-will-make-you-sit-up-and-pay-attention

"The Talent Economy," Frank Kalman, *Talent Economy* magazine, Fall 2016, https://www.
tlnt.com/9-employee-retention-statistics-that-will-make-you-sit-up-and-pay-attention

"Putting a Price on People Problems at Work," Tanya Menon and Leigh Thompson,
Harvard Business Review, August 23, 2016, https://hbr.org/2016/08/
putting-a-price-on-people-problems-at-work

"The State of Candidate Experience in 10 Statistics," Matt Chaney, *Recruiting Daily*, May
11, 2015, http://recruitingdaily.com/the-state-of-candidate-experience-in-10-statistics

Chapter 3

"Employment Branding Matters More Than Ever," Sharlyn Lauby, *HR Bartender*
(blog), July 25, 2012, https://www.hrbartender.com/2012/recruiting/
employment-branding-matters-more-than-ever-case-study

"Employment Branding Is Dead," Sharlyn Lauby, *HR Bartender* (blog), June 26, 2016,
https://www.hrbartender.com/2016/recruiting/employment-branding-dead

"Use Storytelling to Create Employee Engagement," Sharlyn Lauby, *HR Bartender* (blog),
October 29, 2015, https://www.hrbartender.com/2015/recruiting/
use-storytelling-to-create-employee-engagement

"Give Your Business a Boost with Games in the Workplace," Sharlyn Lauby, Mashable,
July 27, 2012, http://mashable.com/2012/07/27/business-games/#0FVFpHe9UsqO

*A Necessary Evil: Managing Employee Activity on Facebook, Twitter, LinkedIn … and the
Hundreds of Other Social Media Sites*, Aliah D. Wright, SHRM, 2013

"50% of Job Seekers Want Purpose, But US Companies Simply Don't Deliver It," Wade
Burgess, *LinkedIn Talent Blog* (blog), December 7, 2016, https://business.linkedin.
com/talent-solutions/blog/trends-and-research/2016/50-percent-of-job-seekers-want-
purpose-but-us-companies-simply-do-not-deliver

"Should You Respond to Negative Online Reviews?," Steve Bates, *SHRM Online*, April
1, 2016, www.shrm.org/resourcesandtools/hr-topics/talent-acquisition/pages/should-
you-respond-to-negative-online-reviews.aspx

Chapter 4

"How Virgin Media Is Turning Great Candidate Experience into a £5.3M Revenue
Stream," HR Open Source, August 1, 2016, https://hros.co/case-study-upload/
hros-case-study-virgin-media-candidate-experience-revenu-stream

"2016 Talent Board North American Candidate Experience Research Report," www.
thetalentboard.org/cande-awards/cande-results

"23 Surprising Stats on Candidate Experience," CareerArc, June 2016 https://www.
careerarc.com/blog/2016/06/candidate-experience-study-infographic

"Corporate Culture and Company Profits Are Not Mutually Exclusive," Sharlyn Lauby, *HR Bartender* (blog), May 19, 2015, https://www.hrbartender.com/2015/recruiting/corporate-culture-and-company-profits-are-not-mutually-exclusive

"Recruiting Bots Are Here to Stay," Dinah Brin, *SHRM Online*, December 16, 2016, www.shrm.org/ResourcesAndTools/hr-topics/technology/Pages/Recruiting-Bots-Are-Here-to-Stay.aspx

"Record Shares of Americans Now Own Smartphones, Have Home Broadband," Pew Research Center, January 12, 2017, http://www.pewresearch.org/fact-tank/2017/01/12/evolution-of-technology/ft_17-01-10_internetfactsheets

"What You Need to Build a Successful Onboarding Program," *Talent Activation Blog*, September 8, 2015, www.silkroad.com/blog/what-you-need-to-build-a-successful-onboarding-program

"SMART-ly Tracking Your Progress," Sharlyn Lauby, *HR Bartender* (blog), April 8, 2015, https://www.hrbartender.com/2015/leadership-and-management/smart-ly-tracking-your-progress

Chapter 5

"The Decline of 'Dynamism'?," Peter Cappelli, *Human Resource Executive* Online, November 30, 2016, www.hreonline.com/HRE/view/story.jhtml?id=534361517

"Workforce Development Should Be Part of Your Recruiting Strategy," Sharlyn Lauby, *HR Bartender* (blog), June 2, 2016, https://www.hrbartender.com/2016/recruiting/workforce-development-part-recruiting-strategy

"The Difference between Knowledge, Skills, and Abilities," Sharlyn Lauby, *HR Bartender* (blog), December 29, 2013, https://www.hrbartender.com/2013/recruiting/the-difference-between-knowledge-skills-and-abilities

"Strategic Planning: What Are the Basics of Environmental Scanning?," *SHRM Online*, November 27, 2012, https://www.shrm.org/resourcesandtools/tools-and-samples/hr-qa/pages/cms_021670.aspx

Essential Meeting Blueprints for Managers, Sharlyn Lauby, Impackt Publishing, 2015

"STEM Crisis or STEM Surplus? Yes and Yes," *Monthly Labor Review*, May 2015, www.bls.gov/opub/mlr/2015/article/stem-crisis-or-stem-surplus-yes-and-yes.htm

"GM and Girls Who Code Partner for After-School STEM Program," Roberto Baldwin, *Engadget*, January 10, 2017, www.engadget.com/2017/01/10/gm-and-girls-who-code-partner-for-after-school-stem-program

"Apprenticeships: One Way to Create a Work-Ready Talent Pool," Kathy Gurchiek, *SHRM Online*, October 24, 2016, https://www.shrm.org/resourcesandtools/hr-topics/organizational-and-employee-development/pages/apprenticeships-one-way-to-create-a-work-ready-talent-pool.aspx

"Finding the middle: How businesses can manage the talent pipeline to close the middle-skills employment gap," Ravi Chanmugam, David Smith and Laila Worrell,

Accenture, www.accenture.com/t20150723T012620__w__/us-en/_acnmedia/
Accenture/Conversion-Assets/DotCom/Documents/Global/PDF/Dualpub3/Accen-
ture-Finding-The-Middle-How-Businesses-Can-Manage-The-Talent-Pipeline-To-
Close-The-Middle-Skills-Employment-Gap.pdf

"Bridging the Skills Gap: Workforce Development Is Everyone's Business,"
Association for Talent Development, 2015, https://www.td.org/insights/
atd-public-policy-council-updates-skills-gap-whitepaper

Chapter 6

"AT&T's Talent Overhaul," John Donovan and Cathy Benko, *Harvard Business Review*,
October 2016, https://hbr.org/2016/10/atts-talent-overhaul

"Building Trust between Your Employees and Freelancers," Jon Younger and Michael
Kearns, *Harvard Business Review*, March 15, 2017, https://hbr.org/2017/03/
building-trust-between-your-employees-and-freelancers

Build, Borrow, or Buy: Solving the Growth Dilemma, Laurence Capron and Will Mitchell,
Harvard Business Review Press, August 2012

"Decision Time: Should Your Company Hire or Outsource," Sharlyn Lauby, *HR Bartender* (blog), March 3, 2015, www.hrbartender.com/2015/recruiting/decision-time-
should-your-company-hire-or-outsource

"Filling Your Talent Needs with 'Build' Recruiting Tactics," Sharlyn Lauby, *Alongside
Blog*, February 17, 2017, https://www.alongside.com/blog
filling-your-talent-needs-with-build-recruiting-tactics

"Using a 'Buy' Recruiting Tactic to Find Talent," Sharlyn Lauby, *Alongside Blog*, January
27, 2017, www.alongside.com/blog/using-a-buy-recruiting-tactic-to-find-talent

"Leveraging 'Borrow' Recruiting Tactics to Meet Your Staffing Needs," Sharlyn Lauby,
Alongside Blog, March 24, 2017, www.alongside.com/blog/leveraging-borrow-
recruiting-tactics-to-meet-your-staffing-needs

"Your Organization Needs a Replacement Plan (Even if They Don't Have a Succession
Plan)," Sharlyn Lauby, *TalentSpace Blog*, March 6, 2017, https://www.halogensoft-
ware.com/blog/your-organization-needs-a-replacement-plan-even-if-they-dont-have-
a-succession-plan

"Being Part of the Succession Plan Isn't an Entitlement," Sharlyn Lauby, *HR
Bartender* (blog), March 5, 2015, www.hrbartender.com/2015/recruiting/
being-part-of-the-succession-plan-isnt-an-entitlement

"5 Steps for Creating Organizational Talent Pools," Sharlyn Lauby, *TalentSpace Blog*,
February 10, 2017, https://www.halogensoftware.com
blog/5-steps-for-creating-organizational-talent-pools

The Employer Handbook (blog), Eric B. Meyer, www.theemployerhandbook.com

"Point-Counterpoint: Should You Tell Employees They're Part of a Succession Plan?," by

Marie LaMarche, and Kim E. Ruyle, *SHRM Online*, January 7, 2015, https://www.shrm.org/hr-today/news/hr-magazine/Pages/010215-sucession-planning.aspx

"Average Cost-per-Hire for Companies Is $4,129, SHRM Survey Finds," *SHRM Online*, August 3, 2016, https://www.shrm.org/about-shrm/press-room/press-releases/pages/human-capital-benchmarking-report.aspx

"7 Activities to Effectively Engage New Hires" (white paper), Sharlyn Lauby, 2016, www.icims.com/sites/www.icims.com/files/public/7%20Activities%20to%20Effectively%20Engage%20New%20Hires%20Updated_0.pdf

"4 Steps to Creating a Successful Social Recruiting Strategy" (white paper), Sharlyn Lauby, www.icims.com/sites/https://www.icims.com/sites/www.icims.com/files/public/7%20Activities%20to%20Effectively%20Engage%20New%20Hires%20Updated_0.pdf

"The Ugly Statistics of Succession Management," Edmond Mellina, HR People + Strategy, July 10, 2015, https://blog.hrps.org/blogpost/1286231/221636/The-Ugly-Statistics-of-Succession-Management-by-Edmond-Mellina

"Baby Boomers Retire," Pew Research Center, DECEMBER 29, 2010, http://www.pewresearch.org/fact-tank/2010/12/29/baby-boomers-retire

"Here's Why The Freelancer Economy Is On The Rise," Brendon Schrader, *Fast Company*, August 10, 2015, www.fastcompany.com/3049532/heres-why-the-freelancer-economy-is-on-the-rise

Chapter 7

"Adidas Group Case Study," LinkedIn Talent Solutions, 2012, business.linkedin.com/content/dam/business/talent-solutions/global/en_us/site/pdf/cs/linkedin_adidas_case_study_us_en_130621.pdf

"Home Depot Social Media Strategy," Findly, 2014, www.findly.com/wp-content/uploads/2014/10/HomeDepot_Social_2014.pdf

"EEO: General: What Is the Difference between EEO, Affirmative Action and Diversity?," *SHRM Online*, August 30, 2016, www.shrm.org/resourcesandtools/tools-and-samples/hr-qa/pages/cms_013810.aspx

"Military Employment Resource Page," *SHRM Online*, https://www.shrm.org/resourcesandtools/hr-topics/talent-acquisition/pages/military-employment-resource-page.aspx

"8 in 10 Employers Lack Recruitment Programs for Veterans," Roy Maurer, *SHRM Online*, May 25, 2015, https://www.shrm.org/resourcesandtools/hr-topics/talent-acquisition/pages/recruitment-programs-veterans.aspx

"USERRA 101," National Veterans' Training Institute, www.nvti.ucdenver.edu/training/userra101Basics.htm

"The Aging Workforce Research Initiative," *SHRM Online*, July 7, 2016, https://www.shrm.org/hr-today/trends-and-forecasting/research-and-surveys/pages/aging-workforce-research-initiative.aspx

The Aging Workforce: Leveraging the Talent of Mature Employees, Cheryl Paullin, SHRM Foundation Effective Practice Guidelines Series, 2014, www.shrm.org/foundation/ourwork/initiatives/the-aging-workforce/Documents/The%20Aging%20Workforce%20Leveraging%20the%20Talents%20of%20Mature%20Employees.pdf

"Hiring Job Seekers with Criminal Histories," Mark Feffer, *SHRM Online*, September 26, 2016, www.shrm.org/hr-today/news/hr-magazine/1016/pages/hiring-job-seekers-with-criminal-histories.aspx

"Do Ban-the-Box Laws Work?," Lisa Nagele-Piazza, *SHRM Online*, January 12, 2017, www.shrm.org/ResourcesAndTools/legal-and-compliance/state-and-local-updates/Pages/Do-Ban-the-Box-Laws-Work.aspx

"Nearly 1 in 5 People Have a Disability in the U.S., Census Bureau Reports," U.S. Census Bureau, July 25, 2012, www.census.gov/newsroom/releases/archives/miscellaneous/cb12-134.html

"Publix Reinforces Reputation for Prioritizing Employment Opportunities for Workers with Disabilities," The Able Trust, www.abletrust.org/business-leader-information/about-my-ability/exemplary-employers

Key Factors that Assist Employers to Recruit, Interview, Hire and Retain People with Disabilities, Patty Born and Randy Dumm, Florida State University, June 2011, www.abletrust.org/sites/default/files/media/docs/Dumm-Born-Final-Report-7-2011.pdf

Global Recruiting Trends 2016, LinkedIn Talent Solutions, business.linkedin.com/content/dam/business/talent-solutions/global/en_us/c/pdfs/GRT16_GlobalRecruiting_100815.pdf

"Employee Well-Being Impacts Your Recruiting Efforts," Sharlyn Lauby, *HR Bartender* (blog), November 29, 2015, www.hrbartender.com/2015/recruiting/employee-well-being-impacts-your-recruiting-efforts

"Employee Referral Programs," Sharlyn Lauby, *HR Bartender* (blog), December 10, 2009, www.hrbartender.com/2009/recruiting/employee-referral-programs

"Boomerang Employees—Can You Go Home Again?," Joyce Maroney, Workforce Institute at Kronos, July 25, 2015, www.workforceinstitute.org/blog/boomerang-employees-can-go-home

"How Extreme Recruiting Is Winning Over Millennial Tech Talent," Steffen Maier, *Entrepreneur*, December 9, 2016, www.entrepreneur.com/article/283348

"Crafting the Perfect Job Ad," Roy Maurer, *SHRM Online*, February 26, 2016, www.shrm.org/resourcesandtools/hr-topics/talent-acquisition/pages/crafting-perfect-job-ad.aspx

"Niche Job Sites Still Valuable as Legacy Boards Fade," Roy Maurer, *SHRM Online*, November 14, 2016, www.shrm.org/resourcesandtools/hr-topics/talent-acquisition/pages/niche-job-sites-monster-careerbuilder.aspx

"Everything HR Needs to Know About SEO," Sharlyn Lauby, *HR Bartender* (blog), June 28, 2015, www.hrbartender.com/2015/recruiting/everything-hr-needs-to-know-about-seo

"Recruiting Firms or Applying Online—Which Is Better?," Sharlyn Lauby, *HR Bartender* (blog), September 23, 2012, www.hrbartender.com/2012/recruiting/recruiting-firms-or-applying-online-which-is-better

"Offered Same Job by Two Different Recruiters—Ask #HR Bartender," Sharlyn Lauby, *HR Bartender* (blog), October 16, 2016, www.hrbartender.com/2016/recruiting/offered-job-two-different-recruiters

"Data Doesn't Lie: Removing These Gendered Keywords Gets You More Applicants," Jeanne Anderson, *ZipRecruiter* (blog), September 19, 2016, www.ziprecruiter.com/blog/removing-gendered-keywords-gets-you-more-applicants

"Are You Limiting Candidates with Biased Job Ads?," Matt Krumrie, *ZipRecruiter* (blog), December 13, 2016, www.ziprecruiter.com/blog/are-you-limiting-candidates-with-biased-job-ads

Chapter 8

"Tell Us Your Worst Job Interview Experiences," Patrick Allen, *Lifehacker* (blog), May 7, 2015, https://lifehacker.com/tell-us-your-worst-job-interview-experiences-1702967168

"What HR Won't Tell You about Online Applications," Sharlyn Lauby, *HR Bartender* (blog), December 6, 2011, www.hrbartender.com/2011/recruiting/what-hr-wont-tell-you-about-online-applications

"Rethinking the Salary History Question," Roy Maurer, *SHRM Online*, February 12, 2016, www.shrm.org/resourcesandtools/hr-topics/talent-acquisition/pages/rethinking-salary-history-question.aspx

"10 Recruiting Tips for First-Time Managers," Sharlyn Lauby, *HR Bartender* (blog), February 26, 2017, www.hrbartender.com/2017/recruiting/10-recruiting-tips-first-time-managers

"How to Do Well at In-Tray and e-Tray exercises," University of Kent, www.kent.ac.uk/careers/interviews/intray.htm

"Do Difficult Job Interviews Lead to More Satisfied Workers? Evidence from Glassdoor Reviews," Andrew Chamberlain and Ayal Chen-Zion, October 29, 2015, www.glassdoor.com/research/studies/interview-difficulty

Chapter 9

"Give Your Interns an Experience They'll Never Forget," Sharlyn Lauby, *HR Bartender* (blog),August 18, 2015, www.hrbartender.com/2015/recruiting/give-your-interns-an-experience-theyll-never-forget

"10 Must-Haves for a Successful Company Intern Program," Sharlyn Lauby, *HR Bartender* (blog), October 10, 2013, www.hrbartender.com/2013/recruiting/10-must-haves-for-a-successful-company-intern-program

"Is 'Cultural Fit' Code For 'Be Like Me'?," Lynda Spiegel, TLNT.com, January 30, 2017, www.eremedia.com/tlnt/is-cultural-fit-code-for-be-like-me

"Should You Hire for Cultural Fit or Adaptability?," Amir Goldberg and Sameer B. Srivastava, *The Water Cooler* (blog), December 6, 2016, rework.withgoogle.com/blog/hire-for-culture-fit-or-adaptability

"Noise: How to Overcome the High, Hidden Cost of Inconsistent Decision Making," Daniel Kahneman, Andrew M. Rosenfield, Linnea Gandhi, and Tom Blaser, *Harvard Business Review*, October 2016, hbr.org/2016/10/noise

"Pre-Employment Tests Can Help HR Hire Faster (and Better)," Sharlyn Lauby, *HR Bartender* (blog), February 7, 2017, www.hrbartender.com/2017/recruiting/pre-employment-tests-hire-faster-better

"The Validity and Utility of Selection Methods in Personnel Psychology: Practical and Theoretical Implications of 85 Years of Research Findings," Frank L. Schmidt and John E. Hunter, *Psychological Bulletin* 124, no. 2 (1998)

Chapter 10

"Case Study: Gonzaga University," HireRight. www.hireright.com/resources/view/case-study-gonzaga-university

"Background Screening Impacts the Candidate Experience," Sharlyn Lauby, *HR Bartender* (blog), September 22, 2015, www.hrbartender.com/2015/strategy-planning/background-screening-impacts-the-candidate-experience

"The Increasing Risks of Background Checks," Kelly O. Scott and Patrick A. Fraioli, Jr., *HR Magazine*, December 2016/January 2017, www.shrm.org/hr-today/news/hr-magazine/1216/pages/the-increasing-risks-of-background-checks-.aspx

"Background Screening Goes with the Workflow," Roy Maurer, *SHRM Online*, October 1, 2016, www.shrm.org/hr-today/news/hr-magazine/1016/pages/making-every-background-check-count.aspx

"Marijuana 101: What #HR Pros Need to Know," Sharlyn Lauby, *HR Bartender* (blog), June 30, 2016, www.hrbartender.com/2016/hr-law-legislation/marijuana-101-hr-business-pros-need-know

Employer's Guide to Medical Marijuana, HireRight, www.hireright.com/resources/view/employers-guide-to-medical-marijuana

Chapter 11

"Defining Employment at Will," Sharlyn Lauby, *HR Bartender* (blog), May 4, 2014, www.hrbartender.com/2014/recruiting/defining-employment-at-will-ask-hr-bartender

"How to Handle Rejection," Sharlyn Lauby, *HR Bartender* (blog), January 27, 2011, https://www.hrbartender.com/2011/recruiting/how-to-handle-rejection/

"How to Create an Offer Letter Without Contractual Implications," *SHRM Online*,

September 1, 2016, www.shrm.org/resourcesandtools/tools-and-samples/how-to-guides/pages/howtocreateanofferletter.aspx

"Beware: Rescinding Job Offers Can Prompt Legal Consequences," Roy Maurer, *SHRM Online*, August 25, 2016, www.shrm.org/resourcesandtools/hr-topics/talent-acquisition/pages/take-care-rescinding-job-offers.aspx

Chapter 12

"Case Study: SilkRoad Technology Helps Streamline Recruiting," Sharlyn Lauby, *HR Bartender* (blog), February 27, 2011, www.hrbartender.com/2011/recruiting/case-study-silkroad-technology-helps-streamline-recruiting

"Pre-Boarding: Bring High Tech and High Touch to Onboarding," Sharlyn Lauby, *HR Bartender* (blog), June 23, 2015, www.hrbartender.com/2015/recruiting/pre-boarding-bring-high-tech-and-high-touch-to-onboarding

Onboarding in a Box: Everything You Need for a Powerful Onboarding Experience, LinkedIn, business.linkedin.com/content/dam/business/talent-solutions/global/en_us/c/pdfs/onboarding-in-a-box-v03-06.pdf

Chapter 13

"Case Study: Accelerating New Employee Productivity at Savis, a CenturyLink Company," Lorri Freifeld, *Training* magazine, November 1, 2012, trainingmag.com/content/case-study-accelerating-new-employee-productivity-savvis-centurylink-company

"Recruiters Must Learn Talent Development (and vice versa)," Sharlyn Lauby, *HR Bartender* (blog), April 24, 2016, www.hrbartender.com/2016/recruiting/recruiters-must-learn-talent-development

"Job Seekers: Social Media is Even More Important Than You Thought," Brooke Torres, The Muse, www.themuse.com/advice/job-seekers-social-media-is-even-more-important-than-you-thought

"Social Recruiting Sets Expectations for Social Training," Sharlyn Lauby, *HR Bartender* (blog), January 29, 2013, www.hrbartender.com/2013/training/social-recruiting-sets-expectations-for-social-training

"How to Build and Implement an Employee Loyalty Program," PaychexWORX, February 15, 2017, https://www.paychex.com/articles/human-resources/build-and-implement-employee-loyalty-program

"Telling Employees What the Policy Says Isn't Training," Sharlyn Lauby, *HR Bartender* (blog), April 23, 2013, www.hrbartender.com/2013/training/telling-employees-what-the-policy-says-isnt-training

"Employee Perceptions of Time Are Important," Sharlyn Lauby, *HR Bartender* (blog), December 11, 2016, www.hrbartender.com/2016/employee-engagement/employee-perceptions-time-important

Chapter 14

"Case Study: On-Boarding Program," August 23, 2012, NorthCoast99, www.north-coast99.org/blog/post/Case-Study-On-Boarding-Program-.aspx

"Employee Turnover Caused By Bad Onboarding Programs," Sharlyn Lauby, *HR Bartender* (blog), May 22, 2012, www.hrbartender.com/2012/recruiting/employee-turnover-caused-by-bad-onboarding-programs

"If You Build It—Strategic Implementation," Sharlyn Lauby, *HR Bartender* (blog), July 4, 2011, www.hrbartender.com/2011/business-and-customers/if-you-build-it-strategic-implementation

"Have We Forgotten the WIIFM?," Sharlyn Lauby, *HR Bartender* (blog), July 25, 2013, www.hrbartender.com/2013/training/have-we-forgotten-the-wiifm

"Onboarding: Your Connection Between Recruiting and Learning," Sharlyn Lauby, *HR Bartender* (blog), June 18, 2017, www.hrbartender.com/2017/recruiting/onboarding-recruiting-learning

On-Boarding Toolkit: Guidance for the Hiring Manager, Johns Hopkins University, hrnt.jhu.edu/working_here/documents/onbhiringmanagerv9.pdf

"Companies Should Include Feedback Training in Onboarding," Sharlyn Lauby, *HR Bartender* (blog), March 14, 2017, www.hrbartender.com/2017/employee-engagement/include-feedback-training-onboarding

Onboarding in a Box, LinkedIn Talent Solutions, business.linkedin.com/content/dam/business/talent-solutions/global/en_us/c/pdfs/onboarding-in-a-box-v03-06.pdf

"9 Employee Retention Statistics That Will Make You Sit Up and Pay Attention," Maren Hogan, TLNT.com, November 30, 2015, www.eremedia.com/tlnt/9-employee-retention-statistics-that-will-make-you-sit-up-and-pay-attention

"Onboarding Key to Retaining, Engaging Talent," Roy Maurer, *SHRM Online*, April 16, 2015, www.shrm.org/resourcesandtools/hr-topics/talent-acquisition/pages/onboarding-key-retaining-engaging-talent.aspx

Chapter 15

"Don't Tell Employees Why the Company Culture Is Great," Sharlyn Lauby, *HR Bartender* (blog), March 16, 2017, www.hrbartender.com/2017/recruiting/dont-tell-company-culture-great

"5 Ways to Build Employee Engagement into the Onboarding Process," Sharlyn Lauby, *HR Bartender* (blog), December 10, 2013, www.hrbartender.com/2013/recruiting/5-ways-to-build-employee-engagement-into-the-onboarding-process

"Prevent Exit Interviews with Stay Interviews," Sharlyn Lauby, *HR Bartender* (blog), June 16, 2015, www.hrbartender.com/2015/recruiting/prevent-exit-interviews-with-stay-interviews

"Tips for Getting the Best Training Feedback," Sharlyn Lauby, *HR Bartender* (blog), December 8, 2011, www.hrbartender.com/2011/training/tips-for-getting-the-best-training-feedback

"6 Steps for Auditing Your Company's Candidate Experience," Sharlyn Lauby, *HR Bartender* (blog), July 29, 2014, www.hrbartender.com/2014/recruiting/6-steps-auditing-companys-candidate-experience

"Mentors or Coaches—Why You Need Both," Sharlyn Lauby, *HR Bartender* (blog), November 18, 2012, www.hrbartender.com/2012/training/mentors-or-coaches-why-you-need-both

"How to Build a Successful Mentoring Program," Sharlyn Lauby, *HR Bartender* (blog), April 21, 2015, www.hrbartender.com/2015/recruiting/how-to-build-a-successful-mentoring-program

How to Build a Successful Mentoring Program, University of North Carolina, Kenan-Flagler Business School, http://onlinemba.unc.edu/wp-content/uploads/How_To_Build_A_Successful_Mentoring_Program.pdf

"Do You Know Why You Were Hired?," Sharlyn Lauby, *HR Bartender* (blog), March 29, 2016, www.hrbartender.com/2016/recruiting/do-you-know-why-you-were-hired

Chapter 16

"Optimize Your Job Ad Messaging: A Recruitment Metrics Case Study," Christopher Brablc, *SmashFly Blog*, May 6, 2010, http://blog.smashfly.com/2010/05/06/optimize-your-recruiting-messaging-a-recruitment-metrics-case-study

"Tips for Getting the Best Training Feedback," Sharlyn Lauby, *HR Bartender* (blog), December 8, 2011, www.hrbartender.com/2011/training/tips-for-getting-the-best-training-feedback

"Measure Training Effectiveness by Results, Not Hours," Sharlyn Lauby, *HR Bartender* (blog), November 17, 2016, https://www.hrbartender.com/2016/training/measure-training-effectiveness/

"Sustainable HR," Sharlyn Lauby, *HR Bartender* (blog), November 25, 2008, www.hrbartender.com/2008/recruiting/sustainable-hr

"6 Steps for Auditing Your Company's Candidate Experience," Sharlyn Lauby, *HR Bartender* (blog), July 29, 2014, www.hrbartender.com/2014/recruiting/6-steps-auditing-companys-candidate-experience

"5 Talent Metrics Every Company Needs to Know," Sharlyn Lauby, *TalentSpace Blog*, June 3, 2015, www.halogensoftware.com/blog/5-talent-metrics-every-company-needs-to-know

How to Measure Human Resource Management (3rd ed.), Jac Fitz-enz, McGraw-Hill Education, 2002

Global Human Capital Trends 2015: Leading in the New World of Work, Deloitte University Press, 2015, www2.deloitte.com/au/en/pages/human-capital/articles/introduction-human-capital-trends-2015.html

"Bots and Crawlers May Represent up to 50% of Web Traffic," Martin Clancy, DeviceAtlas, May 13, 2016, deviceatlas.com/blog/bots-and-crawlers-may-represent-50-web-traffic

Hire with Your Head (3rd ed.), Lou Adler, Wiley, 2007

"The Holy Grail of Recruiting: How to Measure Quality of Hire," Roy Maurer, *SHRM Online*, November 18, 2015, www.shrm.org/resourcesandtools/hr-topics/talent-acquisition/pages/how-to-measure-quality-of-hire.aspx

Chapter 17

"It's Cheaper to Train than Recruit," Sharlyn Lauby, *HR Bartender* (blog), April 5, 2012, www.hrbartender.com/2012/recruiting/its-cheaper-to-train-than-recruit

"The Scientific Method Isn't Just for Scientists," The Workforce Institute at Kronos, March 14, 2014, www.workforceinstitute.org/blog/scientific-method-isnt-just-scientists

"Becoming an Effective Adopter," Sharlyn Lauby, *HR Bartender* (blog), February 20, 2014, www.hrbartender.com/2014/training/becoming-an-effective-adopter

"11 Social Media Recruiting Statistics to Make You Rethink Your Current Strategies," Profiles, March 22, 2016, www.careerprofiles.com/blog/hiring-innovative-talent/11-social-media-recruiting-statistics-to-make-you-rethink-your-current-strategies

"7 Rules to Remember with HR Metrics, Analytics and Data," Sharlyn Lauby, *HR Bartender* (blog), October 12, 2014, www.hrbartender.com/2014/leadership-and-management/7-rules-remember-hr-metrics-analytics-data

About the Author

Sharlyn Lauby, SHRM-SCP, is the author of *HR Bartender* blog and president of ITM Group Inc., a Florida-based training and human resource consulting firm focused on helping companies retain and engage talent.

Before starting ITM Group, Lauby was vice president of human resources for Right Management Consultants, one of the world's largest organizational consulting firms. She has designed and implemented highly successful programs for employee retention, internal and external customer satisfaction, and leadership development.

Media outlets and publications such as *Reuters,* the *New York Times,* ABC News, "Today," *Readers Digest, Men's Health, Mashable,* and the *Wall Street Journal* have sought out her expertise on topics related to human resources and the workplace. She is the author of *Manager Onboarding: 5 Steps for Setting New Leaders Up for Success.*

Lauby launched *HR Bartender* to provide a "friendly place for everyday workplace issues." The blog has been recognized as one of the top 5 business blogs read by HR professionals by the Society for Human Resource Management (SHRM) and best business blog by the Stevie Awards.

She believes strongly in giving to the community. She served by appointment from former Governor Jeb Bush on the Governor's Alliance for the Employment of Citizens with Disabilities. She also served as co-lead of SHRM's Ethics and Corporate Social Responsibility special expertise panel and previously as president of HR Florida, the statewide SHRM affiliate.

Her personal goal in life is to find the best cheeseburger on the planet.

Index

Additional SHRM-Published Books

SHRMStore Books Approved for Recertification Credit

Aligning HR & Business Strategy/Holbeche, 9780750680172 (2009)

Becoming the Evidence-Based Manager/Latham, 9780891063988 (2009)

Being Global/Cabrera, 9781422183229 (2012)

Best Practices in Succession Planning/Linkage, 9780787985790 (2007)

Calculating Success/Hoffmann, 9781422166390 (2012)

Collaborate/Sanker, 9781118114728 (2012)

Deep Dive/Horwath, 9781929774821 (2009)

Effective HR Management/Lawler, 9780804776875 (2012)

Emotional Intelligence/Bradbury, 9780974320625 (2009)

Employee Engagement/Carbonara, 9780071799508 (2012)

From Hello to Goodbye/Walters, 9781586442064 (2011)

Handbook for Strategic HR/Vogelsang, 9780814432495 (2012)

Hidden Drivers of Success/Schiemann, 9781586443337 (2013)

HR at Your Service/Latham, 9781586442477 (2012)

HR Transformation/Ulrich, 9780071638708 (2009)

Lean HR/Lay, 9781481914208 (2013)

Manager 3.0/Karsh, 97808144w32891 (2013)

Managing Employee Turnover/Allen, 9781606493403 (2012)

Managing the Global Workforce/Caliguri, 9781405107327 (2010)

Managing the Mobile Workforce/Clemons, 9780071742207 (2010)

Managing Older Workers/Cappelli, 9781422131657 (2010)

Multipliers/Wiseman, 9780061964398 (2010)

Negotiation at Work/Asherman, 9780814431900 (2012)

Nine Minutes on Monday/Robbins, 9780071801980 (2012)

One Strategy/Sinofsky, 9780470560457 (2009)

People Analytics/Waber, 9780133158311 (2013)

Performance Appraisal Tool Kit/Falcone, 9780814432631 (2013)

Point Counterpoint/Tavis, 9781586442767 (2012)

Practices for Engaging the 21st Century Workforce/Castellano, 9780133086379 (2013)

Proving the Value of HR/Phillips, 9781586442880 (2012)

Reality-Based Leadership/Wakeman, 9780470613504 (2010)

Social Media Strategies/Golden, 9780470633106 (2010)

Talent, Transformations, and Triple Bottom Line/Savitz, 9781118140970 (2013)

The Big Book of HR/Mitchell, 9781601631893 (2012)

The Crowdsourced Performance Review/Mosley, 9780071817981 (2013)

The Definitive Guide to HR Communications/Davis, 9780137061433 (2011)

The e-HR Advantage/Waddill, 9781904838340 (2011)

The Employee Engagement Mindset/Clark, 9780071788298 (2012)

The Global Challenge/Evans, 9780073530376 (2010)

The Global Tango/Trompenaars, 9780071761154 (2010)

The HR Answer Book/Smith, 9780814417171 (2011)

The Manager's Guide to HR/Muller, 9780814433027 (2013)

The Power of Appreciative Inquiry/Whitney, 9781605093284 (2010)

Transformative HR/Boudreau, 9781118036044 (2011)

What If? Short Stories to Spark Diversity Dialogue/Robbins, 9780891062752 (2008)

What Is Global Leadership?/Gundling, 9781904838234 (2011)

Winning the War for Talent/Johnson, 9780730311553 (2011)